MICRO, SMALL, AND MEDIUM ENTERPRISE INSOLVENCY

Micro, Small, and Medium Enterprise Insolvency

A Modular Approach

RONALD DAVIS
Professor Emeritus, Peter A. Allard School of Law, University of British Columbia, Canada

STEPHAN MADAUS
Professor of Civil Law, Civil Procedure and Insolvency Law, Martin Luther University Halle-Wittenberg, Germany

ALBERTO MAZZONI
Professor, Università Cattolica del Sacro Cuore, Milan, Italy

IRIT MEVORACH
Professor of International Commercial Law at the University of Nottingham, UK

RIZWAAN JAMEEL MOKAL
Barrister, South Square Chambers, London, UK

BARBARA ROMAINE
Justice, Queen's Bench, Alberta, Canada

JANIS SARRA
Presidential Distinguished Professor, University of British Columbia; Professor of Law, Peter A. Allard School of Law, UBC, Canada

IGNACIO TIRADO
Professor of Corporate and Insolvency Law, Universidad Autónoma, Madrid, Spain

OXFORD
UNIVERSITY PRESS

OXFORD
UNIVERSITY PRESS

Great Clarendon Street, Oxford, OX2 6DP,
United Kingdom

Oxford University Press is a department of the University of Oxford. It furthers the University's objective of excellence in research, scholarship, and education by publishing worldwide. Oxford is a registered trade mark of Oxford University Press in the UK and in certain other countries

First Edition published in 2018

Published in the United States of America by Oxford University Press
198 Madison Avenue, New York, NY 10016, United States of America

British Library Cataloguing in Publication Data
Data available

Library of Congress Control Number: 2018942413

ISBN 978–0–19–879993–1

Preface

Micro, small, and medium enterprises (MSMEs) are vital to every economy in the world. They comprise the vast majority of businesses, and they account for the greatest proportion of employment globally. MSMEs are also particularly vulnerable to becoming financially or economically distressed. Value is lost when these businesses fail. Entrepreneurs are often left with overwhelming debt, which prevents their skills and energy from being put to new productive uses. While recognized as a significant problem globally, to date there has not been a systematic analysis of how current insolvency law systems are a barrier to allowing MSMEs a timely and effective winding down of the business when they are no longer viable and to relieving entrepreneurs of a crushing burden of debt. There has not been a global strategy to allow a MSME to continue in business under an arrangement with creditors when a viable continuation plan is possible, or to effectively allow entrepreneurs an opportunity for a 'fresh start'.

This volume offers that strategy. It proposes an innovative approach to addressing MSME insolvency that legislative authorities in any jurisdiction may adapt and adopt—a modular framework that permits creditors and other stakeholders in each individual insolvency to deploy the tools necessary to address that insolvency in an effective and timely way.

This volume represents the results of ongoing collaboration of seven scholars in six jurisdictions and one member of the Canadian judiciary. It draws on and refers to a wide range of sources, including international standards and reports and measures available in domestic jurisdictions, as well as our collective experience working in many jurisdictions across the globe.

Acknowledgements

Our sincere thanks go to Jim McCartney for support in many ways, but particularly for his administrative support in the various drafts of the volume—truly a great contribution—as well as for his permanent smile and good spirits, which have been an invaluable help. Thank you also to the individuals who read and provided comments on previous iterations of the draft, including Andres Martinez, Jason Kilborn, and Conor O'Mahony.

Thank you to the following for the opportunity to present work culminating in this volume: Working Group V on International Insolvency Law of the United Nations Commission on International Trade Law; the new working group on MSME insolvency of the World Bank's Insolvency and Creditor/Debtor Regimes Task Force; and INSOL International's Academic Colloquium. We appreciate the contribution to our discussions in London of Andres Martinez, Senior Financial Sector Specialist with the World Bank. Thank you to the *Annual Review of Insolvency Law* at the University of British Columbia for the opportunity to present at its large annual conference and thus allow us another chance to work together in person. We are also grateful to the Universidad Autónoma de Madrid, which hosted the workshop where this project started.

We extend our thanks to Sandy Mulholland and Joanne Forbes for their steadfast administrative support, and the research assistants who checked facts and figures, including Daniel Schipley. Thanks to Dan Parkin and Julia McLaughlin of the Lodge at the Old Dorm on Bowen Island for comfortable accommodation and excellent meals. And who could forget the memorable evening hosted by Joanne Forbes and Greg Crowe at their beautiful home on the island.

We would like to thank our families for their enthusiasm and support. Riz is grateful to Sara, Imani, and Samir for their love and humour and for generally mucking in whenever necessary. Irit would like to thank Carmel, Roni, and Amit, especially for their creations and collaborations with the other cooks in the Bowen Island kitchen. Janis and Ron wish to thank their children Alex, Danielle, and Samantha, and grandchildren Amadea, Jolie, Carmen, and Magdalena, for their continuing love and support. Alberto wishes to thank Mona for her endless patience in continuing to accept postponements of the day in which her most reasonable desires and projects will take priority over his personal and professional ambitions.

Finally, our thanks to Rachel Mullaly and Alex Johnson of Oxford University Press for their excellent help with this project.

Table of Contents

Table of Cases

CANADA

FRANCE

GERMANY

ITALY

UNITED KINGDOM

UNITED STATES

List of Abbreviations

ASEAN	Association of Southeast Asian Nations
BDBC	Business Development Bank of Canada
BIA	Bankruptcy and Insolvency Act (Canada)
BRO	bankruptcy restrictions order (England and Wales)
BRU	bankruptcy restrictions undertaking (England and Wales)
CAIRP	Canadian Association of Insolvency and Restructuring Professionals
CFS	Common Financial Statement (UK)
Comecon	Council for Mutual Economic Assistance
CRO	Irish Companies Registry Office
DRBA	Debtor Rehabilitation and Bankruptcy Act (South Korea)
EiCon	the entrepreneur in control
IFC	International Finance Corporation
IFRS	International Financial Reporting Standards
IMF	International Monetary Fund
IVA	individual voluntary arrangement
MSEs	micro and small enterprises
MSMEs	micro, small, and medium enterprises
ODCE	Irish Office of the Director of Corporate Enforcement
OECD	Organisation for Economic Cooperation and Development
OHADA	Organisation for the Harmonization of Business Laws in Africa
OSB	Office of the Superintendent of Bankruptcy (Canada)
SAL	self-administered liquidation (under Irish Law)
SMEs	small and medium enterprises
SOEs	state-owned enterprise
UNCITRAL	United Nations Commission on International Trade Law
UNIDROIT	International Institute for the Unification of Private Law

List of Contributors

The following notes are summaries of some of the experiences and knowledge brought to this project by the authors.

Prof. Dr Ignacio Tirado, Universidad Autónoma, Madrid, Spain
As of September 2018, Ignacio Tirado is the Secretary General of the International Institute for Unification of Private Law (UNIDROIT). From 2010 to 2012, he worked full-time for the World Bank as Senior Consultant to the Bank's Legal Vice-Presidency. After March 2012, he continued to work part-time as Senior Consultant, first in the Legal Vice-Presidency and, from 2014, in the financial sector. He is co-author of the World Bank's Report on the Observance of Standards and Codes concerning the Debtor/Creditors' Rights and Insolvency Regimes of the following jurisdictions: Mexico, Peru, Paraguay, Kenya, Kosovo, Kazakhstan, Romania, and Bangladesh. Such Reports include assessment and legal reform advice on credit recovery, secured transactions (movable and immovable), banking risk management, credit-reporting systems, and insolvency. He provided technical assistance in legal reform in: Albania (insolvency law reform); Turkey (Financial Sector Assessment Program follow up); Jordan (insolvency law reform); Kazakhstan (with the Ministry of Finance on the reform of the system of corporate (2010–14) and personal (2014–15) insolvency, and design and direction of a judicial training programme (2016–); Thailand (training to state attorneys); Peru (insolvency agency—INDECOPI—and Ministry of Finance: assessment with Business Environment Team; follow-up assistance from ROSC); Kenya (Ministry of Finance and Law Reform Commission; preparation of capacity-building programme for judges and state attorneys; led the legal component of the Completion Report of the Financial and Legal Sector Technical Assistance Project); Poland (Ministry of Justice; assessment of the insolvency system, and work on the reform); the Maldives (elaboration of the Private Sector Legal Scan, including commercial contracts, corporate law, secured transactions, and banking and insolvency law). He worked on the Financial Sector Assessment Program in Paraguay (2011) and Poland (2013). His work with the International Monetary Fund included serving as consultant on insolvency-related matters in Spain in the Article IV Consultation (2013–2016) and adviser to the Financial Sector Assessment Program Team (2017). He was also a Senior Consultant on legal reform for the Pacific Private Sector Development Initiative at the Asian Development Bank. In this capacity, he worked in East Timor on the assessment and reform of the country's secured transactions and insolvency systems.

Dr Rizwaan J. Mokal, South Square Chambers, London, UK
Riz Mokal is a barrister at South Square with a practice extending over all aspects of domestic and cross-border insolvency, restructuring, bank resolution, and trust law. Previously, from 2009 to 2013, Dr Mokal served as Senior Counsel to the World Bank and Head of the Bank's Global Initiative on Insolvency and Creditor/Debtor Regimes. In this capacity, and as Consulting Counsel to the Bank since then, he has worked with the governments of some twenty countries in Africa, Asia, Europe, and the Middle East on reform of insolvency and creditor/debtor systems. His work has involved policy analyses of existing laws and practices, the development of new legislation, and the training of judges, lawyers, insolvency practitioners, central bankers, and other stakeholders. Dr Mokal held the Chair of Law and Legal Theory at University College London until 2016, is currently an Honorary

Professor there and a Visiting Professor at the University of Florence, and has previously held a research position at the University of Cambridge. His scholarship—which ranges over financial sector regulation, insolvency, property and trusts, and legal theory—has influenced law reform in the UK and has been cited with approval by several courts, including the House of Lords, the Australian High Court, and the Courts of Appeal of England and Wales, New Zealand, Ontario, and Victoria. As part of the World Bank's delegation to the United Nations Commission on International Trade Law from 2009 to 2013 and of the United Kingdom delegation since, Dr Mokal has been an active participant in the insolvency law work of the United Nations Commission on International Trade Law (UNCITRAL). He sits on the editorial boards of a number of key publications, including *International Corporate Rescue*, and is a member of the World Bank's Global Insolvency Task Force, the International Insolvency Institute, and the International Exchange of Experience in Insolvency.

Dr Irit Mevorach, University of Nottingham, UK
Dr Irit Mevorach is a Professor of International Commercial Law at the University of Nottingham. Between 1998 and 2003, she practised law at Lipa Meir & Co, Tel Aviv, Israel, as a senior associate in commercial law, and led financing and secured transactions, commercial litigation, and gave advice in corporate restructuring, liquidations, and administrations. Since 2006, Dr Mevorach has been acting as an expert adviser to the UK government's delegation to UNCITRAL and she is the National Correspondent (UK) for Case Law on UNCITRAL Texts (CLOUT). Dr Mevorach was appointed Senior Counsel to the World Bank and worked full-time there between 2013 and 2015. In that capacity, she headed the Bank's Global Initiative on Insolvency and Creditor/Debtor Regimes, has advised the governments of some ten countries in Africa, Asia, Europe, and the Caribbean on reform of business and personal insolvency and creditor/debtor systems, and has participated at the Financial Stability Board, Resolution Legal Expert Group. Dr Mevorach sits on the editorial board of the *Global Restructuring Review* (GRR), and is a member of the World Bank's Global Insolvency Task Force, the International Insolvency Institute, INSOL Europe, and INSOL International. She is the author of *Insolvency within Multinational Enterprise Groups* (Oxford University Press, 2009) and *The Future of Cross-Border Insolvency: Overcoming Biases and Closing Gaps* (Oxford University Press, 2018).

Dr Ronald Davis, Peter A. Allard School of Law, University of British Columbia, Canada
Dr Ronald Davis is Professor Emeritus, University of British Columbia. His research interests are pension law, corporate law, trust law, law and economics, law and society, and insolvency law. He is co-author of *Director and Officer Liability in Corporate Insolvency* (Toronto: LexisNexis, 3rd edn 2015) and is the author of reports on the intersection of insolvency law and pension law for the Ontario Government Commission on Pensions. He has published extensively on pension funds in corporate governance, focusing on the potential exercise of control over these activities by the employee-beneficiaries and whether such control could lead to increased corporate social responsibility. He is the author of books and articles on pension law, corporate governance, and insolvency law, and has presented papers on these topics both nationally and internationally. Professor Davis was called to the Bar of Ontario in 1992, thereafter joining the pension law practice of Koskie Minsky in Toronto. Prior to joining the Allard School of Law in 2003, he taught at the University of Toronto's Law Faculty, as well as Pension and Benefits Law at the Faculty of Law, University of Western Ontario. He has lectured to the Osgoode Hall Law School LLM Specialization in Securities Law Program, as well as to the Investment Management School (sponsored by the Schulich School of Business, York University, and Mercers Consulting), and taught at the Civil Law Symposium of the National Judicial Institute. Since joining the Faculty, Professor Davis has

received the UBC Law Class of '68 Research Award and a University of British Columbia Teaching Development Scholarship.

Prof. Dr Stephan Madaus, Martin Luther University, Halle-Wittenberg, Germany
Dr Madaus is Professor of Civil Law, Civil Procedure, and Insolvency Law at Martin Luther University, Halle-Wittenberg, Germany. In 2017, he prepared an 'In-Depth Analysis' for the European Parliament's Policy Department for Citizens' Rights and Constitutional Affairs at the request of the JURI Committee. It looked at the likely effects on both microenterprises and medium-sized enterprises of the recent European Commission proposed Directive on preventive restructuring frameworks, second chance, and measures to increase the efficiency of restructuring, insolvency, and discharge procedures. It identifies and explains the issues at stake of concerned SMEs related to their capacity as both debtors and creditors. From 2014 to 2017, he led a comparative law analysis of the insolvency and restructuring law and practices in thirteen EU Member States together with Prof. Em. Bob Wessels for the European Law Institute (ELI) in Vienna. The comparative report 'Rescue of Business in Insolvency Law' was approved as an official ELI Instrument in September 2017. It is already available online and will be published by OUP in 2018. Dr Madaus is also a member of the expert group to the German Ministry of Justice for the reform of German insolvency law and is one of three members of a project team that was mandated to evaluate the effects of the 2012 reform for the German Parliament.

Dr Alberto Mazzoni, Università Cattolica del Sacro Cuore, Milan, Italy
Professor Emeritus Alberto Mazzoni's qualifications and teaching positions can be summarized as follows: JD summa cum laude University of Pisa (1965); LLM University of Chicago Law School (1966); Research Fellow at Michigan Law School (1970–1); Professor of Commercial Law at the Universities of Pisa, Genova, Sassari (1974–89); Professor of Commercial Law and International Trade Law, Catholic University of Milan (from 1990 to retirement in 2014); now Professor Emeritus of Commercial Law at the Catholic University of Milan.

Current roles include: President of the Governing Council of UNIDROIT; President of the pre-arbitral Tribunal (Comitato dei Probiviri) of the Milan Stock Exchange; Head of the Italian Delegation at several UNCITRAL Sessions and UNCITRAL Working Groups; Member of the Asian Academy of Comparative Law; Adjunct Professor of the Law School of the University of Macau; Lecturer at the International Arbitration Master Programme at Stockholm University.

Dr Mazzoni's legal career development includes: Associate at Cohen & Meyohas, Paris (1968–70); Associate at White & Case New York (1971–3); Founder and Senior Partner of Mazzoni e Associati, Milan and Rome (1982–2015); now Senior Partner of the law firm Mazzoni Regoli Cariello Pagni.

Justice Barbara Romaine, Court of Queen's Bench, Alberta, Canada
Justice Romaine was appointed to the court in 1997. She practised as a corporate and commercial solicitor for 23 years. She was a partner with the Calgary office of McCarthy Tétrault, involved primarily with national and international project development and financing and securities law. She was President of the Law Society of Alberta in 1997 prior to her appointment. Justice Romaine is a member and former co-chair of the Court's Commercial Practice Group. She is a member of the editorial advisory board of the *Annual Review of Insolvency Law* and has been the co-editor of the *Annual Review of Insolvency Law* for the past five years. She is an International Judicial Affiliate member of the US National Conference of Bankruptcy Judges and a member of the International Insolvency Institute, INSOL

International, the International Women's Insolvency and Restructuring Confederation, the Société de Législation Comparée, the International Exchange of Experience on Insolvency Law, and the Bowen Island MSME Group.

Dr Janis Sarra, Peter A. Allard School of Law, University of British Columbia, Canada
Dr Janis Sarra is Presidential Distinguished Professor, University of British Columbia and Professor of Law, Peter A. Allard School of Law, UBC. In 2015 she held the title of Chair d'État, Collège de France, Paris. She was Director of the Peter Wall Institute for Advanced Studies, UBC and served as Associate Dean of the UBC Faculty of Law. She was founding Director of the National Centre for Business Law and a Senator of the University. She has researched and taught in the areas of insolvency law, corporate and securities law, banking and finance law, law and economics, and contract law. She previously taught advanced corporate law for the Faculty of Law, University of Toronto. Dr Sarra is called to the Bar of Ontario, where she previously served as a commercial and labour arbitrator for many years. She is past director of the Canadian Association of Insolvency and Restructuring Professionals, past director of the Canadian Insolvency Foundation, first INSOL Global Scholar, and member of the Insolvency Institute of Canada, the International Insolvency Institute, INSOL Academics Forum, the European Corporate Governance Network, and UNCITRAL Experts Committee on Cross-Border Corporate Group Insolvencies. Her publications include: *Rescue! The Companies' Creditor Arrangement Act*, (2nd edn, Toronto: Carswell, 2013); *Creditor Rights and the Public Interest, Restructuring Insolvent Corporations* (University of Toronto Press, 2003); *Director and Officer Liability in Corporate Insolvency* (Toronto: LexisNexis, 3rd edn 2015, co-authored with R. B. Davis); and the 2018 *Annotated Bankruptcy and Insolvency Act* (Toronto: Thomson Reuters, 2018); *Failure to Capture the Brass Ring: An Empirical Study of Business Bankruptcies and Proposals under the Canadian Bankruptcy and Insolvency Act in Annual Review of Insolvency Law 2009* (Toronto: Carswell, 2010); and 'An Opportune Moment—Retooling the Bankruptcy and Insolvency Act to Address Micro, Small and Medium Enterprise (MSME) Insolvency in Canada', *Annual Review of Insolvency Law* 2016 (Toronto: Carswell, 2017). She is a member of the Canadian Delegation to UNCITRAL Working Group V on Insolvency Law. In 2017, she received a Lifetime Achievement Award from the Canadian Association of Insolvency and Restructuring Professionals, the Turnaround Management Association, the Annual Review of Insolvency Law, Chordoma Foundation, and the Canadian Cancer Society.

1

Introduction

A. The Modular Approach to MSME Insolvency: An Overview

Micro, small, and medium enterprises (MSMEs or MSME according to context) constitute the bulk and beating heart of virtually all of the world's economies. They are a primary means by which entrepreneurs bring new business propositions to the market and deliver a range of products and services to local economies. They often constitute the most accessible route to employment and typically provide the majority of private sector jobs. They thus deepen and diversify the economy, enhance its resilience, and are key engines of entrepreneurial dynamism and creativity, of wealth and employment.

Whereas larger businesses tend to be robust in a variety of legal and regulatory climates, the ability of MSMEs to survive and thrive is highly sensitive to the quality of their environment. Insolvency regimes,[1] in particular, can have profound effects on whether the social wealth that MSMEs represent is increased, preserved, or destroyed; and on the fairness of distribution of that wealth and those losses. The ability of an economy's commercial lending sector to efficiently work through situations of distress and, in turn, to successfully perform critical financial intermediation functions can be significantly affected by the legal framework governing MSME insolvencies.

Drawing on finance literature, this volume distinguishes between financial and economic distress. A debtor that is unable to meet its obligations as they fall due, but the value of whose assets as a going concern exceeds their piecemeal value, is merely financially distressed. It has a 'going concern surplus' that would be lost if

[1] Two conceptions of insolvency are commonly invoked. 'Cash-flow insolvency' exists when the debtor is unable to meet its payment obligations as they fall due. 'Balance-sheet insolvency' is the state in which the quantum of the debtor's obligations exceeds the value of its assets. References to insolvency in this volume should be understood, depending on context, as including either or both of these notions. 'Imminent insolvency' is the situation where the debtor would be unable to meet future obligations as they fell due; see paragraph 30 of the United Nations Commission on International Trade Law (UNCITRAL) *Legislative Guide on Insolvency Law* (UNCITRAL *Legislative Guide on Insolvency Law*, part two, 25 June 2004) *Guide to Insolvency*. Imminent insolvency characteristically only has legal significance once the entrepreneur discovers or ought reasonably to discover its onset. This is discussed further in Chapter 5. Finally, here, the term 'insolvency' itself is ambiguous between the *factual state* of insolvency defined in one of the foregoing ways and the *legal process* that may be invoked to respond to that factual state. When a reference is intended to the latter legal process, this volume uses terms such as 'insolvency process' and 'insolvency proceedings'.

the relevant assets were to be split from the business. By contrast, an economically distressed debtor is unable to meet its obligations as they fall due and lacks any going concern surplus. That is to say, its stakeholders would receive more value if the assets constituting its business were to be realized piecemeal. In what follows, references to distress as such may, depending on context, suggest financial or economic distress or be intentionally ambiguous between the two.[2]

Different jurisdictions use different terms for entrepreneurs and small-business operators. In this volume, 'entrepreneur' means a natural person trading as a sole proprietor or a member of a partnership, or acting as director or officer of a corporate MSME, who organizes, manages, and/or operates a business enterprise, and who characteristically bears the residual risk irrespective of the MSME's legal form. The term 'debtor' is used to describe the indebted individual entrepreneur, partnership, or corporate entity, particularly one facing actual or imminent insolvency.[3]

Insolvency laws are especially relevant at three critical stages in a MSME's financial life. One key challenge arises when the personal funds of the entrepreneur are no longer sufficient to meet the enterprise's growth potential. Another is when the MSME lacks the resources—financial or technical—to weather a crisis. A third is when the business has failed, often leaving the entrepreneur personally burdened with his obligations. An efficacious insolvency regime would sift through distressed businesses to identify those that remain viable or that have a residual economic or social worth that would be unreasonably destroyed by immediate liquidation,[4] and would provide cost-effective means for their reorganized continuity. Non-viable distressed businesses would be expeditiously dismantled, and their assets recycled to more promising uses. Creditors would receive the highest feasible returns on their claims over an appropriate period, and their resulting confidence in the insolvency regime would to that extent incentivize them to lend more and on more affordable terms. Honest and cooperative entrepreneurs would be extricated from the ruins of a failed business, liberated from obligations that can no longer reasonably be met, and promptly returned to economic productivity. There would be due accountability for any wrongdoing connected with the insolvency.

[2] Rizwaan J. Mokal, *Corporate Insolvency Law—Theory and Application* (Oxford: OUP, 2005) at 194–5.

[3] In some countries with a civil law tradition, the legal term 'entrepreneur' (*imprenditore, empresario,* etc) refers to the person (natural or legal) that acts in the market in its own name and hence bears directly the consequences of its activity. This means, for example, that the director of a company would not be 'legally' an entrepreneur, but only an agent/representative of the entrepreneur (the company). 'Entrepreneur' in that sense would refer to the debtor, that is, to the person with the legal liability for repayment of the debt. In this volume, however, the term 'entrepreneur' is used in a socio-economic manner, as the natural person who masterminds the business activity.

[4] The concept of liquidation is ambiguous in a multitude of ways. It may refer simply to the sale of assets; or to the breakup of a business and piecemeal sale of its constituent assets; or else to the legal process by which an insolvent debtor's business and/or assets are compulsorily sold (usually piecemeal but occasionally as a going concern) in a collective process operating in the interests of creditors as whole. In this volume, context disambiguates references to liquidation. In the text here, for example, the second of the three senses is intended, that is, the dismantling of the debtor's business. This volume also contrasts liquidation with proceedings aimed at the continuation of the distressed MSME business.

Modern insolvency systems typically have been designed with larger enterprises in mind.[5] They assume an extensive insolvency estate of significant worth and the presence of creditors and other stakeholders with sufficient value at stake that participate in and oversee the process. These assumptions undergird mechanisms by which creditors and other stakeholders may ensure that the insolvency process faithfully serves their interests, such as the involvement of an independent professional to run the business undergoing an insolvency process, and extensive judicial oversight.

These assumptions and features are incongruent with reality. The vast majority of businesses entering, and indeed, those in need of, insolvency proceedings are MSMEs, reflecting the general population of businesses and the particular fragility associated with smaller asset bases and relative absence of risk diversification. In a significant portion of MSME insolvencies, little or no value is available for distribution to anyone other than secured creditors, which tend to have effective collection methods under non-insolvency law. Correspondingly, most secured and unsecured creditors, as well as other stakeholders, are rationally disinterested in the insolvency process. In many cases, it is worthwhile for neither the estate nor most stakeholders to engage lawyers to represent them in court. Estates may possess insufficient value even to pay an independent insolvency professional to undertake the legal insolvency process.

Such incongruence between the design of insolvency regimes and the nature of most of the businesses to which they apply leaves the insolvency process unbalanced, inadequately supervised, ineffective, and sometimes simply unfeasible. Policymakers and legislators have often responded through ad hoc changes to the 'standard' regime, such as by shearing some elements of the insolvency process when applied to smaller businesses, shortening statutory timelines, or dispensing with the necessary participation of certain stakeholders. The resulting processes have been marked by arbitrary boundaries, rigid preconditions for availability, and limited effectiveness.

The Modular Approach proposed in this volume systematically rethinks the treatment of MSME insolvency. It is aimed at MSMEs, whether in the form of small legal entities or operated as sole proprietorships. It shares with standard insolvency regimes the core objectives of preserving and maximizing value in the insolvency estate, ensuring distribution over an appropriate period of time of the highest feasible proportion of that value to those individuals and entities entitled to it, providing due accountability for any wrongdoing connected with the insolvency, and enabling discharge of over-indebted natural persons. The Modular

[5] There is a comprehensive body of research on credit networks and relationships; see e.g. Jason Kilborn, 'The 5000-Year Circle of Debt Clemency: From Sumer and Babylon to America and Europe', in *Nederlands Tijdschrift voor Burgerlijk Recht* (2013) 17, 148–52; Gabriele B. Clemens (ed.), *Schuldenlast und Schuldenwert, Kreditnetzwerke in der europäischen Geschichte 1300–1900* (Trier: Kilomedia, 2008 with extensive references to English and French scholarship); David A. Skeel, *Debt's Dominion: A History of Bankruptcy Law in America* (Princeton, NJ: Princeton University Press, 2003); V. Markham Lester, *Victorian Insolvency: Bankruptcy Imprisonment for Debt, and Company Winding-Up in Nineteenth-Century England* (Oxford: Clarendon, 1995).

Approach differs from standard processes, however, in the way it pursues these objectives. Its basic assumption is that the parties to an insolvency case are best placed to select the tools appropriate to that case. The role of the legal regime should be to provide these tools in a maximally flexible way, while creating the correct incentives for their deployment.

Traditionally, insolvency regimes provide particular 'packages' or combinations of these tools and label them 'liquidation' and 'restructuring'. The Modular Approach unpacks those combinations. It assumes a core process, geared towards enabling the entrepreneur to propose how the insolvency process should proceed and to obtain discharge of any unrepayable obligations. The entrepreneur may access any of the full range of insolvency law mechanisms to enable attainment of these objectives. At the same time, creditors and other stakeholders have the right to adequate notice of each step in the process, coupled with the power to override the entrepreneur's choices where a sufficient proportion of them consider it appropriate to do so. In principle, there is no involvement of either an insolvency professional or even a court. The process obtains and retains momentum by virtue of the presumption that stakeholders who have not positively objected to a step in the process have consented to that step and that the failure to exercise procedural rights within the process precludes the relevant stakeholders from objecting to the part of the process to which the unexercised rights relate. Stakeholders are divided into appropriate classes; they must act by stipulated majority by value; and stipulated majorities by value of a class may bind dissenting minorities.

The Modular Approach also responds to differences in the economic, social, and legal circumstances of different countries. It does so by guiding national policymakers with respect to the factors relevant to determining the proper boundaries between standard and MSME insolvency regimes and by identifying three functions: management, administrative, and judicial. The approach explains the costs and benefits of assigning those functions to different entities and proposes options that can fit the circumstances in different countries.

The Modular Approach is designed to provide incentives for the entrepreneur and other stakeholders to select appropriate modules. Under this approach, entrepreneurs have positive incentives to commence the insolvency process in a timely manner. They do not have to declare the debtor insolvent to access the process; they may, in principle, retain management rights; and they have the right to propose how the insolvency process should begin. Entrepreneurs also face negative incentives, such as personal liability, and proportionate legal disabilities that discourage a failure to commence insolvency proceedings in a timely way and/or an abuse of the process.

The Modular Approach acknowledges that in many MSME insolvencies, unsecured creditors are rationally disinterested, given their limited economic stake and the very limited likelihood of any recovery in the process. They need not actively participate in the process if, upon due notice, they do not consider it worth the time and expense of doing so. Their abstention is deemed approval, and the insolvency process may continue apace. Negative incentives for creditor inaction arise because the failure to exercise procedural rights amounts to a waiver of such rights.

Positive incentives arise from the ability of creditors, acting with others who together hold a sufficiently large proportion of the claims against the debtor, to override the entrepreneur's choice of tools and to select a destiny for the business different from the one favoured by the entrepreneur.

B. Structure of the Volume

The structure of this volume is as follows. The rest of this introductory chapter examines the place of MSMEs in the global economy, including challenges for defining MSMEs, and the significance of MSME economic activity. Chapter 2 examines the particular needs of MSMEs in financial distress, analysing why MSME insolvency frameworks should provide a fresh start for natural person entrepreneurs, foster the rehabilitation of viable businesses, prevent further loss of value, and provide cost-effective strategies and mechanisms. Chapter 3 discusses the policy objectives and key components of the Modular Approach, aimed at creating incentives for timely commencement of proceedings, the rescue of viable businesses, the liquidation of non-viable businesses, and the devolvement of choice on stakeholders with the best information and most appropriate incentives for value-maximizing outcomes. Chapter 4 canvasses in detail the design of the Modular Approach, including the basic procedural framework and the due protection of stakeholder rights. This approach offers a menu of modules from which the parties can choose appropriate tools. It also allows national policymakers to choose from a range of options for resolving MSME insolvency and for the involvement of appropriate institutions. Following on from this, chapters 5 and 6 discuss the implementation of the Modular Approach, including the role of key stakeholders and the regulatory and implementation challenges that insolvency systems may face when applying the procedures that the Modular Approach envisages. Chapter 5 focuses on the role and obligations of the MSME entrepreneur, both at times approaching insolvency and during the MSME insolvency process. Chapter 6 considers the position of other stakeholders: unsecured creditors, lenders (including new financiers), the tax authorities, the entrepreneur, or connected persons as guarantors and the MSME employees. Chapter 7 provides examples of how the implementation of the Modular Approach might look in different global economies. Chapter 8 concludes the volume by recapitulating some of its primary themes.

The volume includes three annexes. Annex 1 provides a checklist of actions that should be taken when undertaking a reform of a MSME insolvency regime that incorporates the Modular Approach. Annex 2 describes a survey of trustees and lenders that was commissioned by the Canadian government with the goal of identifying challenges that MSMEs face within Canada's existing insolvency regime. Annex 3 provides sample questions that may be of use when conducting interviews of lawyers who act for insolvent entities and creditors as part of a reform process. We also include an appendix that describes how we began our collaboration and our methodology in completing the volume.

C. MSMEs in the Global Economy

1. No globally consistent definition of MSMEs

There is no globally accepted definition of MSMEs. Across jurisdictions, factors taken as relevant to the identification of this type of business include, among others, annual gross or net revenue, value of assets and/or liabilities, value of sales, legal structure, and number of employees.[6] Table 1.1 illustrates several approaches.

Ardic et al. found that the most common definitions used by regulators are based on the number of employees (the most frequently deployed criterion), sales, and/or loan size.[7] Of sixty-nine countries for which Ardic et al. had data, fifty use the number-of-employees criterion, and thirty-nine out of these fifty also use the other two criteria.[8] A total of forty-one regulators use maximum sales value criterion, fifteen use maximum loan value criterion, and seventeen use the asset volume criterion to define a small and medium enterprise (SME).[9] Figure 1.1 depicts the frequency with which MSMEs are defined by reference to number of employees.

Ardic et al. conclude that the number of employees and sale volumes are likely the most accurate parameters to define an SME, but this information is not always available from lenders. They note that while banks may collect this information at the time of evaluating loan applications, they often do not retain it in their systems.[10] Their study notes that some countries choose to rely on loan size as a proxy for debtor size and thus to define a debtor as a MSME. *Financial Access 2010* reports that only fifteen countries use loan size as relevant to defining an SME; and within this criterion, there is considerable variation among countries.[11]

Ardic et al. also observe that even when MSME data are available, it is extremely difficult to perform a cross-country analysis in the absence of a standard definition as to what constitutes a MSME, given the extent to which definitions vary from country to country.[12]

MSME definitions do not just vary across countries. Different authorities within the same jurisdiction may use different definitions for different purposes. In Canada, for example, Industry Canada defines small business as in Table 1.1, reporting that 98% of the 1.08 million small businesses in Canada in 2013 had one to ninety-nine

[6] Janis Sarra, 'Micro, Small and Medium Insolvent Enterprises: Do We Need Statutory Reform in Canada? First the Data . . . then the Reform', in Janis Sarra and Barbara E. Romaine (eds), *Annual Review of Insolvency Law 2015* (Toronto: Carswell, 2016) (hereafter Sarra, 'Statutory Reform').

[7] Oya Pinar Ardic, Nataliya Mylenko, and Valentina Saltane, 'Small and Medium Enterprises a Cross Country Analysis with a New Data Set' (2012) *Pacific Economic Review*, 17: 4, 498 (hereafter Ardic et al.).

[8] Ibid. [9] Ibid 498–499. [10] Ibid 499. [11] Ibid.

[12] Ibid at 493. An OECD conference on SMEs in 2004 made two key policy recommendations to both member and non-member economies: (i) develop greater international comparability of SME statistics, and (ii) develop a common definition of an SME, citing Second OECD Conference of Ministers Responsible for Small and Medium-Sized Enterprises (Istanbul, 2004) at 4. The conference observes, among other things, that SMEs are commonly defined as registered businesses with fewer than 250 employees (IFC, 2009); the definition still varies from country to country.

Table 1.1 MSME definitions—selected examples

Country/region/entity	Micro	Small	Medium
European Union	Fewer than 10 employees and turnover ≤ € 2 million or balance sheet total of ≤ € 2 million.	Fewer than 50 employees and turnover ≤ € 10 million or balance sheet total of ≤ € 10 million.	Fewer than 250 employees and turnover ≤ € 50 million or balance sheet total of ≤ € 43 million.
United Kingdom	Not defined.	Meets two or more of the following requirements— Turnover not more than £5.6 million. Balance sheet total not more than £2.8 million Number of employees not more than 50.	Meets two or more of the following requirements— Turnover not more than £22.8 million Balance sheet total not more than £11.4 million Number of employees not more than 250.
United States	Not defined.	Engaged in commercial or business activities other than primarily owning or operating real property, with total non-contingent liquidated secured and unsecured debts of $2,566,050 or less. The threshold specified in the Bankruptcy Code adjusts every three years.	Not defined
Canada	With 1 to 4 employees.	With 5 to 99 employees, or in the service industry 5 to 49 employees.	Employing 50 to 499 employees
South Africa	Agricultural with less than 10 employees, other with less than 20 employees; turnover less than R6 million (differentiated by sector).	With less than 50 employees; turnover less than R32 million (differentiated by sector).	Agricultural: with less than 100 employees; other with less than 200 employees; turnover less than R64 million (differentiated by sector)
17 OHADA countries	Not defined.	Sole proprietorship, company, or other legal entity: 0–20 employees, where turnover does not exceed 50,000,000 CFA francs, excluding taxes for 12 months prior.	Not defined
World Bank	With 1 to 4 employees.	With 5 to 30 employees.	With 21 to 100 employees.

Note: See European Union, 'SME Definition—user guide 2015', http://ec.europa.eu/DocsRoom/documents/15582/attachments/1/translations; United Kingdom, ss. 465, 477 of the UK Companies Act, c 46; United States, ch. 1: General Provisions—Section 101 'Definitions'—(51C) and (51D), https://www.usbankruptcycode.org/chapter-1/section-101-definitions; Canada, Innovation, Science and Economic Development Canada, Key Small Business Statistics, June 2016, https://www.ic.gc.ca/eic/site/061.nsf/vwapj/KSBS-PSRPE_June-Juin_2016_eng-V2.pdf/$file/KSBS-PSRPE_June-Juin_2016_eng-V2.pdf. IFC Country Indicators, https://www.smefinanceforum.org/data-sites/msme-country-indicators; Organisation pour l'harmonisation en Afrique du droit des affaires, (Organisation for the Harmonisation of Business Law in Africa) (OHADA), Acte uniforme portant organisation des procédures collectives d'apurement du passif, 2015, (Uniform act on bankruptcy proceedings, 2015), Article 1-3. Note that in some Canadian reports, 'small' is defined as 1–99, thus overlapping with 'micro' definition. Organisation for the Harmonization of Business Laws in Africa (OHADA), Uniform act on bankruptcy proceedings, http://www.ohada.org. Note that in some Canadian reports, 'small' is defined as 1–99, thus overlapping with 'micro' definition.

Sources: European Commission, 2014; UK Companies Act 2006; US Bankruptcy Code; Canada, Market Framework Policy Branch, Industry Canada, 2015; World Bank, 2014; United States Bankruptcy Court services, 2016; Organisation for the Harmonization of Business Laws in Africa (OHADA), Uniform Act on Bankruptcy Proceedings.

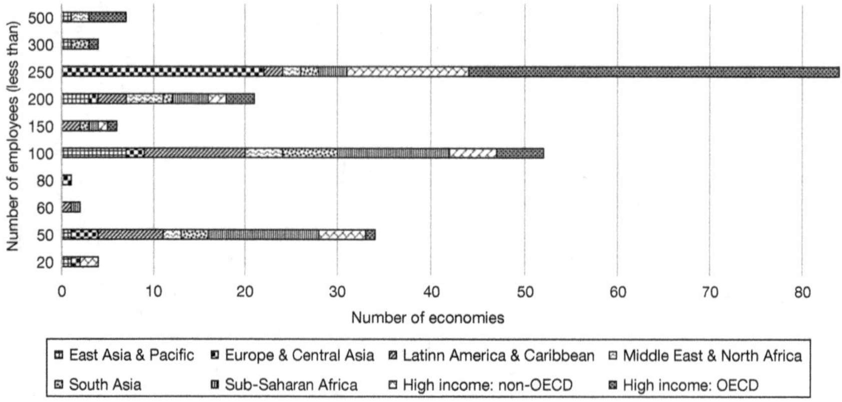

Figure 1.1 Distribution of the MSME 'number of employees' definition.

Note: The number in square brackets following the name of each region signifies the number of economies from that region included in the analysis. The figure uses data from 103 economies. See Kushnir et al., 'MSMEs Around the World' (note 35) 2; IFC, Country Indicators (note 37).

Source: IFC, MSME Country Indicators (note 37).

employees.[13] In contrast, Canada's Office of the Superintendent of Bankruptcy (OSB) defines businesses differently for the purposes of Canada's insolvency legislation as 'any commercial entity or organization other than an individual, or an individual who has incurred 50% or more of total liabilities as a result of operating a business.'[14] Hence, an individual consumer debtor is characterized by the OSB as a business for the purposes of the Bankruptcy and Insolvency Act (BIA), where his or her business-related debts comprise 50% of total debts. This definition is important for the kind of process to which the debtor has access under the BIA.[15]

Also of note is that some jurisdictions use, or are in the process of developing, new definitions that are responsive to particular types of MSME activity. For example, the OHADA (Organisation pour l'harmonisation en Afrique du droit des affaires) countries have introduced new terminology for small entrepreneurs in an effort to promote migration of informal businesses into the formal MSME sector.[16] With support from the World Bank Group, OHADA has revised its general commercial law to introduce the *entreprenant* status. The status can apply to a natural

[13] Industry Canada, Key Small Business Statistics, June 2016.

[14] OSB, *Insolvency Statistics in Canada—March 2017* https://www.ic.gc.ca/eic/site/bsf-osb.nsf/eng/br03747.html. Consumer insolvency is defined as an individual for whom 50% or more of total liabilities relate to consumer goods and services. This lack of alignment of definition has resulted in problems with data analysis.

[15] Bankruptcy and Insolvency Act, RSC 1985, c B-3, as amended (BIA). For a discussion of the Canadian treatment of MSMEs, see Janis Sarra, 'An Opportune Moment—Retooling the Bankruptcy and Insolvency Act to Address Micro, Small and Medium Enterprise (MSME) Insolvency in Canada', in Janis P. Sarra and Barbara E. Romaine (eds), *Annual Review of Insolvency Law 2016* (Toronto: Carswell, 2017) (hereafter Sarra, 'Retooling').

[16] International Finance Corporation, 'An Incentive Package to Encourage Small Business Registration in Benin', http://www.worldbank.org/en/news/feature/2014/03/01/encouraging-small-business-registration-in-benin, March 2014 (hereafter International Finance).

person running a small business who practises any type of limited-turnover activity, be it civil, commercial, artisan, or agricultural.[17]

From an insolvency perspective, a globally uniform definition of a MSME is positively undesirable. MSMEs require special insolvency treatment because standard insolvency proceedings are self-defeatingly resource and time intensive. The costs of extensive involvement in the insolvency process of courts, lawyers, insolvency professionals, creditors, and other stakeholders are not characteristically justified by the benefits of such involvement in the case of MSMEs. This calculus of costs and benefits depends on a myriad of highly jurisdiction-specific factors. The value of routine judicial involvement in the insolvency process depends, among other things, on the number and insolvency expertise of judges, the competing calls on their time, and the availability of other court staff and infrastructure. The fees and expertise of legal and insolvency professionals are important considerations in determining the value each set of these professionals may add to the insolvency process. The degree to which institutional lenders in the country secure their MSME lending and the ways in which commercial counterparties provide trade credit affect the extent to which they and other types of creditors are rationally disinterested in insolvency proceedings. Given these complex and endemic differences amongst jurisdictions, it is inconceivable that a single set of criteria for defining MSMEs would correctly mark the boundary, in all jurisdictions, between the sorts of businesses for which standard court-based insolvency regimes with significant professional and stakeholder involvement would be appropriate and those businesses for which they would not. This is thus a decision best left to the policymakers in each jurisdiction, who are better placed to ascertain the size and other attributes of businesses not well served by their standard insolvency regime.

A crucial definitional issue in respect of micro businesses is that of sole proprietorships. Many jurisdictions define a 'business' as having at least one employee on the payroll.[18] Thus, small business statistics may not count sole proprietorships that do not employ anyone or that employ people as contractors.[19] Further, many small businesses are owned and operated by a single person and may or may not be incorporated. Incorporation of the micro business typically occurs because someone has advised the entrepreneur that incorporation would better protect the entrepreneur's personal assets. In practice, this protection is partial only. Incorporation of a limited liability entity usually precludes the entrepreneur's personal liability for claims such as business tax claims, tort claims against the incorporated entity, and contract counter-party claims. At the same time, micro

[17] Ibid.

[18] Khrystyna Kushnir, Melina Laura Mirmulstein, and Rita Ramalho, 'Counting MSMEs Across the World', IFC 7, http://documents.worldbank.org/curated/en/973331494264489956/text/114823-REVISED-PUBLIC-MSME-Insolvency-report-low-res-final.txt (hereafter Kushnir et al., 'Counting MSMEs').

[19] Sarra, 'Retooling' (n 15). More often, however, sole entrepreneurs with no employees are not excluded from the business count, but rather they are clustered in the group of 'informal businesses' (see, for example, the World Bank Group's Enterprise Finance Gap Methodology, available at https://www.smefinanceforum.org/data-sites/ifc-enterprise-finance-gap).

and small enterprises (MSEs) often cannot get financing unless the entrepreneur guarantees the debt with personal assets.[20] Such guarantees effectively blur the distinction between personal and business debt. It follows, as a matter of practical necessity, that a regime governing MSME insolvency would be required to address the entrepreneur's personal liability.

For similar reasons, a MSME insolvency regime would have to address the entrepreneur's non-business or 'consumer' obligations as well. The boundary between business and consumer obligations is often vague—as when personal credit card loans are invested in the business—and it would not be cost-effective to distinguish between them by investigating the purposes for which a loan was made or the way in which it was spent. In any case, a regime that provided differential treatment for obligations depending on the purposes for which they were incurred would create perverse incentives for the obligations to be disguised. The sensible response is to enable a MSME insolvency regime to deal with all the debts of the natural person entrepreneur. The definition and character of MSMEs require a flexible approach in the design of the insolvency regime.[21]

2. Significance of MSME economic activity

While it has proven difficult to arrive at consistent definitions for MSMEs, there is no denying their immense significance to the global economy. They are a major source of jobs, economic growth, and dynamism in the economy, not least through their potential for utilizing new technologies.[22] The European Economic Area alone has approximately 23 million MSMEs, generating 3.9 trillion euro in value annually and employing 50 million people.[23] In the US, SMEs make up 99% of all firms,[24] employ over 50% of private sector employees, and generate 65% of net new private sector jobs.[25] Similarly, UK MSMEs account for 99.9% of the country's businesses,

[20] See Sarra, ibid.

[21] It is not unusual to find jurisdictions that have some sort of separation of debts and assets depending on the origination of the debts or the use of the assets. These are mostly jurisdictions with a legal framework that stems from the old system of separate European codes (with commercial and civil codes as separate bodies of legislation). However, even in those countries, the dissociated allocation of assets and liabilities is only 'of first degree': at most, certain assets are earmarked for prior payment of tax debts, or, more frequently, assets allocated to one of the two categories must be exhausted before the same creditor can seize assets from the other category. In the end, though, all creditors can access all assets. This earmarking of assets to prior payment of certain debts is being abandoned as countries modernize their legislations. This form of earmarking should not be confused with modern forms of non-recourse funding (see, for example, in Italy, the *patrimoni destinati ad uno specifico affare:* art. 2447 bis of the Italian Civil Code) that are the mainstay of project finance for large entities. This type of structure is not used in the province of MSMEs.

[22] International Finance (n 16).

[23] European Commission, Annual Report, http://ec.europa.eu/growth/smes/business-friendly-environment/performance-review-2016_en. See also European Commission, 'Declaring your enterprise to be an SME', Commission communication—Model declaration on the information relating to the qualification of an enterprise as an SME, Official Journal C 118, 20/05/2003 P. 0005–0015, http://eur-lex.europa.eu/legal-content/EN/TXT/?uri=CELEX:52003XC0520(02).

[24] Defined in their study as firms with fewer than 500 employees, Shahin Firoozmand, Philip Haxel, Euijin Jung, and Kati Suominen, 'State of SME Finance in the United States in 2015', Tradeup and Nextrade Group, March 2015.

[25] Ibid 2.

provide 60% of all private sector employment, and account for 47% of private sector turnover.[26]

The immense significance of MSMEs to the US and European economies is broadly representative of the global picture. Kushnir et al. report that there are 125 million 'formal' MSMEs in 132 countries for which data are collected by the International Finance Corporation (IFC), including 89 million in emerging markets.[27] Formal MSMEs are more common in high-income economies, but in low- and middle-income economies, MSME density is rising at a faster pace.[28] The overwhelming majority of formal MSMEs globally, 83%, are defined as micro enterprises, having one to nine employees.[29] The data collected in most jurisdictions cover only the formal registered sector;[30] it is important to note that, particularly in emerging countries, informal MSMEs often outnumber largely formal ones. For example, in India in 2007, there were fewer than 1.6 million registered MSMEs, but 26 million unregistered.[31]

Globally, studies indicate that there are 31 MSMEs per 1,000 population over the 132 economies for which the IFC collects data.[32] Economies with higher per capita income tend to have more formal MSMEs per 1,000 people. Latin America and the Caribbean have more MSMEs per 1,000 people than non-OECD (Organisation for Economic Co-operation and Development) high-income economies. However, when the countries that are heavily dependent on mineral resources[33] are excluded, the MSME density of non-OECD high-income economies is at a similar level to that of Latin America and the Caribbean.[34] Globally, the number of MSMEs per 1,000 people grew by 6% per year from 2000 to 2009, with Europe and Central Asia experiencing the biggest increase.[35] Figure 1.2, based on the IFC data, illustrates MSME density in relation to population.[36]

Formal MSMEs employ more than one-third of the world's labour force.[37] In Canada, for example, small businesses employ 8.2 million employees, comprising 71% of the total private sector labour force, and accounted for 87.7% of net employment change between 2005 and 2015 (1.2 million jobs).[38] In the European Union,

[26] Department for Business, Energy and Industrial Strategy, *Business population estimate for the UK and regions: 2016 statistical release* (13 October 2016), https://www.gov.uk/government/uploads/system/uploads/attachment_data/file/559219/bpe_2016_statistical_release.pdf.

[27] By formal is meant recognized within the regulatory structures of a country, such as for taxation purposes. Kushnir et al., 'Counting MSMEs' (n 18) 2.

[28] Ibid. [29] Ibid, the authors defining micro as one to nine employees.

[30] Ibid, except for sixteen economies where data is available. [31] Ibid. [32] Ibid.

[33] Which include United Arab Emirates, Qatar, Oman, Kuwait, and Saudi Arabia, ibid 4.

[34] Ibid.

[35] Khrystyna Kushnir, Melina Laura Mirmulstein, and Rita Ramalho, 'Micro, Small, and Medium Enterprises Around the World: How Many Are There, and What Affects the Count?' (2010) MSME Country Indicators 4; https://www.ifc.org/wps/wcm/connect/9ae1dd80495860d6a482b519583b6d16/MSME-CI-AnalysisNote.pdf?MOD=AJPERES (hereafter Kushnir et al. 'MSMEs Around the World'). They suggest that a possible contributing factor may be the accession of the Eastern European economies to the European Union.

[36] Figure 1.2 is taken from the International Financial Corporation ('IFC'), *MSME Country Indicators*, http://www.ifc.org/wps/wcm/connect/Industry_EXT_Content/IFC_External_Corporate_Site/Industries/Financial+Markets/msme+finance/sme+banking/msme-countryindicators.

[37] Kushnir et al. 'MSMEs Around the World' (n 35).

[38] Industry Canada, *Key Small Business Statistics June 2016* (figures are for 2015). The job-creation figures represent the period from 2002–12; https://www.ic.gc.ca/eic/site/061.nsf/vwapj/KSBS-PSRPE_August-Aout2013_eng.pdf/$FILE/KSBS-PSRPE_August-Aout2013_eng.pdf (Industry Canada), discussed in Sarra, 'Statutory Reform' (n 6).

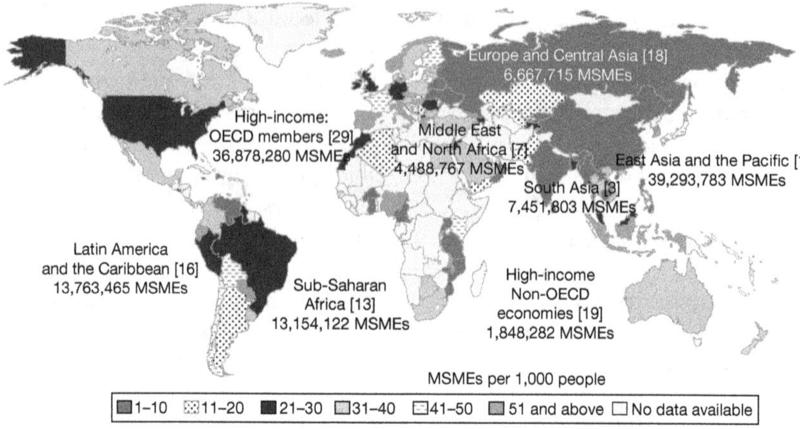

Figure 1.2 MSME density per 1,000 population.
Source: IFC, MSME Country Indicators (note 36).

9.4 million jobs were created in the MSME sector in the twenty-seven European Union countries between 2002 and 2008.[39] From a regional perspective, East Asia and the Pacific have the highest ratio of MSME employment to total employment, driven largely by China, where formal MSMEs account for 80% of total employment.[40] The OECD countries report that MSMEs with fewer than 250 employees account for two-thirds of the formal work force.[41]

Thus, the economic activity of MSMEs is highly significant globally, whether countries are developed or emerging, and whether from the global North or global South. It is therefore critically important that insolvency systems are directly responsive to the specific challenges facing entrepreneurs and their MSMEs. The brief overview in this chapter sets a context for the discussion in the next chapter on why it is timely and necessary to develop a new approach to meet these challenges.

[39] Ardic et al. (n 7) 491. [40] Kushnir et al. 'MSMEs Around the World' (n 35) 4.

[41] Ardic et al. (n 7) 493, citing Beck et al., 2008b; Dietrich, 2010. The numbers are more spectacular in developing nations. According to the World Bank Group, the percentage of full-time labour force originated in microbusinesses in developing nations is around two thirds of the total workforce. See https://www.smefinanceforum.org/data-sites/ifc-enterprise-finance-gap#field-data-sites-tabs-tab-4.

2

The MSME Insolvency Status Quo

This chapter examines specific challenges faced by micro, small, and medium enterprises (MSMEs or MSME according to context). These challenges arise from factors such as size, lack of available collateral, undiversified nature, and lack of suitable external governance mechanisms, all of which contribute to a high MSME failure rate. This chapter discusses the need for cost-effective insolvency regimes tailored to the specific circumstances of MSMEs and the problems inherent in the development of such regimes. It also summarizes key features of existing insolvency law that attempt to address MSME insolvency and why such efforts are often inadequate.

A. Size and Susceptibility

Just as MSMEs are significant contributors to the global economy, they also fail in significant numbers. The Organisation for Economic Co-operation and Development (OECD) has observed that MSMEs are particularly vulnerable to macroeconomic and financial shocks, reporting that MSME insolvencies in Denmark, Italy, Spain, and Ireland exceeded 25% of total insolvencies in 2007–8.[1] A US study found that in 1999, 80% of US firms that filed for bankruptcy reported assets under 1 million USD, and 88% reported employing fewer than twenty people.[2]

One reason why most insolvency proceedings involve MSMEs is simply that they constitute the largest proportion of private sector businesses. In addition, however, smaller businesses may lack the types of physical assets acceptable to financial lenders as collateral. MSMEs tend to be relatively undiversified as to both suppliers and customers and suffer higher default risk upon the loss of a significant counterparty, or even from late payments. MSMEs also tend to be overrepresented in economic sectors characterized by discretionary spending, such as hospitality and construction.[3] They may lack suitable internal governance mechanisms and may be unable to

[1] Organisation for Economic Co-operation and Development, 'The Impact of the Global Crisis on SME and Entrepreneurship Financing and Policy Responses', 2009 (OECD).

[2] Elizabeth Warren, Jay L. Westbrook, 'Financial Characteristics of Business in Bankruptcy' (1999) *American Bankruptcy Law Journal*, 73: 499–589.

[3] See e.g. Paul Orton, Jake Ansell, and Galina Andreeva, 'Exploring the Performance of Small- and Medium-Sized Enterprises through the Credit Crunch' (2015) *Journal of the Operational Research Society* 66(4): 657–63.

afford specialist credit- and risk-management expertise.[4] These limitations not only constrain MSME growth potential, but give rise to significant vulnerability, especially, but not only, in times of stress or crisis.[5] They may result in untimely filing of insolvency proceedings, failure to prevent further downward spiralling of finances, failure to deal with operational and financial deficiencies, and a lack of resources to hire effective expertise to deal with the insolvency. Such limitations relating to small-scale business likely explain MSMEs' particular vulnerability to insolvency.

In addition to internal factors contributing to distress, there are also issues external to the MSME itself, in particular, the issue of the obligations of institutional lenders, which is discussed in Chapter 6.

B. The Importance of Insolvency Law

Insolvency regimes that are responsive to the needs of MSMEs are crucial. Insolvency law is broadly recognized as an essential tool in a properly functioning economic framework.[6] A balance of mechanisms that allow for timely and effective liquidation, but also for a fresh start for entrepreneurs and rehabilitation of viable businesses, tends to enhance creditor recoveries and confidence. In turn, such mechanisms can stimulate greater volumes of lending,[7] at longer maturity periods,[8] at lower cost,[9] and with lower levels of collateral.[10] They can also offer an effective framework for the

[4] For a literature survey revealing mixed evidence on the relationship between corporate governance quality, debtor size, and incidence of debtor failure; see Ibtehal Orabi Awad and Ibrahim Raslan Hegazy, 'Reviewing the Implications of Corporate Governance, Corporate Social Responsibility on Corporate Failure in the Literature: Developing Countries' (2016) *Journal of Emerging Trends in Economics and Management Sciences (JETEMS)*, 7.1: 22–230.

[5] MSMEs are generally vulnerable, independently of the existence of an economic crisis in the jurisdiction. Economic literature has shown that the survival of a business is directly related to its size, in part because the larger enterprises have more and cheaper access to financial capital (see the classic analysis of David B. Audretsch, 'New Firm Survival and the Technological Regime' (1991) *The Review of Economics and Statistics*, 73: 441 et seq.). In the United States, for example, only about 50% of new small businesses survive beyond the fourth year, and around 40% beyond the fifth: see, with similar data and results, Brian Headd, 'Redefining Business Success: Distinguishing between Closure and Failure' (2003) in *Small Business Economics*, 21: 51 et seq; and Hanas A. Cader and John c. Leatherman, 'Small Business Survival and Sample Selection Bias' (2011) in *Small Business Economics*, 37: 155 et seq.

For a more in-depth treatment of these issues concerning microbusinesses, see Louis Gullifer and Igancio Tirado, 'Financing Microbusinesses and UNCITRAL's Model Law on Secured Transactions' (2017) *Uniform Law Review*, 22(4).

[6] The Financial Stability Board, which monitors the global financial system, recognizes 'Insolvency and Creditor Rights' as one of fourteen policy domains 'designated as key for sound financial systems', in which internationally recognized 'best practice standards' are considered as 'deserving of priority implementation depending on country circumstances.' Financial Stability Board, *Key Standards for Sound Financial Systems* (http://www.fsb.org/what-we-do/about-the-compendium-of-standards/key_standards/, accessed 7 March 2016).

[7] Joseph P.H. Fan, Sheridan Titman, and Garry Twite, 'An International Comparison of Capital Structure and Debt Maturity Choices' (2012) *Journal of Financial and Quantitative Analysis*, 47(1): 23–56.

[8] Ibid.

[9] See e.g. Jun Qian and Philip E. Strahan, 'How Laws and Institutions Shape Financial Contracts: The Case of Bank Loans' (2007) *The Journal of Finance*, 1 Dec, 62(6): 2803–34.

[10] Sergey A. Davydenko and Julian R. Franks, 'Do Bankruptcy Codes Matter? A Study of Defaults in France, Germany, and the UK' (2008) *The Journal of Finance*, 1 Apr, 63(2): 565–608.

creation of new business activity.[11] Credible restructuring schemes can ensure that businesses with viable going-forward business plans can survive, in turn preserving jobs, supply contracts, customer goodwill, and economic stability more generally.[12] From a macrofinancial perspective, effective insolvency laws enable financial institutions to resolve problem assets more effectively, thereby freeing up provisioned funds, strengthening investors' perception of financial sector stability, improving the ability of banks to lend, and thus particularly benefitting small and medium enterprises in many economies where such businesses are particularly dependent on bank funding.[13] The World Bank Group has observed that effective insolvency systems enhance predictability and thus lender confidence in loan recovery on default, which encourages more lending and leads to financial inclusion for more businesses.[14]

Of significance for MSMEs globally are both the formal legal rules and informal societal rules and practice norms that affect entrepreneurs, including the design of insolvency laws, the structure of capital markets, and the perception of stigma related to personal responsibility when a business starts to fail.[15] Cost-effective insolvency proceedings can encourage inefficient firms to exit, encourage greater entrepreneurial activity and new firm creation, and result in greater returns to creditors.[16] Timely resolution of distress can reduce uncertainty for entrepreneurs, creditors, and management, and improve asset value and transparency.[17] An effective functioning MSME insolvency regime can alleviate the downside risk of a venture, in turn increasing the number and variety of people pursuing entrepreneurial activities.[18] It can benefit lenders because of certainty in recovery rules, in turn increasing confidence in lending.

Nor are insolvency regimes only relevant to one end of the MSME life cycle. Access to credit is particularly important for MSMEs. The global MSME lending volume is estimated to be 10 trillion USD, of which 70% is in high-income OECD

[11] See e.g. John Armour and Douglas J. Cumming, 'Bankruptcy Law and Entrepreneurship' (2008) *American Law and Economics Review*, 10(2): 303–50, (hereafter Armour and Cumming), and Seung H. Lee, Yasuhiro Yamakawa, Mike W. Peng, and Jay B. Barney, 'How Do Bankruptcy Laws Affect Entrepreneurship Development Around the World?' (2011) *Journal of Business Venturing*, 26(5): 505–20.

[12] See e.g. Edith S. Hotchkiss, Kose John, Robert M. Mooradian, and Karin Thorburn, 'Bankruptcy and the Resolution of Financial Distress' (2011) in *Handbook of Empirical Corporate Finance: Empirical Corporate Finance*, 2: 235.

[13] Shekhar Aiyar, Wolfgang Bergthaler, Jose M. Garrido, Anna Ilyina, Andreas Jobst, Keneth Kang, Dmitriy Kovtun, Yan Liu, Dermot Monaghan, and Marina Moretti, 'A Strategy for Resolving Europe's Problem Loans' (IMF Staff Discussion Note, SDN/15/19, September 2015).

[14] Antonia Menezes (2014) 'Debt Resolution and Business Exit: Insolvency Reform for Credit Entrepreneurship and Growth'. Public policy for the private sector: Note no. 343, Washington, DC; World Bank Group, at 3.

[15] Seung H. Lee, Mike W. Peng, and Jay B. Barney, 'Bankruptcy Law and Entrepreneurship Development: A Real Options Perspective', (2007) *Academy of Management Review*, 32(1): 257–72 (hereafter Lee et al.); Mike W Peng, 'Institutional Transitions And Strategic Choices', (2003) *Academy of Management Review*, 28(2): 275–96.

[16] Elena Cirmizi, Leora Klapper, and Mahesh Uttamchandani (2010) 'The Challenges of Bankruptcy Reform', Policy Research Working Paper 5448, World Bank Development Research Group Finance and Private Sector Development Team, 4 (hereafter Cirmizi et al.).

[17] Ibid 5. [18] Lee et al. (n 15).

countries.[19] On average, small and medium enterprise loans constitute 13% of GDP in developed countries and 3% in developing countries.[20] In a survey of 130,000 firms in 135 countries, the World Bank Group found that there is unmet demand for bank loans and lines of credit in developing regions, particularly Africa.[21] The survey found that, while almost 60% of businesses require a loan at some point, just over a third of businesses have a loan or line of credit.[22] The survey results revealed that well-designed insolvency laws are a factor in accessing credit, directly related to creditor confidence in the ability to recover.[23] In turn, access to credit can assist with fostering entrepreneurship and the creation of new business activity.

Unsurprisingly, the effectiveness of insolvency laws varies among countries around the world.[24] According to a survey on debt enforcement in eighty-eight countries, referenced by a World Bank Research Paper, many existing insolvency procedures are time-consuming, costly, and inefficient in being able to preserve the business as a going concern. In only 36% of countries is the business likely to be preserved as a going concern, and an average of 48% of the business's value is lost in debt enforcement.[25] The World Bank Group *Doing Business 2017* report found that the secured creditor recovery rate in distress scenarios is one of the most valuable measures for doing business, as failure is part of taking risks and there needs to be a well-developed system in place for closing businesses that do not succeed.[26]

The World Bank also examined MSMEs that had defaulted on bank loans and found that differences in the level of creditor rights in insolvency in different jurisdictions had an impact on lending terms, particularly terms used by bank creditors, and that legislative reform regarding liquidation led to a decrease in interest rates, although reorganization reform had the opposite effect.[27] Moreover, a research study for the International Monetary Fund (IMF) reports that six years after the commencement of the global financial crisis, the problems of high levels of corporate

[19] Oya Pinar Ardic, Nataliya Mylenko, and Valentina Saltane 2, 'Small and Medium Enterprises: A Cross Country Analysis with a New Data Set' (2012) *Pacific Economic Review*, 17: 4, 494.

[20] Ibid.

[21] The World Bank Group, 'Debt Resolution and Business Exit', *Viewpoint* July 2014, http://documents.worldbank.org/curated/en/912041468178733220/pdf/907590VIEWPOIN003430Debt0Resolution.pdf at 3 (hereafter World Bank 'Debt Resolution').

[22] Ibid. [23] Ibid.

[24] See e.g. Oscar Couwenberg, 'Survival Rates in Bankruptcy Systems: Overlooking the Evidence' (2001) *European Journal of Law and Economics*, 1 Nov; 12(3): 253–73; and Stijn Claessens and Leora F. Klapper, 'Bankruptcy Around the World: Explanations of Its Relative Use' (2005) *American Law and Economics Review*, 20 Mar; 7(1): 253–83.

[25] Cirmizi et al. (n 16) 6.

[26] World Bank 'Doing Business 2017', http://www.doingbusiness.org/~/media/WBG/DoingBusiness/Documents/Annual-Reports/English/DB17-Report.pdf. The recovery rate is recorded as cents on the dollar recovered by secured creditors through judicial reorganization, liquidation, or debt-enforcement (foreclosure or receivership) proceedings. The calculation takes into account the outcome: whether the business emerges from the proceedings as a going concern or the assets are sold piecemeal.

[27] Cirmizi et al. (n 16) 3.

debt and non-performing loans persist in several European countries.[28] It found that SMEs in general are more leveraged and reliant on bank financing than large firms and have significantly higher non-performing loan ratios. It also found that, given the large number of SMEs and their small size and heavy reliance on collateral, SME loan restructuring is more costly and riskier for banks than restructuring lending to large firms, and current frameworks are ill-suited to SMEs, both in the ways they limit restructuring options and in how they prevent speedy enforcement against collateral and subsequent exit.[29]

C. One Size or Strategy for MSME Insolvency Will Not Fit All

The public policy in many jurisdictions is to encourage the formation and growth of MSMEs, yet that policy does not necessarily align with the treatment financially distressed MSMEs receive. Insolvency processes in many countries are too expensive and unwieldy for MSMEs. As noted previously, the broad range of definitions for MSMEs across jurisdictions is highly problematic in terms of conceptualizing one insolvency framework that is responsive to the multiple different challenges facing MSMEs. One size does not fit all.

Often, on MSME insolvency, there are few or no assets to realize. Liquidation is the most prevalent outcome, which can result in loss of value to creditors and debtors. Insolvency regimes not designed to address MSME failure can fail to distinguish viable businesses from non-viable ones.

Owners of small businesses usually need to secure business loans with their personal assets or personal guarantees, creating a convergence and blurring of distinctions between personal and business liability in practice, a factor not accounted for in most insolvency law regimes globally. Researchers have observed that while the personal guarantee of a firm's owner might encourage a level of financial discipline in countries without a personal insolvency framework, a single business failure can doom an owner to a lifetime of outstanding debt,[30] effectively preventing such individuals from re-entering the market as experienced entrepreneurs.[31] Evidence suggests that exactly the opposite approach better serves standard public policy objectives. One study that compared self-employment in fifteen countries in Europe and North America from 1990–2005 found that the more forgiving the personal

[28] Wolfgang Bergthaler, Kenneth Kang, Yan Liu, and Dermot Monaghan, 'Tracking Small and Medium Sized Enterprise Problem Loans in Europe', European Department, Legal Department, and Monetary and Capital Markets Department, International Monetary Fund, March 2015, 6. See also Adrian Alter and Selim Elekdag, 'Emerging Market Corporate Leverage and Global Financial Conditions', IMF Working Paper, December 2016, https://www.imf.org/external/pubs/ft/wp/2016/wp16243.pdf, which reports that the debt of nonfinancial firms in emerging markets has quadrupled over the past decade.

[29] Ibid.

[30] Mahesh Uttamchandani and Antonia Menezes (2010), 'Freedom to Fail: Why Small Business Insolvency Regimes are Critical for Emerging Markets', *International Corporate Rescue*, no. 4, vol. 7. Chase Cambria Publishing Co., http://www.chasecambria.com/site/journal/article.php?id=488.

[31] Armour and Cumming (n 11).

insolvency laws, measured particularly by reference to the time a bankrupt individual has to wait to be discharged from pre-insolvency debts, combined with ready access to limited liability protections—the more entrepreneurial activity was enhanced.[32]

The failure to recognize this convergence of personal and business debt means that debtors may have access to effective liquidation or rehabilitation schemes only if they fit within very specific criteria. For example, in Canada a highly streamlined mechanism for MSME businesses exists under Division II consumer proposal provisions of the Bankruptcy and Insolvency Act (BIA), accessible to self-employed individuals and sole proprietors whose debts are less than 250,000 CAD (approximately 200,000 USD), excluding a mortgage or hypothec on the individual's principal residence, if 50% or more of their debts are business related.[33] But these mechanisms are not available where the individual has incorporated the business.

D. The International Regulatory and Policy Context

As noted, modern insolvency laws have tended to be designed with larger entities in mind. They generally envisage two key comprehensive types of proceedings, one for liquidation and another for reorganization. Such proceedings involve insolvency professionals, the supervision of the court, and other oversight mechanisms, such as a creditors' committee. These proceedings are often unwieldy and too expensive for smaller businesses. They may also lack adequate mechanisms to deal with the effect of business insolvency on individual entrepreneurs, particularly on their ability to make a fresh start.

More recent efforts have increasingly been oriented toward smaller-scale debtors. Legal systems around the world have attempted to introduce or reform their insolvency laws in terms of their application to individual consumers, and the notions of a discharge from remaining unpaid debt and a fresh start for debtors are gaining traction. An IMF Working Paper from 2013 noted, for example, that:

> Estonia, Iceland, Italy, Latvia, Lithuania, and Poland adopted or amended the personal insolvency law. The Irish Parliament recently adopted an entirely new personal insolvency law to, inter alia, shorten the discharge period from 12 years to 3 years subject to certain conditions. The German government is also considering a reform of the personal insolvency regime that includes a shortening of the discharge period.[34]

[32] Ibid, citing John Armour (2008).

[33] Janis Sarra, 'An Opportune Moment—Retooling the Bankruptcy and Insolvency Act to Address Micro, Small and Medium Enterprise (MSME) Insolvency in Canada', in Janis P. Sarra and Barbara E. Romaine (eds), *Annual Review of Insolvency Law 2016* (Toronto: Carswell, 2017) (hereafter Sarra, 'Retooling').

[34] See Yan Liu and Christoph B. Rosenberg, 'Dealing with Private Debt Distress in the Wake of the European Financial Crisis: A Review of the Economics and Legal Toolbox,' IMF Working Paper WP/13/44 (February 2013), 14. Since then, for example, the Irish law has been enacted and is in force, and in 2014 Germany reduced discharge periods for debtors that are able to pay procedural costs (five years) or 35% of claims (three years). Austria introduced amendments to its personal bankruptcy process in 2017 aimed at facilitating debt relief and allowing individuals whose businesses fail a more rapid fresh start. The changes to the law include a significant shortening of the debt-settlement process that can lead to a discharge from residual debt, and the removal of the requirement that a certain minimum has been paid at the end of the period before a discharge can be granted.

Additionally, new proceedings and tools to prevent insolvency are being contemplated, whereby the debtor may be able to access an insolvency process more quickly and at an early stage. Notably, several European countries have reformed their laws in recent years to provide more rescue oriented solutions. For example, Germany reformed its restructuring regime in 2012; Spain introduced the 'homologated refinancing agreements' and the 'out-of-court agreements on payments', a MSME-specific procedure, in 2013 (with further substantial amendments in 2015) and Romania generally modernized its insolvency law in 2014, including preventive mechanisms, the concordat and the ad hoc mandate.[35]

At the regional level, the EU Commission has identified a need for reform and harmonization of aspects of the insolvency regimes of Member States. In 2016 the Commission made 'a proposal for a Directive on preventive restructuring frameworks, second chance and measures to increase the efficiency of restructuring, insolvency and discharge procedures and amending Directive 2012/30/EU (EU proposal for a Directive on preventive restructuring frameworks and second chance).[36] The proposal's main aim is 'to enhance the rescue culture in the EU'.[37] It seeks to encourage entrepreneurial activity by avoiding stigmatization of business failure and by providing an opportunity for a second chance.[38]

These developments internationally will likely have important implications for MSMEs, yet they are not tailored for MSMEs. Consumer insolvency laws address a subset of MSMEs that are not incorporated, and they might not address the business aspects of the distress situation adequately. Restructuring frameworks aimed at preventing insolvency may enhance the feasibility of business continuation, yet fail to benefit MSMEs because they lack mechanisms geared toward their specific needs and vulnerabilities.

In Africa, a number of countries such as Kenya (2015), Malawi (2014), Mauritius (2009), the Seychelles (2013), and Uganda (2011) have revised their insolvency regimes, enacting a unified insolvency law that covers individuals,

[35] Ibid, p 11, noting that:

> Corporate insolvency reforms undertaken in the wake of the recent financial crisis focus on better supporting the early rescue of viable firms.... Recognizing the importance of insolvency law in tackling the economic consequences of over indebtedness, several European countries including Latvia, Moldova, Portugal and Ukraine ... have introduced fast track court approval procedures.... Italy, Moldova and Serbia also introduced pre-packaged procedures, which provide for expeditious court approval of pre-negotiated restructuring plans that bind minority creditors.

[36] COM(2016) 723 final. The proposal followed the earlier recommendations on a new approach to business failure and insolvency (European Commission, Recommendation of 12 March 2014 on a new approach to business failure and insolvency, C(2014) 1500 final).

[37] Ibid. p. 6.

[38] Ibid. The European Directive proposal has, however, been criticized for not devoting enough attention to MSMEs. In fact, most of its provisions are clearly designed for large corporations. An analysis of the Proposal with regard to MSMEs, commissioned by the European Parliament, can be read at: Stephan Madaus, 'The Impact on SMEs of the Proposal of Preventive Restructuring, Second Chance and Improvement Measures', available at http://www.europarl.europa.eu/thinktank/en/document.html?reference=IPOL_IDA(2017)583151.

unincorporated businesses, and corporations.[39] The goal is to provide lenders with more certainty and predictability with respect to recovery on defaulted loans and thereby to increase confidence in lending to MSMEs.[40] New insolvency laws in Malawi, the Seychelles, and Zimbabwe have created the individual voluntary arrangement (IVA), modelled on the UK procedure. A natural person business owner can enter into an arrangement with his or her creditors on a voluntary basis, aimed at a quick and inexpensive procedure that avoids the debtor being declared formally bankrupt.[41] Uganda and Kenya[42] also have similar provisions, which permit a debtor to obtain an interim order, the effect of which is to temporarily suspend enforcement against the debtor for a few weeks.[43] In order to be granted an interim order, the debtor has to commit to presenting a proposal of a plan of arrangement to the creditors, which is then considered at a creditors' meeting. Kenya's law sets out an even more expedited process where a person lacks any realisable assets.[44] Most of these laws exempt the tools and equipment necessary to the bankrupt's employment or business from liquidation.[45] However, some of these statutes impose limits on debtors' activities, such as prohibiting them from taking part in the management or control of any business, with a penalty of up to two years' imprisonment in case of contravention.[46] Such provisions work against a fresh start for entrepreneurs and create a disincentive to commence insolvency proceedings. Martinez observes that several African jurisdictions have the objective of releasing the debtor from ongoing debt obligations, essential for debtors to continue to contribute to the economy after an insolvency process, but that some laws leave discharge to the discretion of the court after hearing the views or recommendation of the official receiver, making it possible that a debtor's future income is destined to remain committed to the repayment of the old debts for an indefinite period of time.[47]

In 2015 the Organisation for the Harmonization of Business Laws in Africa (OHADA), comprising seventeen West African States, adopted a revised uniform insolvency law, directly applicable in all member state jurisdictions, which provides for a new simplified regulation of MSMEs.[48] The OHADA insolvency

[39] Andrés Martinez, 'Micro, Small and Medium Enterprise Insolvency in Africa: A Comparative Study', paper presented at UNCITRAL's 50th Anniversary Colloquium, available at http://www.uncitral.org/pdf/english/congress/Papers_for_Programme/135-MARTINEZ-SME_Enterprise_Insolvency_in_Africa.pdf (hereafter Martinez). Lesotho and Zimbabwe are also currently drafting unified insolvency legislation.

[40] World Bank, 'Debt Resolution' (n 21).

[41] Martinez (n 39). In Malawi, the provisions dealing with individual voluntary arrangements also contain a provision allowing for a fast-tracked individual voluntary arrangement.

[42] Ibid, citing Article 31 Uganda's insolvency law (2011) and Article 161 (2) Kenya Insolvency Act (2015).

[43] Ibid. [44] Ibid at 6.

[45] For example, the Seychelles' new insolvency law exempts 'tools, books, vehicles and other items of equipment as are necessary to the bankrupt for use personally by him or her in his or her employment business or vocation' up to a specified maximum value. Art. 28 (2) Seychelles insolvency act (2013), discussed in Martinez (n 39) at 7.

[46] Ibid at 7, citing Art. 152 Kenya Insolvency Act (2015).

[47] Ibid, citing Art. 42 (3) Uganda's insolvency law (2011).

[48] Organisation pour l'harmonisation en Afrique du droit des affaires, (Organisation for the Harmonisation of Business Law in Africa) (OHADA), Acte uniforme portant organisation des procédures collectives d'apurement du passif, 2015, (Uniform act on bankruptcy proceedings, 2015).

law specifically includes small businesses and natural person owners of unincorporated businesses and applies to every natural person undertaking an independent professional, civil, commercial, artisanal, or agricultural activity, as well as every legal person in private law, including public enterprises. MSMEs have the option of selecting simplified proceedings, but are not obliged to do so. The simplified proceedings apply to three of the four procedures set out in the law, *règlement préventif* (preventive settlement); *redressement judiciaire* (reorganization), and *liquidation des biens* (liquidation).

Pursuant to L'Acte uniforme portant organisation des procédures collectives d'apurement du passif, 2015, the simplified provisions for *règlement préventif* provide that any small business may open proceedings before the business is in a state of insolvency. The procedure can be opened even if no plan has yet been developed; the debtor must disclose its financial situation, but there is no requirement for audited and comprehensive cashflow or other financial statements.[49] The restructuring plan must be prepared by the debtor with the assistance of the administrator and can have more simplified content than a plan under general proceedings. An agreement with creditors must be reached within two months, with a possible brief extension of fifteen days. Under *redressement judiciaire*, the filing must be made by an insolvent debtor within thirty days of insolvency, using the cashflow test (but with fewer documents required), and must be accompanied by a sworn statement attesting that the debtor meets the conditions of a simplified reorganization. The reorganization plan must be filed, with the assistance of an administrator, within forty-five days of the declaration of insolvency and can be limited to payment terms, debt relief, and the possible guarantees that the entrepreneur must make to ensure its execution.[50] A simplified *liquidation des biens* is also available where the debtor files a sworn statement attesting that it meets the relevant conditions for a simplified liquidation proceeding, but the debtor is ineligible if it owns any immovable property. The liquidator, within thirty days, may prepare and file a report with the competent court.

To date, there is little experience with the OHADA law, and thus its effectiveness cannot yet be evaluated.[51] Martinez suggests that the OHADA model focuses more on the business aspects of the entrepreneur, in an attempt to achieve a higher survival rate of businesses as going concerns, whereas new Southern and Eastern African laws seem to focus more on the entrepreneur as a natural person and, therefore, on discharge, but have less regard to rescue or sale of an individual's business as a going concern.[52] Martinez also observes that creditors in Africa suffer as a result of lengthy proceedings, often resulting in no return to creditors. The OHADA legislation, if implemented effectively across the OHADA countries, offers some potential to reduce costs and delays.[53] To date, however, there is a lack of infrastructure to support the law in many of the jurisdictions.

In the Asia Pacific region, some legal systems have introduced proceedings designed specifically for MSMEs. For example, the Republic of South Korea introduced

[49] Article 6-1, OHADA.
[50] Article 145-3, OHADA; Martinez (n 39) 8.
[51] Martinez (n 39) 10.
[52] Ibid.
[53] Ibid.

summary rehabilitation proceedings for small business debtors, including individuals and corporations, as part of its consolidated Debtor Rehabilitation and Bankruptcy Act (DRBA), effective 1 July 2015.[54] The process is available where pre-petition debts do not exceed KRW 3 billion.[55] Only the debtor is entitled to petition for commencement,[56] and only unsecured pre-commencement claims are subject to the proceedings. Presumptively, a trustee is not appointed, and the debtor, a principal of the debtor, or the debtor's representative is deemed to be the trustee. A court-appointed examiner undertakes an examination of the debtor's business and property, and reports in a simplified form. For incorporated MSMEs, a certified accountant is appointed to perform this task. The requirement for acceptance of a proposed plan has been relaxed,[57] and if the plan is not accepted by all classes of creditors, the court has authority to implement a form of cram-down to approve the plan if certain conditions are met. The term 'cram-down' refers to the legal authority of a court to approve a restructuring of debt in a bankruptcy despite objections from creditors. The Ministry of Justice reports that the goal is to complete the process from the time of the petition for commencement to approval of the plan within 100 days, although the court can extend the timing for a specified period.[58] The repayment period can extend up to ten years. Creditors vote on the proposed plan, and the court must subsequently approve it.[59]

The Korean system is helpful in that it expressly creates a regime for MSME insolvency. However, its effectiveness may be limited because only unsecured debts fall within its ambit, whereas MSME assets are often completely encumbered by secured interests, and restructuring of secured claims is almost always critical to continuation. The court's ability to override creditor rejection of a plan may also prove problematic, given that the court would possess neither debtor-specific information nor sector-specific expertise. Also, ten years is a long period for repayment, and experience will be needed with the new legislation to determine how frequently an extended period is imposed.

In Japan, the Bankruptcy Act[60] does not provide any special proceedings for MSMEs. However, in practice, the Tokyo District Court has sought to relieve parties of overly rigid requirements by creating a simplified procedure, 'small administration', under the Civil Rehabilitation Act.[61] The debtor can file a petition for

[54] Ministry of Justice, Republic of South Korea, Presentation to UNCITRAL Working Group V on 'Special Rehabilitation Proceedings for MSMEs', 10 May 2017. The new law was aimed at lowering the costs of procedures and expanding the scope of small business debtors, at 6. Debtor Rehabilitation and Bankruptcy Act (DRBA) Ministry of Justice, Republic of South Korea, ch. 2, subch. 9.

[55] 3 billion South Korean won (KRW) is approximately 3 million USD, Article 15-3, ibid. at 2.

[56] Ibid. at 7. However, the petition will be rejected if the debtor has received a discharge within the previous five years.

[57] The plan is deemed to be accepted by the class of unsecured rehabilitation creditors if either (i) at least two thirds by value of the unsecured creditors or (ii) more than one half by value and more than one half by number of the unsecured creditors have accepted the plan. Ibid 8.

[58] Ibid 10. [59] Ibid.

[60] Bankruptcy Act (Act No 75 of 2 June 2004, as last amended by Act No 109 of 15 December 2006).

[61] Etsuko Sugiyama, 'Insolvency Proceedings for MSMEs in Japan', Presentation to UNCITRAL Working Group V, 10 May 2017. Japanese insolvency systems are primarily regulated by the Bankruptcy Act of 2004, Civil Rehabilitation Act (Act no. 225 of 22 December 1999, hereafter Civil Rehabilitation Act), and Corporate Reorganization Act of 2002. The Bankruptcy Act regulates the procedure for

simplified rehabilitation, after the period for filing proofs of claims has expired and before the investigation has started, and the court can make an order of simplified rehabilitation, in which there is no investigation. The holders of the filed claims that account for three-fifths or more of the value of the total filed claims must have consented, in writing, to a proposed rehabilitation plan submitted by the debtor and consented to the proceedings for investigation and determination of rehabilitation claims not being performed.[62] The court, on making an order of simplified rehabilitation, makes an order to refer a proposed rehabilitation plan to a resolution by creditors. Public notice must be given regarding the date of a creditors' meeting.[63] Where the holder of a filed rehabilitation claim who has not attended a creditors' meeting has consented to the commencement of simplified proceedings, it is deemed to have attended the creditors' meeting and consented to the proposed rehabilitation plan.[64]

In terms of liquidation, when the debtor is represented by a lawyer, the Tokyo District Court quickly conducts a hearing of the debtor and decides if it can prepay 200,000 yen [1,829 USD].[65] If so, the court orders the commencement of insolvency proceedings and appoints a trustee, who investigates the debtor's assets and submits a report to the court. Based on this report, the court implements liquidating distribution or makes an order of discontinuance. If the debtor cannot prepay 200,000 yen, the court orders discontinuance of the proceedings.[66] Japan has thus tried to address the challenges facing MSMEs, but arguably, absent a statutory framework, there is a lack of transparency and certainty in the regime. Deemed approval by creditors not attending the creditors' meeting is, however, a helpful feature that may mitigate the high threshold requirement of three-fifths of the value of claims needed to support the proposed plan.

Spain in 2013 introduced, and in 2015 revised, the 'out-of-court agreement on payments', a procedure designed for insolvent MSMEs.[67] This procedure consists of a relatively nimble out-of-court procedure, with limited paperwork and the use of predesigned templates, channelled through the Commercial Registry and Chambers of Commerce,[68] with the intervention of insolvency professionals labelled 'mediators' (*mediador concursal*), whose role stretches well beyond mere mediation. The initiative is assigned only to the debtor, who starts the procedure by requesting the appointment of a mediator from the Commercial Registry of its domicile or an authorized Chamber of Commerce. Once all formal requirements are satisfied, a mediator is

liquidating the property of debtors, the Civil Rehabilitation Act regulates the procedure for rehabilitating debtors, and the Corporate Reorganization Act regulates the procedure for reorganizing stock companies. Both the Bankruptcy Act and Civil Rehabilitation Act are applicable to individuals as well as corporations. However, the Corporate Reorganization Act is applicable only to stock companies, see Articles 1 and 2, Corporate Reorganization Act.

[62] Article 211(1) Order of Simplified Rehabilitation, Civil Rehabilitation Act.

[63] Article 212, Civil Rehabilitation Act (n 61)

[64] Article 214(3), Civil Rehabilitation Act (n 61).

[65] Currency exchange rate as of 24 August 2017.

[66] Sugiyama (n 61).

[67] The debtor may be a sole entrepreneur or a legal entity with an estimated debt of less than 5 million euros (art 231 IL).

[68] Individual debtors who are not entrepreneurs will trigger the procedure through a notary public who may also act as mediator.

appointed from a list in pre-established order. The court will be notified of the commencement of the negotiation period and a stay of execution will commence. The mediator will check the documents submitted by the debtor and contact creditors, summoning them to a meeting within two months of the appointment. All creditors except public creditors are involved in this procedure. The mediator will draft a plan, obtain the debtor's agreement, and share the plan with creditors ahead of the meeting. The content of the plan is open and flexible, although the majorities required to approve the plan increase or decrease depending on the level of sacrifice envisaged in the plan. If passed, the agreement also binds non-participating and dissenting creditors, including secured creditors, and the agreement cannot be bypassed in a subsequent insolvency. The law tackles the problem of passivity of creditors, common in the insolvency of MSMEs, in a stern fashion: those creditors that have been notified and have not attended the meeting or otherwise expressly supported or rejected the plan will suffer the subordination of their claims in case of subsequent insolvency proceedings.[69] If this procedure fails to result in an approved plan, Spain's insolvency law provides for abbreviated in-court insolvency proceedings.

The Irish statutory advisory group on company law in its June 2017 report has proposed a new form of liquidation called self-administered liquidation (SAL), intended in particular for very small incorporated businesses that do not have the funds to undergo the usual liquidator-led liquidation process.[70] Directors of such companies may, subject to certain safeguards, apply to the Companies Registration Office (CRO) with a liquidation proposal. The CRO would then publish the application and proposal. From that point on, the directors' only role would be to wind up the company and not to trade in it other than specifically with a view to maximizing the value of its assets in the interests of its creditors. Creditors and members would have thirty days to object to the proposal, and the CRO would report any such objection to the Office of the Director of Corporate Enforcement (ODCE). The ODCE would investigate the objection and may permit the SAL to continue in its original or a modified form. The directors would then have a year to realize any assets, distribute the proceeds amongst creditors, and report back to the ODCE. Alternatively, the proposal suggests that the ODCE could call a creditors' meeting to consider the appointment of a liquidator, or it may instigate an investigation into the company's affairs. The proposed SAL, while restricted only to small companies and not intended as a comprehensive insolvency framework, has the potential, if implemented with due regard to concerns about possible misuse, to help reduce the number of unresolved cases of 'zombie' insolvent companies.[71]

[69] Article 237 IL.

[70] Company Law Review Group, 'Report on the Protection of Employees and Unsecured Creditors', June 2017, https://dbei.gov.ie/en/Publications/Publication-files/CLRG-Report-on-the-Protection-of-Employees-and-Unsecured-Creditors.pdf, 66, and Appendix 7 at 137 et seq.

[71] 'Zombie companies' are companies that are non-viable but have not been liquidated or restructured. The European Central Bank provides the following definition: 'We define a firm as zombie whenever (i) its return on assets is negative, (ii) its net investments are negative, and (iii) its debt servicing capacity (defined as EBITDA over financial debt) is lower than 5% for (iv) at least two consecutive years.' European Central Bank Working Paper, Manuela Storz, Michael Koetter, Ralph Setzer, and Andreas Westphal, 'Do we want these two to tango? On zombie firms and stressed banks in Europe',

E. Existing International Tools

At the global level, the efforts of organizations such as the United Nations Commission on International Trade Law (UNCITRAL) and the World Bank Group have contributed significantly to creating model insolvency legislation and best practice guidance and to helping governments implement reforms.[72] Nevertheless, there are currently insufficient tools to address MSME insolvency. UNCITRAL, which has led international policy development in the insolvency arena, only makes brief mention of small businesses in its four-part *Legislative Guide on Insolvency Law*.[73] The *Legislative Guide* is aimed at providing a comprehensive statement of the key objectives and principles that should be reflected in a state's insolvency laws. While it provides a valuable reference tool for national legislative authorities in reviewing the adequacy of their laws and regulations or enacting new ones, and discusses the obstacles facing small creditors in terms of barriers to participation,[74] there is no specific attention paid to MSMEs.

Part one of the *Legislative Guide*discusses the key objectives of an insolvency law, the types of mechanisms available, and the institutional framework required to support an effective insolvency regime. It does not address the particular challenges facing MSMEs that are highlighted in this volume, aside from a brief note that the costs and fees associated with accessing insolvency proceedings may be of particular importance in the case of small- and medium-sized businesses.[75]

Part two of the *Legislative Guide* deals with core features of an effective insolvency law, including standardized commencement criteria, stays, post-commencement finance, participation of creditors, expedited reorganization proceedings, simplified claims procedures, conversion of reorganization to liquidation, and clear rules for the discharge of the debtor and closure of insolvency proceedings. While these elements are directly relevant to MSMEs, the assumption is that debtor companies have the financial and human resources to undertake the processes envisioned, which is not the reality for the vast majority of insolvent MSMEs.

The *Legislative Guide* does refer to cost burdens that will deter creditors and discourage commencement of proceedings, 'of particular importance in the case of insolvency of small and medium-size businesses'.[76] It also notes the issue of overlap of consumer and small business debt:

> One issue that may need to be taken into account in considering discharge of natural persons engaged in a business undertaking is the intersection of business indebtedness with consumer

October 2017, available at https://www.ecb.europa.eu/pub/pdf/scpwps/ecb.wp2104.en.pdf?0167b3eada64c9757df8e6e0b866b3a1.

[72] United Nations Commission on International Trade Law (UNCITRAL), *Legislative Guide on Insolvency Law*, 2005, United Nations Publication No.E.05.V.10 (hereafter *Legislative Guide*; additional parts were added in 2010 and 2013); World Bank, Principles on Effective Insolvency and Creditor/Debtor Regimes (revised May 2016, http://pubdocs.worldbank.org/en/919511468425523509/ICR-Principles-Insolvency-Creditor-Debtor-Regimes-2016.pdf; hereafter World Bank Principles). The *Legislative Guide*, together with the World Bank Principles, form the insolvency standard.

[73] Ibid. [74] Ibid 25. [75] Ibid 57. [76] Ibid 63, repeated at 162.

indebtedness. Recognizing that different approaches are taken to the insolvency of natural persons (in some States a natural person cannot be declared bankrupt at all, while in others there is a requirement for the person to have acted in the capacity of a 'merchant') and that many States do not have a developed consumer insolvency system, a number of States have insolvency laws that seek to distinguish between those who are simply consumer debtors and those whose liabilities arise from small businesses. Since consumer credit is often used to finance small business either as start-up capital or for operating funds, it may not always be possible to separate the debts into clear categories. For that reason, where a legal system recognizes both consumer and business debt, it may not be feasible to have rules on the business debts of natural persons that differ from the rules applicable to consumer debts.[77]

Part three of the *Legislative Guide* addresses the treatment of enterprise groups in insolvency, both nationally and internationally. It is not directly applicable to the overwhelming majority of MSMEs, and there is no specific reference to smaller debtor companies in this part.

Part four of the *Legislative Guide* focuses on the obligations that might be imposed on the directors and officers responsible for making decisions when an enterprise faces or becomes insolvent. In this part, the only reference to MSMEs is to family members and senior employees of small, family-owned companies being considered de facto directors; some criteria for that assessment, and potential resultant liability, are mentioned.[78] The UNCITRAL Model Law on Cross-Border Insolvency (1997) and its Guide to Enactment make no reference to MSMEs.

Hence, the UNCITRAL *legislative guides* and other policies, while comprehensive, closely reflect how insolvency systems have been designed in many states. As noted previously, such systems have been designed with larger enterprises in mind, assuming an insolvency estate of significant worth, and the presence of creditors and other stakeholders with sufficient value at stake that they actively participate in the process to work out a solution to the debtor's financial distress.

In April 2014, after an extensive and thorough preliminary analysis, UNCITRAL's Insolvency Working Group V declared that:

> The mechanisms provided by the *Legislative Guide* were not sufficient to address all of the needs of MSMEs; thorough treatment of the issues would require both a consideration of matters not yet addressed in the *Legislative Guide* as well as the tailoring of solutions already in the *Legislative Guide* to specifically address MSMEs.[79]

The Working Group observed, as an example, that 'the application of elements of the insolvency law, such as creditor committees, the central role of the courts and extensive involvement of insolvency professionals, might not be appropriate for MSME regimes.'[80]

The World Bank Group while it has dedicated considerable resources to the financing and education of MSMEs, also does not have a specific approach to MSME insolvency that addresses some of the problems previously identified. Its extensive

[77] Ibid 284–6. [78] Ibid, Part IV, 16.

[79] See https://documents-dds-ny.un.org/doc/UNDOC/LTD/V14/011/39/PDF/V1401139.pdf?OpenElement.

[80] See https://documents-dds-ny.un.org/doc/UNDOC/GEN/V14/028/64/PDF/V1402864.pdf?OpenElement.

studies acknowledge that MSMEs are collectively the largest employers in many low-income countries and, as such, face barriers in access to capital and financial services. The World Bank Group has developed a wide range of available instruments to help meet the challenge of MSME finance, including data analysis, financing, risk-sharing, technical assistance, and a financial inclusion support framework. It works globally with standard-setting bodies to develop guidelines, standards, and good practices.[81] To date, no similar instruments and policies have been developed, however, expressly aimed at MSME insolvency.

The 'World Bank Insolvency and Creditor/Debtor Regimes Task Force, Report of the Working Group on the Treatment of the Insolvency of Natural Persons' has addressed specific issues arising in consumer bankruptcies.[82] In that regard, the Report briefly mentions the overlap of consumer and business credit in small businesses. In 2017, however, both UNCITRAL and the World Bank Group expressed their intention to focus more on the topic of MSME insolvency in future deliberations.[83]

Having canvassed the structure and limits of the current treatment of MSME insolvency in various regions, including recent developments in the law of several jurisdictions, the next chapter identifies principles and objectives in the design of an effective approach to MSME insolvency.

[81] The World Bank Principles do not contain any specific principles concerning MSMEs.

[82] The World Bank, 'World Bank Group Insolvency and Creditor/Debtor Regimes Task Force, Working Group on the Treatment of the Insolvency of Natural Persons, Report on the Treatment of the Insolvency of Natural Persons', http://siteresources.worldbank.org/INTGILD/Resources/WBInsolvencyOfNaturalPersonsReport_01_11_13.pdf.

[83] See World Bank, 'World Bank Group Insolvency and Creditor/Debtor Regimes Task Force, Working Group on the Treatment of MSME Insolvency, Report on the Treatment of MSME Insolvency', 2017, http://documents.worldbank.org/curated/en/973331494264489956/pdf/114823-REVISED-PUBLIC-MSME-Insolvency-report-low-res-final.pdf; UNCITRAL, Insolvency of micro, small and medium-sized enterprises, Note by the Secretariat, Working Group V, Fifty-first session, New York, 10–19 May 2017, https://documents-dds-ny.un.org/doc/UNDOC/LTD/V18/009/85/PDF/V1800985.pdf?OpenElement.

3

Principles and Objectives Guiding the Modular Approach to MSME Insolvency

This volume offers the design of a flourishing micro, small, and medium enterprises (MSMEs or MSME according to context) insolvency regime. It advocates principles and processes that would provide an apt response to the insolvency of such businesses. This advocacy in its very nature is 'normative': concerned not so much with what the law of whatever jurisdiction is, as with what it ought to be. A key question in evaluating such a normative approach is identifying the standards by which to assess this advocacy. How have the particular principles and processes explained in this volume come to be adopted? How can they be assessed by the reader?

Our normative approach is to treat fairness as the overarching standard: a judgement both on the law and on the behaviour of the parties subject to it. Fairness is a fundamental principle of an effective insolvency system. One way of testing for the fairness of the law is to regard it as fair insofar as it treats the interests of all those individuals subject to it with equal concern. The law should not countenance favourable treatment simply on the basis of gender, race, ethnicity, tribe, family, sexual orientation, wealth, social status, or political affiliation. Nor should anyone be condemned to unfavourable treatment simply because of lack of wealth, experience, expertise, or other resources. These premises have become truisms in some societies, are rejected or controversial in others, and are everywhere honoured in the breach at least as often as in the observance. They are nevertheless the fundamental ideals to which the following argument is committed and by which it seeks to be judged. This volume's normative proposals envisage a regime that aspires in good faith to treat all of its subjects with equal concern in the foregoing sense. A reader who rejects this fundamental commitment will find inhospitable terrain.

This chapter explicates what equal concern implies in the MSME insolvency context. It identifies the elements of such equal concern and how it might be operationalized. The chapter adopts and makes use of the distinction between the substantive goals of the law and its procedural goals.[1] A substantive goal pursued in good faith by the relevant branch of the law confers ultimate justification upon it. The requirement of equal concern is here treated as the law's primary substantive goal: it

[1] See Rizwaan J. Mokal, 'On Fairness and Efficiency' (2003), *Modern Law Review* 66: 452–7 (hereafter Mokal, 'Fairness').

would be a compelling justification of a MSME insolvency regime that it respects the equal standing of all those individuals subject to it. The chapter shows that fairness, understood in this way, undergirds distinctive features of current insolvency regimes. Procedural goals relate to process; to the way the law goes about pursuing substantive goals. This chapter explains the relationship between substantive and procedural goals and introduces the concept of transaction cost-efficiency, a primary procedural goal. Several other procedural goals of the law are also described. They include accessibility, transparency, timeliness, certainty, and accountability. The chapter concludes by analysing the distinctive challenges that must be overcome by an insolvency regime oriented towards MSMEs.

A. Relevance of Insolvency Law Policy to Distressed MSMEs

Insolvency law and its underlying policy framework are an indispensable component of any economy that countenances debt. Insolvency law determines the governance of insolvent businesses during the period in which a given business's entrepreneurs are trying to determine the best strategy to address its distress.[2] Insolvency law also plays a broad social and economic role in overall economic planning, in that the survival of distressed businesses and the economic activity that they generate are important objectives of the system.[3] Many countries with developed insolvency regimes reflect core objectives of preserving and maximizing the value of the insolvency estate, ensuring fair distribution over an appropriate period of time of the highest feasible proportion of that value to creditors and other stakeholders, and providing remedies for any wrongdoing connected with the insolvency.[4] Critically important to these objectives are timely and effective mechanisms to address enterprise distress, be it on a piecemeal liquidation or going-concern basis. Effective implementation of these objectives is often in tension with the private sectional interests of particular stakeholders, for example, the senior creditor desirous of maximizing recovery and unwilling to take any further risk irrespective of the potential for survival; or the entrepreneur unwilling to admit the business is not viable and thus unwilling to wind it down, who operates the business on increasingly unfavourable terms. The deferral of dealing with distress in turn depletes value that may have been made available to other creditors in a speedy liquidation.

Insolvency frameworks are characteristically designed to prevent further loss of value from the insolvency estate. Such a loss may occur in two scenarios. First, a viable business may suffer piecemeal liquidation, resulting in the loss of any remaining

[2] Janis Sarra, *Creditor Rights and the Public Interest, Restructuring Insolvent Corporations* (Toronto: University of Toronto Press, 2003) (hereafter Sarra, *Creditor Rights*).

[3] Karen Gross, *Failure and Forgiveness: Rebalancing the Bankruptcy System* (New Haven: Yale University Press, 1997) (hereafter Gross).

[4] On value preservation and distribution, see Rizwaan J. Mokal, 'Liquidity, Systemic Risk, and the Bankruptcy Treatment of Financial Contracts', *10 Brook J Corp Fin & Com L* (2015), 18 and 32–5; and on accountability, Rizwaan J. Mokal, *Corporate Insolvency Law—Theory and Application* (London: Oxford University Press, 2005), chapters 8 and 9 (hereafter Mokal, *Corporate Insolvency Law*).

going-concern surplus. Second, a non-viable business may be restructured and subsequently fail, which results in additional losses of reinvested value that should instead have been recycled into viable businesses.[5] In order to prevent both types of error, any insolvency framework must include a decision-making procedure that sifts viable from non-viable businesses and that facilitates rescue of the former and speedy liquidation of the latter.

Some jurisdictions offer liquidation, discharge from over-indebtedness, and a fresh start for insolvent natural persons, including individual entrepreneurs, allowing these individuals to re-enter the market and create or take advantage of new entrepreneurial opportunities. Different systems set different time periods for discharge, and many specify that a certain amount of indebtedness must be repaid as a precondition to discharge. These requirements reflect different normative choices by countries regarding what should be required for rehabilitation from insolvency. Other insolvency systems do not provide any such relief for natural person debtors, including individual entrepreneurs. The result is that these individuals carry the full amount of their debts over the long term and are thus often unable to free themselves of the crushing burden of debt, even where failure of the business was not due to any culpable behaviour on their part.

Where an insolvent enterprise's business is viable, a statutory restructuring mechanism provides an opportunity for the debtor to negotiate a solution to the financial distress with its creditors. Such negotiated solutions, often referred to as 'workouts', can include compromises of the amount of claims owing or timing of payments, refinancing agreements, conversion of debt to equity, the injection of new equity investment in the firm, or changes in the business structure.[6] Restructuring can result in arrangements that are a hybrid of these strategies, such as liquidation on a going-concern basis or liquidation of part of the business in order to finance restructuring of the rest of the enterprise and a disposal of underperforming assets, or a mix of liquidation and going-forward business.[7]

A business may be merely financially distressed, that is to say, worth more as a going concern notwithstanding its inability to meet current financial obligations, than if its assets are liquidated on a piecemeal basis to satisfy creditors' claims. Where a debtor can restructure, preservation of ongoing value, such as the skilled workforce, supply arrangements, customer base, and other goodwill, adds extra value over and above the aggregate realizable value of individual tangible or intangible assets. Alternatively, sale of the enterprise on a going-concern basis to pre-filing creditors or new third parties may be the solution, especially if the new owner brings

[5] See Robert Hansen and Randall Thomas, 'Auctions in Bankruptcy: Theoretical Analysis and Practical Guidance' (1998) 18 *Intl Rev L & Econ* 159, 177, describing both types of errors. The second scenario additionally involves a transfer of value from creditors, whose legal rights are not fully honoured in the insolvency, to other stakeholders (particularly managers, employees, and perhaps equity owners), none of whom has legal rights to the continuation of their particular positions in the non-viable distressed business, yet who benefit from its continuation.

[6] Janis Sarra, *Rescue! The Companies' Creditors Arrangement Act*, 2nd edn (Toronto: Carswell, 2013) at 4 (hereafter Sarra, *Rescue*).

[7] Ibid.

operational expertise, management skills, liquidity, access to reserve capital, and other benefits to the business. An effective insolvency process assists with controlling and allocating the collective action and transaction costs among the firm's diverse creditors, thus ensuring more value is extracted from the firm.[8]

The majority of distressed MSMEs will end up being liquidated. This outcome is a logical and defensible consequence of the operation of a market economy where the debtor is economically distressed. Yet it is unknown how many debtors are merely financially distressed and ought to and could survive if an effective insolvency process was in place to assess the scope and reasons for the distress and to canvass possible avenues for its resolution. Moreover, liquidation could be made much more accessible, leading to more timely responses to economic distress, freeing up skills and effort to create new value in the marketplace, and enabling the assets of the business to be put to alternative and better uses.

Against this backdrop, a helpful approach to the design of a MSME insolvency law framework is to consider the fundamental principles that underpin resolution of insolvency for smaller businesses and how those principles can apply to the development and implementation of an approach responsive to the particular challenges faced by MSMEs.[9]

B. Fairness as an Overarching Principle

1. Existing analyses

There is a rich theoretical literature addressing the structure and operation of insolvency law. Historically, there have been advocates for 'debtor-oriented' regimes[10] and advocates for 'creditor-oriented' ones.[11] There are stakeholder theories of insolvency law and enterprise wealth maximization theories.[12] A key divide exists between those theories favouring and those opposing the distributive inertness of insolvency law. The former approach requires insolvency law to respect the parties' pre-insolvency entitlements.[13] On this view, most prominently associated with the so-called creditors' bargain, the objective of insolvency law should be to preserve and maximize the insolvency estate and distribute it according to the rights for which creditors and

[8] Ibid. [9] These challenges were discussed in the previous chapter.

[10] Gross (n 3) 80. Elizabeth Warren, 'Bankruptcy Policymaking in an Imperfect World' (1993) 92 *Michigan LR* 336 (hereafter Warren).

[11] Thomas Jackson, *The Logic and Limits of Bankruptcy Law* (Cambridge, MA: Harvard University Press, 1986); Douglas Baird, 'Loss Distribution, Forum Shopping, and Bankruptcy: A Reply to Warren' (1987) 54 *U Chicago LR* 775.

[12] Vanessa Finch, *Corporate Insolvency Law—Perspectives and Principles* (Cambridge: Cambridge University Press, 2002) (hereafter Finch); Warren (n 10); George G. Triantis and Ronald J. Daniels, 'The Role of Debt in Interactive Corporate Governance' (1985), 83 *Cal Law Review* 1073; Michael C. Jensen and William H. Meckling, 'Theory of the Firm: Managerial Behaviour, Agency Cost and Ownership Structure' (1976), 3 *Journal of Fin Econ* 305.

[13] Thomas Jackson, 'Translating Assets and Liabilities in the Bankruptcy Forum', in Jagdeep S. Bhandari and Lawrence A. Weiss (eds), *Corporate Bankruptcy: Economic and Legal Perspectives* (Cambridge: Cambridge University Press, 1996) (hereafter Jackson, 'Translating Assets').

equity holders have bargained prior to the insolvency event.[14] Scholars opposed to this approach suggest that insolvency law should recognize the interests of some parties that do not hold formal rights prior to insolvency because creditors with formal rights rarely bear the full costs of the debtor's insolvency.[15] On this view, employees and others have an economic interest at stake in their employer's insolvency, and the insolvency regime should appropriately distribute the residual value of the debtor's estate having regard to those interests and investments.[16]

This volume conceptualizes MSME insolvency law as a scheme of fair social cooperation in the particular circumstances of MSME insolvency. One way that the principles and processes constituting the scheme would be fair would be for them to respect the right to equal concern of each person affected by such circumstances. Each affected person is regarded as willing and able to cooperate if each of them has a reasonable expectation that they can pursue their self-interest bound by the same set of principles acceptable to all.[17] Importantly, having one's interests accorded equal concern in the choice of insolvency law principles does *not* equate to being given identical treatment under insolvency law.[18] To show equal concern towards each of the law's subjects may require *differential* legal treatment responding to relevant *differences* amongst them, such as their relative inability to influence the debtor, diversify their risk, obtain protection against or exit from insolvency scenarios, their particular vulnerability to insolvency harm, and their choices and effort.[19]

One way of testing whether an insolvency regime displays equal concern has been developed by Rizwaan Mokal. Drawing on the work of John Rawls,[20] Mokal sets up a hypothetical choice position in which all those affected by peculiar insolvency circumstances and thus to be subjected to insolvency processes shaped by insolvency law principles are regarded as possessing identical information about the world and the range of options available, but, critically, no information about their own identity, attributes, interests, or stake in any particular insolvency. They are then required to agree on the design of the insolvency regime. This 'dramatic ignorance' built into the choice position operationalizes the egalitarian requirement that no one should accord more weight to a principle or a process on the basis of individual or group interest, nor discount it on the basis of personal or communal prejudice. The choice

[14] Jackson, 'Translating Assets' (n 13); Douglas Baird and Thomas Jackson, 'Corporate Reorganization and the treatment of Diverse Ownership Interests: A Comment on Adequate Protection of Secured Creditors' (1984) 51 *Univ. of Chicago Law Rev.* 97.

[15] Finch (n 12).

[16] See, for example, Elizabeth Warren, 'Bankruptcy Policy' (1987) 54 *Univ. of Chicago Law Rev.* 775.

[17] Mokal, *Corporate Insolvency Law* (n 4), chapters 1 and 3.

[18] Ibid 10, citing Ronald Dworkin, *Sovereign Virtue: The Theory and Practice of Equality* (Cambridge, MA: Harvard University Press, 2000), 11.

[19] Mokal, 'Fairness' (n 1) (2003) *MLR* 452, 459; and Mokal, *Corporate Insolvency Law* (n 4) 9, 84–5, 119–20, 126–7, 308–10, etc. See also Warren (n 10), and Irit Mevorach, *Insolvency within Multinational Enterprise Groups* (Oxford: Oxford University Press, 2009) 113–19 (hereafter Mevorach).

[20] John Rawls, *A Theory of Justice* Cambridge (MA: Harvard University Press, 1971), and *Political Liberalism* (New York: Columbia University Press, 1996). See also, Janis Sarra, 'Embedding Fairness as a Fundamental Norm in Financial Markets', in Janis Sarra (ed.) *An Exploration of Fairness, Interdisciplinary Inquiries in Law, Science and the Humanities* (Toronto, Carswell, 2013) 193–240.

position thereby ensures that each person's concerns are given equal weight by every participant in the bargain, since each has an equal chance of discovering that a particular set of interests is in fact their own.[21] Mokal observes that if parties do not know who they will turn out to be once the state of dramatic ignorance is removed, they must equally take into account the interests of all the actual people they might find themselves to be.[22]

In the choice position, each of the debtor's stakeholders seeks to ensure that the insolvent's assets are used so as to benefit them.[23] Employees would prefer to have their jobs and economic livelihood protected; trade suppliers would prefer to have ongoing arrangements of supplies and services with the debtor, rather than receiving only the discounted value of their pre-filing claims; and directors, owners, principals, and equity-holders would prefer the debtor to continue operating and to retain their investments of time and resources. The role of insolvency law is to mediate fairly amongst these competing, even conflicting, preferences and to facilitate fair cooperation to the maximal extent. Because of dramatic ignorance, Mokal argues, the bargaining parties would not choose principles that imposed burdens on anyone that they themselves would not reasonably wish to face. Instead, the parties would propose principles others could reasonably accept. They would do so by taking into account the consequences of those principles being mutually recognized, of the effect of the application of those principles upon their conceptions of themselves of all those to whom they would apply, and upon their motivation to act from those principles.[24]

Another manifestation of equal concern is that like cases should be treated alike. Hence, the principles of insolvency law should ensure that the law as a whole treats similarly placed individuals similarly. This approach limits the scope of insolvency law to exclude distributive issues not peculiar to the circumstances of insolvency.[25] For example, if workers surplus to their *solvent* employer's requirements may be made redundant on that basis alone, then the same should presumptively hold even if the employer is *in*solvent. Correspondingly, if workers deserve protection against dismissal even though they are judged not to be required by the employer, then this protection should be implemented generally, and not merely restricted to the minority of workers whose employer becomes subject to insolvency law.[26] In this context, the concern about equality of treatment requires identifying which branch of the law should address a particular issue so as to show equal concern to all those individuals or entities affected by that issue.

The same set of stakeholders may have multiple types of interest, of which some, but not others, ought to properly be addressed by insolvency law. Landlords, for example, have fixed claims for rent arrears owed by the MSME or for capital improvements made to the debtor's leased property. They may also have an interest in the MSME debtor continuing in business, given the possible future upside potential of continued rental income. At the same time, there may be one or more issues that the landlord is concerned about, such as the debtor's violation of environmental

[21] Mokal, *Corporate Insolvency Law* (n 4) 80–1. [22] Ibid 81.
[23] Ibid 80. [24] Ibid 75. [25] Ibid 64. [26] Ibid 65.

standards regarding emissions or water contamination on the landlord's leased premises, that are not related to insolvency law per se and for which the landlord might be held vicariously liable under environmental or other remedial legislation. In such instances, addressing it within insolvency law alone could create indefensible discrepancy within the law as to essentially similarly placed persons.

This analysis does not imply that insolvency law should not address distributive issues. To the contrary, to do so is part of this law's *raison d'être*. By definition, an insolvent debtor's estate lacks the value to fully satisfy the claims against it. This lack of assets tends to give rise to one of two scenarios. Pre insolvency, certain creditors may obtain rights, typically proprietary security, that allow them to seize and realize some or all of the debtor's assets so as to obtain discharge of their claim, and these rights may trump those of some or all other creditors. Further or alternatively, once the debtor becomes distressed, there may be a 'race' to obtain judgment against it and to enforce that judgment against the debtor's assets. Both scenarios tend to favour sophisticated and well-resourced repeat players, such as banks, and others connected with the debtor by significant ownership or control, such as the principals, directors, equity-holders, and connected entities. Correspondingly, in both scenarios, insolvency loss is disproportionately and thus inequitably placed upon weaker, less sophisticated creditors, and upon those stakeholders unconnected with the debtor. Such an outcome would be anathema to the parties bargaining in dramatic ignorance about insolvency law principles.

Moreover, both scenarios tend to fail to preserve value. A fully secured creditor may only be interested in liquidating the assets, and the race to enforce claims may destroy the possibility of a rational decision about the business's future. Either way, a viable going-concern solution—either reorganization or sale of the going concern—may be lost, even though it would return more value to the stakeholders as a group than a breakup sale.[27] Two primary objectives of insolvency law are thus to create mechanisms to ensure that value is not unnecessarily lost when a debtor becomes insolvent, and to distribute that preserved value and the corresponding insolvency loss in a normatively defensible manner. An effective insolvency regime would also thereby advance societal goals of fostering entrepreneurial activity and preventing the loss of economic activity and jobs where appropriate.

To be clear, then, this volume advocates a key distributive role for insolvency law *in relation to issues peculiar to insolvency*, but opposes any such role where the result would be arbitrary distinctions and thus equality violation amongst similarly placed persons.

Further, in seeking to identify the proper ambit of insolvency law, it should be taken into account that the law affects the interests of those individuals and businesses that plan for insolvency and in the expectation that insolvency law might come to govern them, yet who end up never in fact facing peculiar insolvency issues. The interests of such parties, who make plans, demand rights, and accept liabilities in the shadow of insolvency law, must legitimately figure in the choice of principles to govern that law.[28] Similarly, Irit Mevorach

[27] Sarra, *Creditor Rights* (n 2). [28] Mokal, *Corporate Insolvency Law* (n 4) 734.

suggests that respecting pre-insolvency entitlements and providing adequate incentives and measures to enhance pre-insolvency efficiency are critically important features of a well-designed system.[29] Forecast costs of distress affect not only those firms that have entered into the insolvency process, but also those enterprises and parties contracting with them that might potentially go into insolvency.[30] Other things equal, insolvency law should translate pre-insolvency assets and liabilities into the insolvency forum with minimal dislocation, so that such creditors can rely on their rights and create appropriate arrangements to suit their particular needs.[31]

In summary, insolvency law principles must accord equal concern to the interests of all those stakeholders affected by issues peculiar to insolvency. Such principles must guide the creation of insolvency law tools and processes that reflect society's policy choices within the complex combination of corporate, employment, environmental, property, tax, tort, and welfare laws, amongst which insolvency law must find its place. Insolvency law must duly recognize existing commercial and other relationships and must create ascertainable and transparent rules that parties understand before they enter into the credit arrangement.

2. Extant insolvency mechanisms to achieve fairness

Fairness is the foundation of the Modular Approach proposed in this volume. The discussion in this subsection demonstrates that it already shapes key distinctive features of extant insolvency regimes. The Modular Approach does not invent the requirement of fairness; rather, it seeks to systemize and generalize it across the entire range of responses to MSME distress.

Two distinctive features of insolvency regimes illustrate the point. The first feature is statutory payment priorities. Most modern insolvency systems recognize some preferences for parties particularly vulnerable to the loss of the value of their claims, particularly employees. As Janis Sarra has observed, employees face information asymmetries and lack of diversification of their investments in the debtor; they are often the last creditors to know of the business's financial distress and the least able to protect themselves in advance from the losses associated with the business failing.[32] In a study Sarra conducted of sixty-two jurisdictions, 89% had some form of statutory priority for employee wages claims, and 55% had a wage guarantee fund.[33] These protections reflect fairness principles in recognizing that not all creditors are equally disadvantaged by business failure, and thus it is important to place specific protections in insolvency law for more vulnerable claimants.

Advocates of the creditors' bargain suggest that the insolvency system should not address the vulnerability of specific stakeholders; rather, remedial legislation,

[29] Mevorach (n 19) 109. [30] Ibid 110.

[31] Ibid 111, citing Douglas G. Baird, 'Bankruptcy's Uncontested Axioms' (1998) 108 *Yale Law Journal* 573 at 580–2.

[32] Janis Sarra, *Employee and Pension Claims During Company Insolvency, A Comparative Study of 62 Jurisdictions*, (Toronto: Thomson Carswell, 2008) 4.

[33] Ibid 10.

such as employment standards and pension benefits legislation, can more appropriately address the vulnerability of employees and other stakeholders.[34] However, arguably, they take this position confident that such protections are unlikely to be implemented or that insolvency legislation will override this remedial legislation. Advocates for the creditors' bargain suggest that principles underpinning the insolvency regime should reflect the hypothetical pre-insolvency bargain constructed from the rational self-interest of creditors to maximize their realizations and that any departure from the terms of this bargain would be unfair as well as inefficient.[35] This position is flatly contradicted by the distributive priorities granted under many insolvency laws for employee and related claims in the event of a debtor's insolvency. Since all the creditors of a solvent debtor are characteristically paid in full, non-insolvency law does not address the issue definitionally peculiar to insolvency itself: namely, who should bear how much loss when a debtor is rendered terminally unable to meet its obligations.[36] Employee claimants are almost uniquely vulnerable to harm in their employer's insolvency. Employees cannot diversify by working for many more than one employer and may have no insurance because they are unable to join a union that would obtain such insurance for its members. Employees may have had no influence on the terms on which they were employed and therefore became creditors involuntarily and might be unable quickly to find work upon being deprived of their job when their employer becomes insolvent. They may be owed wages for weeks or months, having supplied services to their employer when it was in distress without demanding payment on time, in the hope of the employer's recovery. For all these reasons, employee creditors may suffer serious harm if deprived of too great a proportion of what they are owed. Equality of concern for the interests of different creditor types should therefore accord greater priority to employee claims over those claims held by other, less vulnerable claimants.[37]

The UNCITRAL *Legislative Guide on Insolvency Law (Legislative Guide)* also embeds notions of fair and equitable treatment of creditors.[38] It does not suggest a pure translation of pre-insolvency rights to the insolvency law, but rather, observes that insolvency law should ensure *equitable treatment of similarly situated creditors*, providing for a distribution on their claim in accordance with their relative ranking and interests.[39] The *Legislative Guide* recognizes that all creditors do not need to be treated identically, but in a manner that reflects the different bargains they have struck with the debtor.[40] The *Legislative Guide* also specifies that even though the principle of equitable treatment may be modified by social policy on priorities and give way to the prerogatives pertaining to holders of claims or interests that arise, for example, by operation of law, it retains

[34] For a critique of this approach, see Sarra, *Creditor Rights* (n 2).

[35] Jackson, 'Translating Assets' (n 13).

[36] Mokal, *Corporate Insolvency Law* (n 4) 118, citing Roy Goode, *Principles of Corporate Insolvency Law* (London: Sweet & Maxwell, 2005) 39.

[37] This discussion is a close paraphrase of Mokal, *Corporate Insolvency Law* (n 4) 119. See also, Sarra, *Creditor Rights* (n 2).

[38] UNCITRAL *Legislative Guide on Insolvency Law*, https://www.uncitral.org/pdf/english/texts/insolven/05-80722_Ebook.pdf at part one, ch. I, at 13 (hereafter *Legislative Guide*)

[39] Ibid 11. [40] Ibid.

its significance in terms of equitable and fair treatment. Thus, the *Legislative Guide* considers the principle of equitable treatment in a multi-layered way, both prescribing equal treatment to creditors according to prior entitlements and referring to equality among creditors of preferred classes as created by insolvency law, while also accepting that the concept is subject to social decisions on priorities, leaving it to national law to determine distributive issues.[41]

The treatment of employee claims in Canadian insolvency proceedings provides a reasonably representative example. Employees are given a limited statutory super-priority for their wage and pension claims, to a specified amount, on a debtor filing insolvency proceedings, whether a restructuring or a liquidation. The priority charge for wage claims applies to cash, accounts receivable, and inventory, or the proceeds from any dealing with those assets.[42] Unlike unpaid wage claims, the super-priority for pension amounts is not limited to the aforementioned asset categories, but rather, is a charge against all of the assets of the debtor.[43] The legislation, enacted in 2009, was aimed at addressing a specific social need: losses to employees and pensioners when employers were paying down other debts in the period leading up to insolvency, instead of making remittances for pensions or keeping up with the payroll. The Canadian Parliament sought to readjust the incentives at work when debtors are on the eve of insolvency. The rules are transparent, and creditors lend to debtors understanding that these statutory preferences exist if the debtor becomes insolvent. Owners and directors also understand the need to meet these priorities in the period leading up to insolvency.

Insolvency law's avoidance or 'clawback' mechanisms provide the second example. Different insolvency law regimes opt for different mechanisms for clawing assets back into the insolvency estate, including statutory provisions addressing transfers at undervalue, preferences, and fraudulent transactions. While the timelines differ across jurisdictions—as do approaches in terms of requiring objective versus subjective intent and differing standards for arm's-length versus non-arm's-length transactions—frameworks are often aimed at both the fairness principle and at maximizing the value of the debtor's assets available to meet creditors' claims. Some jurisdictions impose absolute liability, while others provide defences, particularly for fair value for third parties receiving the assets if the exchange has taken place in good faith and without the third parties' knowledge that the transaction was a violation of insolvency law. The principles underlying these mechanisms are the fair and equal treatment of creditors when the firm is on the eve of insolvency, with the goal of maximizing the value of the assets to be shared among creditors and reducing transaction costs in establishing such claims. These mechanisms are designed to prevent the debtor from depleting its assets in the pre-insolvency period, or attempting to evade payment obligations on insolvency. They also work to prevent undue pressure by powerful creditors on the debtor to direct assets away from other

[41] Mevorach (n 19) 122.
[42] Bankruptcy and Insolvency Act, RSC 1985, c B-3, as amended (BIA) at s 81.3.
[43] Ibid s 85.1.

creditors in a period of distress, perhaps even precipitating insolvency as a result of a preferential payment.[44]

Mokal argues that avoidance rules mediate amongst three insolvency law objectives.[45] The first, already mentioned, is the distribution of insolvency value and loss in a normatively defensible manner. This objective explains the very existence of avoidance rules as rooted in the protection of weak and vulnerable claimants. Sophisticated and well-resourced parties do not need the protection of avoidance rules and instead would bargain pre-insolvency to protect themselves through proprietary security, contractual covenants, and other mechanisms. Nor are such rules needed by claimants connected with the debtor by ownership or control; in fact, such claimants would tend to prefer the freedom of engineering preferential or undervalue transactions to themselves. Again, then, equal concern for different types of claimant argues in favour of mechanisms protecting some, but that may be redundant for or disfavoured by others. The second objective at play is maximization of the value in the insolvency estate, which undergirds protection to otherwise avoidable transactions that nevertheless benefit the insolvency estate in the net present value sense. The third objective is that of finality of transactions, and it affords protection to parties who have performed due diligence before entering into the transaction even if the transaction is otherwise voidable and subsequently turns out not to have added value to the estate of the subsequently insolvent party. This objective manifests equal concern for the interests of solvent counterparties and also incentivizes them pre-insolvency to discover and abstain from entering into transactions that are potentially avoidable in the first place.

Mevorach observes that setting aside transactions entered into near default is another way of tackling opportunistic behaviour by managers pursued collectively rather than by creditors individually.[46] She notes that the *Legislative Guide* also suggests that equitable treatment permeates many aspects of insolvency law, including provisions to set aside acts and transactions and recapture value for the insolvency estate. Insolvency law should address problems of fraud and favouritism that may arise in cases of distress by providing that acts and transactions detrimental to equitable treatment of creditors can be avoided.[47]

3. Respecting legislative choices

The demands of fairness characteristically preclude some possible rules or ways of structuring legal institutions, such as those that are based on morally arbitrary discrimination amongst stakeholders. Fairness does not, however, dictate exactly what rule or type of institution must be put in place. Tax law provides a salient example. A fair

[44] Both the debtor's and powerful creditors' perverse incentives are discussed in Mokal, *Corporate Insolvency Law* (n 4) 306–8.

[45] Ibid 308–12 and 330–8.

[46] Mevorach (n 19) 108.

[47] Ibid 123, citing the *Legislative Guide* (n 38), part two, ch. II, para. 150, explaining that many insolvency laws include avoidance provisions. See also Jay L. Westbrook, 'Locating the Eye of the Financial Storm' (2007) 32 *Brook J Int'l L*, 1019, 1021.

distribution of the benefits and burdens of a decent social security net may rule out excessively low tax rates for the wealthy and excessively high rates for the poor. This approach would still leave considerable latitude for legislative choice: fairness would not dictate that value added tax should be levied at exactly 17.5% rather than 18%, nor that the top rate of income tax should be 45% rather than 50%. By analogy, the Modular Approach advocated in this volume is designed to acknowledge significant policy and legislative discretion being exercised by the authorities of each jurisdiction.

Indeed, fairness itself requires according weight being given to the policy and legislative choices of such authorities, which may legitimately speak on behalf of the political communities they represent and govern. It is partly the acknowledgement of this dimension of fairness that justifies the modularity of the Modular Approach: it is in the first instance for national authorities to decide exactly what modules to make available to parties in particular MSME insolvency cases, how to fine-tune the modules for their country's particular circumstances, and in which institutions to vest the various functions that must be performed.

Fairness, then, is the substantive foundational principle of the Modular Approach. A MSME insolvency regime should be structured according to fair principles. It must also, however, be responsive to a variety of second-order principles that, while subordinate to fairness, guide the regime's operations and processes. These procedural principles are discussed next.

4. The role of efficiency

The first procedural goal is efficiency. This volume discusses and rejects the Pareto and Kaldor–Hicks conceptions of efficiency and instead draws on the tool of transaction cost-efficiency,[48] which is an indispensable procedural goal.[49]

A transaction is 'Pareto-efficient' if its occurrence satisfies the preference of at least one person and does not violate anyone else's preference. A transaction that consists of taking away an entitlement from A and vesting it in B may be Pareto-efficient so long as B fully compensates A for the loss as judged by A themselves and yet B is better off because of the transaction as judged by B. The same transaction is 'Kaldor–Hicks-efficient' if B *could have* fully compensated A, regardless of whether compensation actually occurs.

Both these conceptions of efficiency are defective, and there are several reasons for this. First, Pareto efficiency is unattainable, since even the most trivial transaction tends to create uncompensated losses. Second, and since any departure from the status quo tends to be inefficient, such efficiency favours stasis. Third, and turning to Kaldor–Hicks, this conception would support the infliction of severe harm, for example, legal discrimination, on a small and unpopular group so long

[48] Paul Milgrom and John Roberts, *Economics, Organization and Management* (New Jersey: Prentice-Hall, 1992).

[49] The discussion in this section draws on Mokal, 'Fairness' (n 1) 454–9; Mokal, *Corporate Insolvency Law* (n 4) 20–6; and Mokal, 'Contractarianism, Contractualism, and the Law of Corporate Insolvency' (2007) *Singapore Journal of Legal Studies* 51, 53–9.

as this discrimination satisfied the strongly held preferences of a sufficiently large other group. This violation of the egalitarian requirement of equal concern renders this version of efficiency morally odious. Fourth, both conceptions are subject to endowment effects. Both require preference satisfaction, but preferences are in significant part a product of the initial distribution of wealth and natural endowments. Both of these conceptions imply that to attain efficiency in either sense may have little normative merit unless that initial distribution of resources is itself normatively meritorious. This approach also implies that both types of efficiency are indeterminate, it being possible at least in principle either to take the initial resource distribution as given and attain efficiency by satisfying the resulting preferences, or to alter resource distribution, thus altering the pattern of preferences. It suggests that either of these approaches will attain efficiency by satisfying these new preferences. Efficiency analysis itself has no resources for choosing between these possibilities. Fifth and finally, both types of efficiency treat preferences as morally basic or foundational: their satisfaction is regarded as a source of value, but there can be no assessment of the worth of different preferences themselves. Efficiency analysis cannot help choose between a preference for hurting and another for healing. On any plausible view, this theoretical approach is manifestly inconsistent with the basic structure of morality. For all these reasons, this volume rejects both Pareto and Kaldor–Hicks efficiency.

The procedural conception of efficiency favoured instead is grounded in the acknowledgement that the implementation of any given set of substantive goals, in this case of a MSME insolvency regime, would need resources. Transaction cost-efficiency requires that the chosen set of substantive goals be implemented in the least costly feasible manner. Given a stock of resources available for the implementation of the chosen set of substantive goals, transaction cost-efficiency demands that the resources be deployed so as to implement these goals to the maximal feasible extent.

Transaction cost-efficiency seeks the minimization of the sum of two types of cost, both premised on the existence of information asymmetry amongst the relevant parties. Coordination costs arise from the limits on the cognitive capacities of those individuals engaged in a common project for selecting the mutually optimal response to circumstances. Therefore, resources have to be expended in remedying limitations and/or in ameliorating their consequences. Motivation costs arise from the fact that even those individuals engaged in a common project have only overlapping but not coterminous interests, and that resources must be deployed in order to better align those interests or ameliorate the consequences of the misalignment.

However, to reiterate, substantive goals such as fairness concern the law's ultimate ends and, as such, can neither compete with, nor be traded off against, procedural goals such as transaction cost-efficiency, which are about means.[50]

[50] See e.g. Mokal, 'Fairness' (n 1) 458; Mokal, *Corporate Insolvency Law* (n 4) 458–9.

5. Aspects of an efficient process

An efficient process for MSME insolvency would be accessible without unnecessary barriers, would provide due transparency and certainty for stakeholders, and would require accountability in relation to the entrepreneur's acts and omissions. It would ensure progress in a timely manner from commencement to resolution. The presence of these features results in a fair process overall.

a. Accessibility

Many insolvency systems create processes for commencing insolvency proceedings that require either court involvement, filing of detailed financial information, and/or the opinion or support of an insolvency professional prior to commencement. These requirements, while important, may impede accessibility for MSMEs because of the expense of court appearances and the previously identified problems of inadequate financial records and insufficient resources to engage an insolvency professional. Insolvency systems need to address these barriers to filing in order to reduce both coordination and motivation costs. Micro and small businesses, in particular, need to easily access the process to assist with resolution of distress, at the same time as building in protections to maintain the integrity of the credit system. Several other features of a well-designed insolvency process would enhance accessibility, including a moratorium on creditor claim enforcement and the availability of funding for the process. These are considered in Chapters 4 and 6.

b. Transparency

Transparency is an important procedural goal.[51] It is required for fairness to all stakeholders, and for the purpose of reducing both coordination and motivation costs, each of which is premised on information asymmetry and thus diminish in line with such asymmetry. Transparency has several aspects: transparency with respect to the financial situation of the debtor, transparency in processes to resolve insolvency, and transparency of outcomes.

Starting with transparency of the MSME's financial situation, the question, disregarding contractual obligations of disclosure, is what is fair for creditors and other stakeholders to know and when. Using Mokal's dramatic ignorance approach, stakeholders would seek to strike a balance between the debtor's ability to manage its financial affairs without interference and with due regard for privacy and commercial confidentiality, and creditors' and others' right to know when a business is financially distressed so that they are able to take self-help action in the absence of a collective process. The difficulty in striking this balance, however, is that MSMEs, particularly micro and small businesses, frequently have inefficient—and in some countries virtually non-existent—record keeping, such that not even the

[51] Sarra, *Rescue* (n 6).

entrepreneurs themselves notice the slide into insolvency. Moreover, once the entrepreneur understands that the enterprise is insolvent, transparency for other stakeholders may be difficult to bring about when the financial records are incomplete and cannot now be made adequate.

One question, therefore, addressed in the chapters that follow, is how a simple form of financial status reporting could be devised that would be cost-effective for MSMEs and would assist creditors and other stakeholders in assessing their debtor's status and what options these stakeholders have in response. Another concern is the need for transparency for debtors, creditors, and other stakeholders regarding the mechanisms in place to address the insolvency. The availability of such mechanisms may not be visible to MSME debtors and their less sophisticated creditors. Thus, in addition to system design, the question is how that system can be made transparent through public education, such as web-based education, or as a requirement of new business licensing.

In terms of process transparency, creditors should receive timely and effective notice of the insolvency in cases both of liquidation and proposed plans for the continuation of the business. They should be informed of the financial condition of the debtor and of the MSME's prospects going forward, to enable them to make an informed judgment in respect of any proposed actions. Creditors and other stakeholders with an interest in the insolvent MSME debtor are best placed to select the tools appropriate to that case. The role of the legal regime should be to provide these tools in a maximally flexible way, while creating the correct incentives for their deployment. On liquidation, transparency may also mean minimizing the risk of illegitimate self-dealing by the entrepreneur, such as the transfer of business assets at undervalue to related parties.

Transparency includes embedding a right for creditors to receive notice of issues that affect their interests and affording them an opportunity to be heard. This notice does not, it is worth pointing out, imply a normative conceptualization that creditors are now the only residual 'owners' of the business. It is not necessarily a transfer of decision authority to creditors. Transparency should allow creditors to monitor the debtor's financials during the insolvency process, and some jurisdictions actually provide for formal creditors' committees to undertake that role.

A third requirement is transparency in respect of outcomes. A properly functioning system requires that stakeholders with a direct interest in the MSME insolvency understand the compromises and trade-offs being made in working out the options for addressing the debtor's insolvency. Creditors are legitimately entitled to the assurance that their treatment has been fair in the circumstances, and if the resolution is a continuation plan, that they are receiving at least the liquidation value of their claims going forward.

c. *Certainty*

Another consideration is that the insolvency regime must create sufficient legal certainty with respect to the recovery of debts from the insolvency estate in order to allow lending to proceed on reasonable terms, including the factoring in of interest rates. Certainty in commercial credit relationships is important to the functioning of a society. That certainty includes both legal certainty on the actual content of the rules and practical certainty on the ability of the process to ensure timely and adequate enforcement of claims if the debtor defaults on the credit arrangement. Certainty during the insolvency process directly affects the availability of credit for businesses that are not yet insolvent and those that are unlikely to become so. Creditors wish to know their respective rights and remedies, should the debtor be unable to meet contractual obligations, be they loan payments, payments for goods and services, or source deductions for pensions, taxes, etc. Lack of certainty can increase monitoring costs both prior to and during insolvency, as each individual stakeholder will need to monitor the debtor if there is no certainty regarding the collective process.

Certainty and predictability are identified in the *Legislative Guide* as critically important in promoting economic stability, in fostering lending and investment, and in providing a backdrop against which relative rights and risks can be assessed in a timely manner at the point of insolvency.[52]

Certainty in the insolvency system and in its practical administration also speaks to the need to make clear to creditors, well in advance of insolvency, what the hierarchy of claims will be in the insolvency process. That hierarchy informs the decision whether or not to grant credit, at what interest rate, and, where the creditor has the bargaining power, whether to require security. Certainty also speaks to creditors understanding how their contractual claims will be treated in insolvency, in terms of the hierarchy that will affect the amount that a creditor is likely to recover under various approaches to liquidation or business continuation. Where countries have made normative decisions to protect involuntary creditors—such as particular types of claimants harmed by a tort committed by the business, or employees, or pensioners—the statutory framework signals to creditors that their claims may be subordinated to these claims during insolvency because of the value that a society has placed on those claims or the recognition that a society has in terms of the distributive consequences of insolvency on particular creditors or other stakeholders.

With particular reference to MSME insolvency, certainty also entails having a process that is simplified and easy to work with. Mevorach further observes in a different context that certainty and predictability of insolvency law rules support minimization of transaction costs pre insolvency, which in turn may facilitate the provision of credit, since potential lenders can easily identify and rely with confidence on the rules provided by the insolvency regime in pricing the transaction and calculating their risk.[53] Certainty may also enhance consensual dispute resolutions between the debtor and its creditors, in some cases preventing entry into insolvency proceedings.[54]

[52] *Legislative Guide* (n 38), part one, ch 1, at paras 4, 11–13.

[53] Mevorach (n 19) 111.

[54] Ibid.

d. Timeliness

The efficacy of an insolvency process may turn on the timeliness with which the process is commenced. An effective insolvency process reduces transaction costs by encouraging debtors to initiate rescue or liquidation proceedings in a timely manner. Delayed commencement may result in the depletion or destruction of value and perhaps of the going concern, as the debtor's assets are seized by secured and judgment creditors and/or misapplied by the debtor's managers, in either case unimpaired by an insolvency stay. Once a MSME slides into distress, value can quickly be lost if the debtor fails to address the financial distress in a timely manner.

Equally, premature commencement of insolvency proceedings may destroy the most realistic options for turning around the distressed business by stigmatizing the debtor in the eyes of its counterparties, who might assume that it was no longer viable and might thereafter refuse to do business with it on ordinary commercial terms or at all.

There must be incentives for entrepreneurs to commence an insolvency process at the appropriate time, and the range of mechanisms for creating such incentives is canvassed in Chapter 5. Incentives for the entrepreneur to make the decision to enter insolvency proceedings or to work with their creditors to resolve the financial distress must take account of the fact that on the eve of insolvency, creditors, including employees, may not understand the scope of the financial distress, that is, its seriousness, underlying causes, and possible methods of resolution. A delicate balance must be struck. Too onerous a burden will result in entrepreneurs being unwilling to risk carrying on business and will discourage entrepreneurial activity. Yet without incentives, entrepreneurs will delay filing, leaving few or no assets for creditors to realize on their claims.

The individualistic debt-collection mechanisms offered by non-insolvency law operate on a 'first come, first served' basis, with claims being met roughly in the order in which they are pressed. Other things equal, this system encourages a 'race to collect' against distressed debtors, where their creditors anticipate that they would not be able to meet their obligations in full. Creditors then have incentives to rush to enforce claims, and a disorderly and value-destructive dismantling of the debtor's business may follow. In order to preserve the estate and enable a value-maximizing decision to be made about its future, insolvency law imposes restrictions on individualistic claim enforcement and compels creditors into a collective realization and distribution process. Armour observes that enhancing after-insolvency cost-efficiency requires collective decision-making that will be rapid and accurate, and will minimize strategic behaviour as a result of heterogeneous priorities, effectively dealing with the diversity of stakeholders' interests.[55] This approach is in the interests of creditors, indeed also those of other stakeholders, as a group.[56] Timeliness

[55] John Armour, 'The Law and Economics of Corporation Insolvency: A Review' (2001) ESRC Centre for Business Research, University of Cambridge, Working Paper No. 197, 20–5.

[56] Mevorach (n 19) 108; Philippe Aghion, Oliver Hart, and John Moore, 'The Economics of Bankruptcy Reform' (1992) 8 *J L Econ & Org* 523, 525–6; Michelle J. White, 'Corporate Bankruptcy as a Filtering Device: Chapter 11 Reorganizations and Out-of-Court Debt Restructurings' (1994) 10 *J L Econ & Org* 268.

here requires expediting commencement of the insolvency process, notice to creditors, and ultimate resolution of the insolvency.

The collective process should not, however, be invoked as a tactic merely to delay creditors. Timeliness also means that creditors need to be able to enforce their security interests with reasonable expedition; hence, it is important to achieve a balance between enforcement, stays, and timing of proceedings, so not as to give the debtor or a senior creditor unreasonable power or leverage in the process. A stay may not be necessary at all where key creditors agree to a plan for the debtor going forward and there is no need to stay other creditors' claims as they are being met in full under a continuation plan.

e. *Accountability*

Accountability as a process is premised on the existence of information asymmetry, which needs to be structurally addressed in the insolvency framework. Accountability is a function of both coordination and motivation costs. The entrepreneur may be regarded as an agent of the other stakeholders in the business, whose acts and omissions affect their interests in relation to it. Accountability is required because these interests may be harmed by the entrepreneur's incompetence or poor judgement. Here, accountability serves to reduce coordination costs. Further, the harm to stakeholder interests may result from the entrepreneur's fraud, cheating, or shirking, and accountability controls motivation costs.[57]

6. The specific challenges of MSME insolvencies

The procedure of the Modular Approach developed in Chapter 4 addresses the specific challenges unique to the insolvency of a MSME. While issues like the timely commencement of proceedings are challenges to the design of all insolvency frameworks, the characteristics of MSMEs raise some distinctive challenges. Some of these challenges become more complex and difficult to overcome, the smaller the business.

a. *Determining viability*

Every insolvency framework should be designed to effectively maximize value in, and to prevent unnecessary losses from, the insolvency estate. Typically, such losses may occur in two scenarios: (1) a viable business is dismantled in a piecemeal liquidation, which results in the loss of any remaining going-concern surplus; and (2) a non-viable business is continued and subsequently fails, which results in additional losses of the reinvested value that should instead have been invested in other, viable ventures.[58] There is also a potential third scenario that may trigger the occurrence

[57] This paragraph draws on Mokal, 'Fairness' (n 1).

[58] See n 5.

of unnecessary and unreasonable losses—the 'no-assets' case, which is a regular phenomenon in MSME insolvencies. Here, liquidation would produce nil returns to creditors. By contrast, allowing the business to continue may return some value to creditors and would significantly reduce social costs by enabling self-employment and economic survival for the entrepreneur and their family.

Starting with this third category, the Modular Approach permits continuation of the distressed business if the entrepreneur is willing to continue and the creditors provide actual or deemed consent. In principled terms, party autonomy trumps the implications of strict valuation analysis. The decision of whether to continue or liquidate the business, and how to do so, should, in principle, always be left to the parties who possess the best information about the business, its management, its competitors, and the state of the economic sector in which it operates. Such information is likely to be critical to the assessment of the reasonableness of the expectations concerning the distressed enterprise's viability.

The entrepreneur characteristically possesses private information as to the business's viability. Similarly, the business's creditors, considered as a group, also possess debtor- and sector-specific information to a greater degree than any other stakeholder group. Creditors as a group also have legal rights to repayment, which are unlikely to be honoured fully by the distressed debtor. In this important sense, they have the residual claim against the debtor and stand to gain from the maximization of the value of its business and to lose if a chance to maximize that value is missed. Creditors as a group thus possess incentives to pick whichever option—liquidation or continuation—likely maximizes the value of the business. Crucially, however, a well-designed insolvency regime would acknowledge and respond to the fact that not all types of creditor possess such value-maximizing incentives.[59]

The process may be conceptualized as consisting of two steps. The first is to propose the best way in which the value in the insolvency estate may be maximized. This step includes not merely deciding whether to liquidate or to continue the business, but, if the latter, also identifying the optimal terms on which the continuation may occur. The Modular Approach seeks to capitalize on this private information possessed by the debtor as to the business's viability by giving the entrepreneur the opportunity of proposing how the insolvency should be addressed, while, presumptively, running the business and thus retaining the most current information about its status and prospects.

The second step in determining viability is to make the ultimate decision on whether to pursue continuation on the basis of one or more proposed plans, or to consign the business to liquidation. The Modular Approach seeks to capitalize on properly incentivized creditors as a group to identify and support the option that is most likely to maximize the value of the business.

[59] A well-known example is secured creditors whose collateral has sufficient value to ensure full repayment regardless of the maximization of the overall value of the business.

In general, no other stakeholder group is likely to be better placed than creditors to make the liquidate/continue decision. The entrepreneur, any other equity owners, and employees *qua* employees,[60] all can be expected to have a bias in favour of continuation, which for them is a one-sided bet. These groups tend to have little to lose and something to gain from opting for continuation, regardless of the business's viability. Courts and other state authorities have no personal incentive to choose the value-maximizing option, and they, like employees and many equity owners, may lack knowledge of the business, its competitors, and/or the relevant economic sector. Similarly, the entrepreneurs cannot be expected to make a credible decision about whether they bear some responsibility for the business's distress, nor about their own ability to turn around the business's fortunes. Since there is significant overlap between ownership and control in most MSMEs, the same points apply to equity owners. Further, no other stakeholder group has legal rights at risk in the debtor's insolvency: equity holders are not entitled to payment from the business unless creditors are paid in full, and employees are not entitled to maintain their status once they are redundant to their employer's requirements.

In summary, the decision as to whether to attempt a continuation of the business or to provide for its speedy liquidation is, in principle, best vested primarily in creditors as a group. In the MSME context in particular, however, most creditors are likely a dispersed group with small individual stakes in the outcome. MSME insolvency regimes must be built on the understanding that it would often be rational for such creditors not to participate actively in their debtor's insolvency proceedings. The decision as to whether or not the debtor should be allowed to continue to operate should not be held hostage to creditor participation that is irrational in principle and non-existent in practice. The Modular Approach responds to these considerations in a number of ways, as described in Chapter 4.

b. Reducing the burdens on parties' knowledge and capabilities

Most stakeholders in any insolvency process are unlikely to have extensive expertise in restructuring or liquidation. In larger estates where significant value is at stake, the debtor and some stakeholders can address such deficiencies through the engagement of appropriate expertise. However, such services are often prohibitive financially for MSMEs, especially in the case of micro-enterprises. The Modular Approach responds by providing for 'off-the-shelf' continuation and liquidation plans requiring minimal customization, to be proposed by the entrepreneur in the first instance, for creditors' consideration. The plans would provide both for the deployment of the business's assets with a view to value maximization and for the distribution of that value to those stakeholders entitled to it. The creation and presentation of these plans are discussed in Chapter 4. Entitlements and the priorities among them would be provided for by law and must be respected unless the relevant claimants agreed

[60] Distinguishable from employees as creditors, who have all the rights of creditors as set out in the relevant insolvency, employment, and other related legislation.

to different treatment, subject always to fulfilment of the requirements in the particular jurisdiction, such as effective notice, majority voting, the cram-down of some creditors' rights by class, and deemed approval, etc.

c. *Responding to creditor passivity*

The limited resources in MSME insolvencies lead to very limited expectations for unsecured creditors regarding any substantial distribution in right of their claims. Thus, unsecured creditors often have little incentive to incur further costs with regard to the insolvent debtor by participating actively in negotiations or court proceedings and incurring the required travel and communication costs and investment of time. Overall, it is often rational for creditors not to participate unless a particular creditor has a special interest in the result of the proceedings, most notably because it is personally connected to the debtor as a family member or employee.

As for secured creditors, most jurisdictions afford them effective non-insolvency routes by which to enforce their security interests. Even where effective mechanisms do not exist, the low value of the collateral may not justify extensive secured creditor engagement in the process beyond immediate liquidation of the collateral. Again, secured creditors are usually not interested in participating in a process geared towards continuation or even a going-concern sale.

This apathy can lead to minimal participation by creditors in the process, other than creditors filing a claim. To the extent that there is a potential for greater value preservation, and that potential is stymied by non-participation by creditors, even where participation only requires consent to a plan or proposal, the resulting uncertainty for other creditors and the debtor concerning whether to invest resources in a going-concern solution is destructive of economic value. One method for increasing the certainty in MSME insolvency proceedings is to invert the dynamic in the absence of timely objection by deeming consent to have been given to what is proposed. Using this procedure, rationally apathetic creditors need only expend minimal resources to indicate their opposition, while more motivated creditors can still pursue value-enhancing avenues without having their efforts wasted in the absence of a positive response from one creditor. The need to incentivize participation is considered in the design of the Modular Approach's procedures in Chapter 4. Additional tools and incentives are contemplated in Chapter 6, which addresses the role and position of creditors in the regime for MSMEs in distress.

d. *Funding the business through the insolvency process*

Even a business that was, in principle, viable at the point of commencement of the insolvency process may wither on the vine unless watered with adequate funding. The Modular Approach responds both by reducing the need for financing and by ensuring the flow of value through the insolvency estate. The most significant drain on an insolvent entity's resources arises from the fees of insolvency and legal professionals. As is described in Chapter 4, the Modular Approach dispenses with both to the extent practicable, leaving it to the parties in the given case to seek involvement of such professionals if the benefits exceed the costs. As to funding the business undergoing the insolvency process, Chapter 6 provides a discussion of the various possible options for the financing of distressed businesses, differentiating among stages of the business and addressing both out-of-court and in-court situations. The Modular Approach prevents counterparties' attempts to terminate both financial and trade contracts, so long as their interests can be adequately protected. In practice, this prohibition means that the financial lender or trade supplier may not exercise an *ipso facto* clause entitling it to terminate its relationship with the now insolvent business nor demand higher 'ransom' rates for its finance, goods, or services, so long as the insolvent entity is able to muster sufficient funds to cure existing contractual breaches and to meet future obligations on time. Such an approach gives the insolvent business the best practicable chance of trading out of its insolvency.

e. *Providing for due accountability*

An effective MSME insolvency regime allows the entrepreneur options to address the MSME's financial distress, and continuing such a business can benefit debtors, their families, their employees, and society. In many instances, an investigation of the debtor's conduct is not necessary, as the entrepreneur has acted with integrity and is continuing to deal with creditors in good faith and in an accountable manner. However, these same benefits to family and others can create moral hazard by incentivizing entrepreneurs to act carelessly or even fraudulently in a way more likely to precipitate business failure. More than any other regime, a MSME insolvency framework must therefore ensure that it provides an effective mechanism to detect fraud or other impropriety. Dishonest or reckless entrepreneurs do not deserve to remain in business or to benefit from a quick discharge.

Insolvency, by definition, involves breach of creditors' rights, and typically also results in destruction of productive capacity and loss of employment. Cost-effective investigations of the circumstances of the insolvency serve both private and public interests. They ensure that the creditors and other stakeholders in a given case recoup what they are owed to the maximum extent practicable. They also reinforce commercial morality by assuring market participants that legal processes, including limited liability (if applicable) and insolvency law itself, are not being abused.

Micro- and small-business insolvency cases typically have few or no unencumbered assets, which leaves little or no resources to fund a credible independent investigation. The limited resources in MSME cases require a mechanism that unearths fraudulent or reckless behaviour of the entrepreneur without a lengthy and costly investigation. Any public agency or trustee would be overburdened by the sheer number of cases to review, especially in times of an economic crisis with insolvencies mounting up. As is discussed in Chapter 4, there are various possible options in terms of who might initiate proceedings for misbehaviour, including creditors, insolvency professionals, and other agencies. Chapter 5 also includes a discussion of challenges to access to information, including funding limitations. While any public investigator and any court investigation would require efforts to detect such information, such cases could be properly handled by a framework that allows and incentivizes all those creditors and other stakeholders who possess relevant facts to present them before a decision to rescue a business or discharge a debtor is made, providing due accountability in the process. In addition, the decision to discharge should be reversible for a period of time if information relating to debtor misbehaviour emerges after proceedings have ended.

f. *Providing for discharge of overindebted natural persons*

Opinion is changing with respect to the treatment of natural person entrepreneurs who have taken risks and suffered insolvency. Legislators increasingly seek to incentivize such persons, previously stigmatized and excluded from productive activity, to bring their experience and expertise back to productive use.[61] Quick and predictable debt relief is a powerful incentive for people running a troubled business to take steps to address distress in a timely manner. It provides for an exit option in a distress situation, allowing entrepreneurs to either shut down or restructure their business at an early stage, thus reducing the incentive to take excessive risks in a final attempt to turn the business around. At the same time, the threat of denying debt relief works as a powerful disincentive for those entrepreneurs who act fraudulently or attempt to misuse the regime, for example, by forging or concealing information about their business or their assets; this is discussed further in Chapter 5.

g. *The institutional context*

The resource scarcity characterizing the MSME insolvency context necessitates reconsideration of the functions to be vested in particular institutions. The question is how to balance the costs versus the benefits of features such as extensive mandatory involvement of creditors, insolvency professionals, and the courts. As previously noted, where this balance lies would be highly sensitive to the attributes of the economy and legal system. With that in mind, the Modular Approach assumes that national authorities would draw upon some combination of these parameters to define the types of enterprise that would be required or permitted to make use of the special features described in this volume, and also those features that would fall beyond the ambit of this approach.

The operation of any insolvency system requires the performance of three types of function. Someone must manage the business through the insolvency process. This management function includes ordinary commercial decisions, commercially informed choices about which of the available legal tools to deploy, and negotiations with creditors and other stakeholders to obtain a desirable conclusion to the

[61] See for the latter: *Legislative Guide* (n 38) part two, III, A, para 32. See also EU proposal COM(2016) 723 final (EU proposal for a Directive on preventative restructuring frameworks and second chance) Recital 37, Art 1 and Title III; World Bank Natural Persons Report, 2014 Working Paper, World Bank, 25–40.

insolvency process. Oversight of the process is critical to ensure that deadlines are being met, notices duly provided, and disclosures duly made. This oversight is the administrative function. Finally, the judicial function ensures that the law has been correctly applied, reasonable findings of fact have been reached, and that the parties have all been treated fairly.

The Modular Approach enables national policymakers to choose the range of options described in Chapter 4 to make available to parties in their jurisdiction. One legal system may require certain decisions in every individual case to be vested in the court. Another jurisdiction may, by contrast, allow court involvement to be dispensed with altogether in the individual case, unless fraud is suspected or a critical party is being uncooperative. Instead, the judicial function might be vested in an administrative agency, or in a regulated insolvency professional, in each case acting in a quasi-judicial capacity. National legislators would make the decision in view of their own constitutional arrangements and their own assessment of the relative abilities and availability of courts, administrative bodies, and private sector professionals. Similarly, a national legislature may decide to vest the management function in an administrative agency, or alternatively, permit the entrepreneur to remain in place. Finally, the administrative function may be vested in a public body or a private sector office holder.

Further, and subject to national authorities' design decisions, the Modular Approach devolves choices about the precise form of the insolvency process applied to a particular business to those stakeholders with the best information about the business and an appropriate stake in a value-maximizing outcome. The Modular Approach provides an essential 'core' process in each case, and allows relevant stakeholders to invoke additional tools or 'modules' if and when the benefits of wielding those tools in the particular case outweigh the costs. For example, the legislature may provide for the management function to be performed by the entrepreneur. In a simple case, the entrepreneur will steer the business through the process. In less straightforward cases, however, a requisite proportion of stakeholders may express their distrust in the entrepreneur's competence or integrity by seeking to obtain the entrepreneur's removal and replacement by an independent insolvency professional. Similarly, a legal system may envisage no court involvement in the standard case, while permitting stakeholders to invoke the court's help if and as considered necessary. Again, the assumption is that the stakeholder would only do so if the dispute is of sufficient value to it to make the costs of instructing legal professionals worthwhile. A description of these stakeholder-initiated modules is set out in Chapter 4.

In summary, fairness is the defining principle and primary substantive objective of the Modular Approach. In this instance, fairness requires treating the interests of all those stakeholders affected by issues specific to MSME insolvency with equal concern. While fairness cannot dictate uniquely correct rules, it does constrain and guide the design of the MSME insolvency framework. The Modular Approach draws inspiration from the fact that fairness can be identified as the governing critical feature of existing insolvency regimes.

This volume describes not merely the substantive rules constituting the Modular Approach, but also the process by which it is operationalized. While fairness determines substantive content, transaction cost-efficiency governs process. Accessibility, transparency, certainty, accountability, and timeliness are the key dimensions of such efficiency, not least in the treatment of MSME insolvency.

The Modular Approach is designed to meet the demands of fairness and of transaction cost-efficiency. It seeks to generate incentives for relevant parties to bring about timely commencement of the insolvency process; to sift through distressed businesses to identify and rescue viable ones, liquidate non-viable ones, and permit continuation where parties agree; to do so without making unrealistic demands on parties' capabilities and knowledge; to respond to the rational indifference to the process of creditors and other stakeholders; to provide for the funding of the business undergoing the process; to provide for accountability for any wrongdoing related to the insolvency; and to enable overindebted natural person entrepreneurs to be discharged.

4

Procedure under the Modular Approach

The Modular Approach is modular in two respects. First, it provides for a simple, clear-cut default process to liquidate or continue a MSME. At the same time, it allows flexibility, recognizing the diversity in size and needs of micro, small, and medium enterprises. The default process can be altered wherever stakeholders select specific modules to meet their particular needs. Second, the Approach also leaves open to lawmakers in each jurisdiction the choice of modules to make available to stakeholders and their allocation of responsibilities in relation to such modules. Based on local values, constitutional requirements, and economic circumstances, legislators may choose not to enact all of the offered modules. Countries may also make decisions about the most suitable institutions to perform essential roles in liquidation and continuation proceedings.[1] Overall, the Modular Approach offers a flexible, simple, and cost-effective framework for MSMEs in distress with roughly as much complexity and cost as is called for by each case.

This chapter outlines the core aspects of the procedural framework of the Modular Approach and describes the modules by which the framework may be adapted. This design offers significant legislative leeway and also provides guidelines for implementing the Modular Approach in a specific jurisdiction.

The procedural framework of the Modular Approach consists of a default 'core', complemented by a combination of additional mechanisms or 'modules' selected in each case by relevant stakeholders. It thus unpacks the many tools traditionally available under restructuring and liquidation processes. Starting from a core of presumptively essential elements, it enables parties to the specific case, acting with appropriate incentives, to select whichever combination of modules is suitable to that case, given the nature and type of debtor and assets, the causes of distress, and the perceived prospects for viability and rehabilitation of the debtor.

Figures 4.1 to 4.5 map the Modular Approach process by presenting a visual outline of the overall approach for both liquidation and continuation procedures, and by then offering an illustration of each procedure, followed by a diagram of how the various modules interact with the continuation procedure. The text boxes throughout the chapter summarize, in point form, the most important elements of the modular option being discussed.

[1] The relevant factors influencing a legislator's decision on the venue of proceedings are discussed in detail in Section C.2.b. of this chapter.

Micro, Small, and Medium Enterprise Insolvency. First Edition. Ronald Davis, Stephan Madaus, Alberto Mazzoni, Irit Mevorach, Rizwaan J. Mokal, Barbara Romaine, Janis Sarra, & Ignacio Tirado. Published 2018 by Oxford University Press.

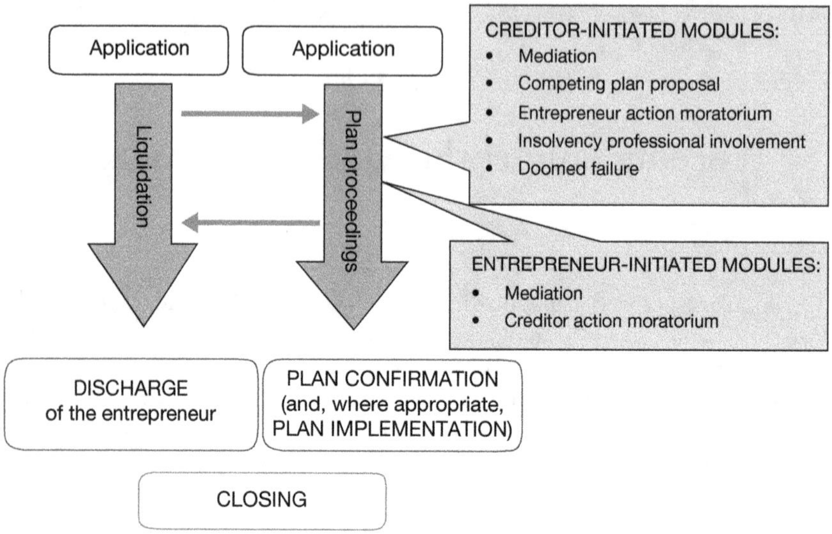

Figure 4.1 the Modular Approach—overview.

A. The Procedural Framework

The Modular Approach consists of two basic options: *automatic liquidation* and *continuation proceedings*. It adjusts the features of 'standard' liquidation and restructuring procedures typical of modern insolvency frameworks to the specific needs and circumstances of MSMEs. From an entrepreneur's perspective, both options may offer value in the situation of a business in distress. A visual overview of the Modular Approach is provided in Figure 4.1 above.

The liquidation option offers the entrepreneur a way to walk away from the business in an orderly manner, discharged of debt. It allows the entrepreneur to re-allocate skills and energy to a new business idea or to seek employment. An efficient liquidation of distressed businesses also clears the ground for more successful competitors. Both effects should support economic growth.

The business continuation option allows the entrepreneur to continue the business while addressing the factors that are the cause of its financial and/or economic distress. The reasons for a business crisis may be internal, such as the loss of a key customer, sickness, or divorce; or it may as well be external, such as distress precipitated by a larger economic downturn or recession. The continuation process provides a coordinated way to address these issues in a manner that respects the peculiarities of MSMEs. At the same time, the implementation of modules allows for the adequate protection of creditor interests in any specific case.

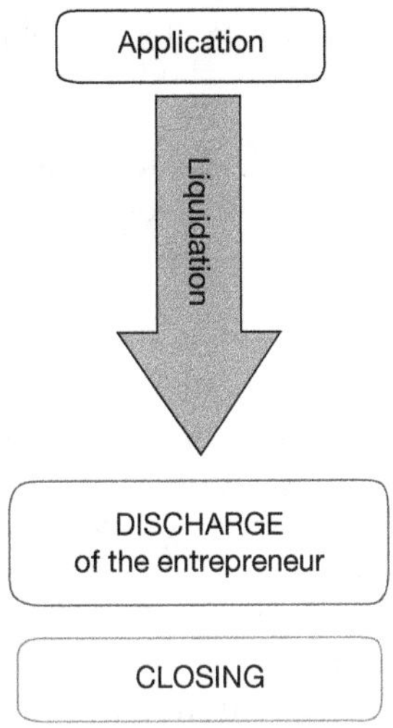

Figure 4.2 Option 1: automatic liquidation and discharge proceedings—overview.

1. Automatic liquidation proceedings and statutory discharge

a. Function and effects

Automatic liquidation and discharge proceedings offer an exit for the entrepreneur who is either not able or not willing to continue the troubled small business. They facilitate the shutting down of the business and selling of its assets piece by piece, but also allow for a takeover bid for the business generating a going-concern value. The entrepreneur is losing the business in any case. In order to make a fresh start without the business, a discharge of debt is essential. A discharge has proven to be an economic and psychological precondition to reintegrating failed entrepreneurs into the economy. A visual overview of automatic liquidation and discharge proceeding is provided in Figure 4.2 above.

In addition, a rescue-oriented approach for viable businesses can only function effectively if it is coupled with a cost-efficient liquidation process for non-viable businesses. The liquidation option works as a default option and provides an exit in restructuring negotiations. Against this backdrop of liquidation as the default option, creditors may negotiate and agree to a rescue plan.

Automatic liquidation and discharge proceedings would provide some key effects, as follows.

i. Default rule

For insolvent MSMEs, automatic liquidation and discharge proceedings provide the default route. If the debtor is insolvent and no continuation plan is brought forward by either the debtor or any creditor, or if a proposed plan does not obtain the requisite approvals, and unless a modified continuation plan obtains judicial authority approval, the debtor's business should be liquidated. Here, the business can be sold on a going-concern basis or can be wound up in a piecemeal liquidation. It should be easy to initiate such proceedings for insolvent businesses, and a competent authority would have to determine the insolvency of a debtor only in the rare case of an involuntary filing and the debtor's opposition.

ii. Stay if requested

Automatic liquidation and discharge proceedings are only protected by a short stay if such a stay is requested with the application to commence proceedings. The need for court involvement to order a stay is an unnecessary cost in most cases where a lack of unencumbered assets would cause rational creditor passivity due to the probability of unrecovered collection costs. If requested, a short stay would be imposed automatically and affect enforcement actions of all creditors, including public or statutorily preferential creditors. Such a stay may be useful in cases where selling the business as a going concern requires protection from enforcement actions. The requested stay would last for a specified short period commonly needed in a specific jurisdiction to organize the transfer of a MSME business, and it would expire automatically.

iii. Discharge of natural person debtor

In most economies, a great majority of micro and small businesses take the form of sole proprietorships or small partnerships with no separate legal personality. The entrepreneurs at the heart of such businesses are personally liable for the enterprise's obligations. Fraud and bad faith apart,[2] and as long as such debtors cooperate with the insolvency process in a timely manner, there are both fairness and efficiency-based reasons[3] for affording them an early and full discharge from their liabilities, which would encompass all business-related claims, including public or preferential claims.[4] Such discharge is a core element of the Modular Approach. Where the business is incorporated, but owned and operated by one individual, often the individual has personally guaranteed the debt and is likely to become personally insolvent as a result of the failure of the business. The Modular Approach provides a mechanism to link the individual's insolvency and discharge with the legal entity's insolvency, as discussed in Section A.1.e. of this chapter.

iv. Fundamental rights

The position of creditors is protected under fundamental rights relating to protection of property, and due process or fair trial, in most jurisdictions. Such safeguards

[2] For further discussion, see Chapter 5, Section B.3.

[3] See World Bank, *Natural Persons Report*, 2014 Working Paper, World Bank, 25–40 delineating the host of benefits to debtors and to society from providing relief to honest but unfortunate debtors. Available at: http://siteresources.worldbank.org/INTGILD/Resources/WBInsolvencyOfNaturalPersonsReport_01_11_13.pdf.

[4] The full discharge of the debts of an individual entrepreneur may be subject to a limited number of exceptions, often concerning socially sensitive claims (e.g. debts for alimony, debts to compensate physical damage, etc).

need to be respected. They include effective notice and access to a court or other decision authority where creditors' rights are being infringed:

- *Publication and notices*: Public notice of the commencement of automatic liquidation and discharge proceedings must be given through publication, as appropriate: in an official gazette, news media, relevant online sources, and in edicts in court houses, business chambers, etc. Legislators should be careful to consider cost barriers to effective notice in deciding what kind of public notice is required in their jurisdiction.[5] In addition, each known creditor and any other relevant stakeholder must be individually notified through an appropriate, cost-efficient method, such as postal services and/or electronic mail, about the resulting effect of a discharge that impairs their legal position. Notice given through reasonably cost-effective methods—including publicly, and, where appropriate, to the last reasonably known or registered address of a stakeholder—should be deemed to have been received by that stakeholder.[6]
- *Involvement of the court*: The infringement of creditors' property rights requires the consent of the property owner or the involvement of the court in many jurisdictions. The Modular Approach reflects these safeguards.

b. Application

The debtor, as well as creditors, may be entitled to initiate proceedings according to the relevant test under local law.[7] Creditors should have a competing right to apply, as it may be expected that some debtors, because of incompetence and/or perverse incentives, may not commence the insolvency process in a timely manner.

Commencement of proceedings puts the enterprise on the route to liquidation unless continuation plan proceedings are initiated immediately. In the case of failed continuation proceedings, liquidation proceedings would be initiated or would resume automatically.

c. Liquidation and distribution

The competent institution, be it a secured lender, an insolvency professional, or a public or self-regulatory authority, may seize the debtor's assets and seek their value-maximizing disposal on its own without the consent of a court or a creditors' representative, as a going concern if possible or else by means of piecemeal sale. The debtor itself may manage a quick liquidation under supervision of a regulatory authority in

[5] For example, in some OECD countries, notice in newspapers can cost thousands of dollars, which an MSME may not have; thus, it is important to take advantage of Web-based notice and public notice mechanisms where they are available.

[6] The importance of ensuring that a proper system of 'deemed notification' is included cannot be overstated. In many developing jurisdictions, notifications are one of the main challenges of formal insolvency proceedings. Debtors are able to delay proceedings for months and even escape the consequences of an insolvency process simply by ensuring that there is no effective way to notify creditors (or even there is no way for them tp be notified).

[7] Whether and when there should be a duty to file is discussed in Chapter 5, Section A.

specific jurisdictions.[8] Proceeds of such a sale or auction would be used to (a) cover administrative costs of the acting institution and subsequently (subject to discharge of any debt enjoying a higher priority in relation to the proceeds) (b) discharge the secured debt, and (c) pay other outstanding liabilities if there is remaining value. A process of filing claims would only be initiated if a distribution to other classes of creditors is probable. Any creditor who disagrees with the way the competent institution handles the process may not delay proceedings, but would be able to involve a supervisory institution, possibly a court,[9] for review and, if appropriate, damages.

d. A special challenge in a MSME liquidation— a significant disputed or unpaid claim

A common problem in the liquidation of MSMEs, especially in the case of micro and small enterprises, is that a single disputed or unpaid claim is the main asset of the business. Litigating and/or collecting the claim could significantly delay the completion of proceedings and raise costs. If a discharge is to depend on the termination of liquidation proceedings, such discharge would also be delayed. The solution to the latter problem is simple: the order to discharge a debtor must not require a completed liquidation of all assets, but should be available after the debtor turns all of its non-exempt assets over to the liquidating authority. Several options can be considered for handling the disputed claim:

1. The most natural solution in a liquidation process would be to sell the claim, which would probably mean accepting a significant discount on the nominal value, provided that there is a buyer at all. It would be consistent with the idea of a quick and low-cost procedure.
2. A second legislative option would be to allow for a quick and, if required by constitutional law, preliminary judicial determination and subsequent collection by the liquidating authority.
3. A separation of assets would be the third option. Here, pursuit of the disputed or unpaid claim would be removed from the estate through transfer, which would allow the termination of formal liquidation proceedings. The transferee would afterwards be responsible for litigating and collecting the claim.

Each of these options would allow for a speedy liquidation despite the fact that the value of the main asset is uncertain. It would be up to the specific jurisdiction to decide on a preferred option.

e. Discharge of the entrepreneur

The Modular Approach creates the presumption that an honest and cooperative entrepreneur would be personally discharged from liabilities on the lapse of a

[8] See, for example, the Country Example, European/Central Asian Emerging Nation, Section D in Chapter 7.

[9] See Section C.2.b. of this chapter.

stipulated period—for example twelve months, from the commencement of the liquidation process—automatically and without the need for judicial intervention. Discharge would include all dischargeable claims and may be opposed by a stakeholder. In jurisdictions in which such automatic discharge is unconstitutional or is considered undesirable, the entrepreneur herself or the institution performing the management function may, on the conclusion of the stipulated period, apply to the judicial or administrative authority for a discharge. In either case, discharge occurs unless the relevant authority finds the entrepreneur to have been fraudulent, to have acted in bad faith, to have culpably made incomplete disclosure, or to have been uncooperative.[10]

A typical insolvency case of a non-viable MSME would look like this:

- Application by the debtor or a creditor to a competent institution to commence liquidation
- Notice to appropriate parties
- Initiation of sales process by that institution
- Process of filing claims if creditors can expect value
- Mediation and/or resolution of any claims disputes
- Closing of sales process and distribution of proceeds
- Review of decisions, only upon request and only for damages
- Automatic discharge from remaining debt one year after the application

2. Continuation proceedings

a. Function and effects

Continuation proceedings provide a second option to the entrepreneur when her business is in distress. If the entrepreneur or a creditor intends to prevent a liquidation, they may opt for continuation proceedings, even before an application for liquidation proceedings is filed. Figure 4.3 provides a visual image of continuation proceedings aimed at developing a plan, illustrating the relationship between plan proceedings and liquidation proceedings, discussed in detail in this section.

The continuation option would enable the entrepreneur to retain control of the assets, to continue the business, and to propose and enforce a continuation plan that has sufficient creditor support, following a process that is cost-efficient. The Modular Approach creates positive incentives while respecting creditors' fundamental rights.

Continuation proceedings would possess some key attributes:

i. Entrepreneur retaining control

The entrepreneur remains at the helm of the business after commencement, making day-to-day, ordinary decisions about the deployment of the constitutive productive

[10] See Chapter 5, Section B.3.

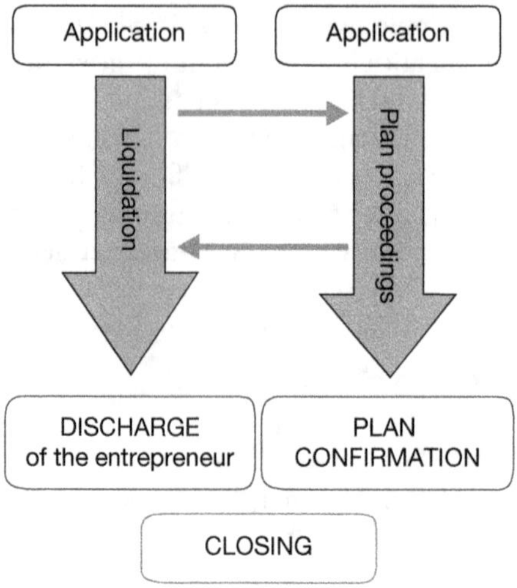

Figure 4.3 Option 2: continuation proceedings—overview.

factors. This option has three primary justifications. First, experience indicates that a concern of entrepreneurs that they will be displaced from the helm creates a powerful disincentive to commence the insolvency process in a timely manner. Second, the continuing presence of the debtor's pre-distress decisionmakers may be critical to the MSME's viability, because they frequently have access to important private information about the debtor's finances and operations; they have existing relationships with counterparties; and/or because their continued participation may be necessary to effectively balance the costs of decision-making and residual risk-bearing. Third, a significant reason that MSMEs call for a distinctive insolvency treatment is that the value at stake is often not sufficient to justify the full panoply of insolvency mechanisms, such as paying for the expertise of an insolvency professional.

ii. The 'continuation plan'

The core assumption of the Modular Approach is that the debtor would propose a plan to some or all of its creditors in order to address the distress and avoid a liquidation. The plan's intended objective is to continue the business and, by doing so, to maximize its value for the benefit of all relevant stakeholders as a group. In most cases, the debtor would present a restructuring plan that would leave the business in their hands while changing the composition, conditions, or structure of a debtor's liabilities. Such a plan, for instance, would include an extension of payment or a 'haircut', that is, a compromise of amounts claimed by creditors. It could also provide for a debt-restructuring procedure under a payment-auction mechanism.[11] In

[11] The ACCORD scheme provides an example. See Donald Hausch and S. Ramachandran, 'Systemic Financial Distress and Auction-based Bankruptcy Reorganization', (2009) 18 *Int'l Rev. Econ & Fin.* 366 ff.

some cases, the debtor may value taking control of a going-concern sale, in contrast to such a sale process pursued under the liquidation option. The continuation plan would also cover such transfer plans.

iii. Minimization of costs

MSMEs and most of their creditors are characteristically unable to spare many resources to commence or participate in the insolvency process. In recognition of this reality, the Modular Approach seeks to minimize commencement and participation costs. The process is designed to minimize complexity, to vest discretion in decisionmakers only where it is conducive to achieving the objectives of the Modular Approach, and thereby to maximize certainty. The following list is illustrative of the ways in which the Modular Approach works to minimize costs and resolve the financial distress in a timely manner.

- *Administrative costs of the procedure*: The process may be initiated and continued online, for example, through voting on a proposed plan, in those economies in which an Internet-based process is a realistic low-cost possibility. Parties participate in the first instance by using standard forms, including a standard statement of affairs and/or a financial statement.
- *Length of the procedure*: The institution discharging administrative functions for the continuation proceedings should enforce strict and brief timelines.

iv. Incentivizing creditor participation

For the reasons explored previously, creditor apathy is a common occurrence in MSME insolvency. The Modular Approach addresses this challenge by providing two types of consequences if duly notified parties fail to respond:

- *'Scream or die'*: Creditors notified of a plan must review whether the plan reflects their claims or rights correctly and object if that is not the case. If no objection is raised within the stipulated period, the content of the plan is presumptively regarded as being correct and any creditor whose claim is not listed is regarded as having waived that claim. Thus the 'scream' is the opportunity to object, and the 'die' is the loss of the ability to later complain if creditors do not object within the time period specified.
- *'Deemed approval'*: In addition, when creditors and other stakeholders are entitled to vote on a plan, a failure to vote within the stipulated period is deemed a vote in favour of the plan. Court approval of the plan would only be required if the plan is not accepted by all creditors and stakeholders according to their actual or 'deemed' votes in accordance with the threshold set under national law.

Such incentivizing measures respond to the disinterest of creditors in MSME continuation proceedings by raising the cost and consequences of a failure to participate. Passive stakeholders risk being bound to a plan that reflects neither their initial claim nor their preferred outcome. At the same time, such measures allow these stakeholders to profit from the additional value created by the proposed plan without incurring additional participation costs to ensure its acceptance.

v. Fundamental rights

As already mentioned for liquidation and discharge proceedings, the position of creditors and equity holders is protected under fundamental rights relating to protection of property, due process, or fair trial in most jurisdictions. Such safeguards need to be respected by implementing efficient means for providing notice of the commencement of continuation proceedings, as well as information about a continuation plan that impairs the creditors' legal position. Notice given through reasonably cost-effective methods—including publicly, and, where appropriate, to the last reasonably known address of a stakeholder—should be deemed to have been received by that stakeholder.

- *Involvement of the court*: The infringement of property rights of creditors and equity holders usually requires the consent of the property owner or the involvement of the court. These safeguards are reflected in the Modular Approach. While a consensual plan would not generally need to be sanctioned by a court, objections by creditors or other stakeholders (in other words, a contested plan) would create the need for a court to review, and, if appropriate, sanction the plan.

If such a sanction order is granted, it should not be subject to appeal in jurisdictions in which the right to appeal a judicial decision affecting legal rights is not required by constitutional law, for instance, in Germany.[12] This limit on appeal rights streamlines the process and limits the cost burden in MSME cases. Jurisdictions that guarantee a right to appeal any court decision should at least limit delay by not providing for an automatic stay pending appeal, or by placing limits on the right to appeal based on factors such as the importance of the issue to the practice generally, the prima facie merits of the appeal, or prejudice to the parties.

b. Application

Continuation proceedings can be initiated by the debtor or a creditor before or after an application for liquidation is filed.

c. Entrepreneur's application

The entrepreneur, in principle, possesses private information about the state of the business and its prospects and viability. The Modular Approach seeks to create positive and negative incentives for the entrepreneur to capitalize on this information

[12] Although it varies from country to country, the right to appeal (right to access a second instance) is deemed a fundamental right only in criminal law matters. Such, for example, is the approach of the European Convention on Human Rights, Protocol No. 7 to the Convention for the Protection of Human Rights and Fundamental Freedoms (Strasbourg), 22 November 1984, Article 2.

to make a timely commencement decision. Control over commencement timing may itself constitute a positive incentive. Therefore, the entrepreneur may initiate stand-alone continuation proceedings any time. In addition, the entrepreneur may also respond to a creditor's application for liquidation proceedings by filing for continuation proceedings within a short period (for example, one or two weeks), which would stay the liquidation process.

The Modular Approach allows jurisdictions to consider two different thresholds before the entrepreneur is able to commence continuation proceedings. One option is to require that the entrepreneur's application is supported by the proposal of a continuation plan, in order to ensure that initiating continuation proceedings is useful and not just an attempt to escape pressure from creditors. The other approach is to recognize that it may be too difficult for the entrepreneur to draw up a plausible plan prior to commencing the proceeding, and the MSME may need a short 'breathing space', created by a moratorium of a week or two, to work with creditors to devise a continuation plan. If no plan is presented in time, the application would be rejected. As noted in the introductory chapter of this volume, the term entrepreneur refers to sole proprietors, partners, and directors and officers of incorporated businesses—all the natural persons authorized to make decisions on behalf of the business. Thus, the 'entrepreneur's application' referred to here is also applicable to directors and officers of an incorporated small or medium enterprise as the mechanism to commence a continuation plan proceeding.

A continuation plan should be drafted by the entrepreneur. This task may, however, be beyond the capacity of many individuals running small businesses. The legal framework should, therefore, offer advice and education on this matter.[13] Assigning the task of plan design to a third party instead would contradict the objective of cost-efficiency, as this party would require remuneration. Instead, the use of official standardised forms and interactive templates that automatically generate plan content, such as classes or lists, from the information entered, offers a modern and cost-efficient alternative that most MSMEs should be able to use, as they typically have a very limited number of creditors, business partners, or employees, and a simple capital structure.

An entrepreneur's application for continuation proceedings that is supported by a plan should not require a declaration of a state of insolvency. Avoiding this requirement creates an incentive to filing and minimizes stigma. To require the debtor to be declared insolvent as a precondition to making use of the continuation process can inflict reputational harm on the entrepreneur and her business and may thus retard the prospects of its rehabilitation and create disincentives for the entrepreneur to commence the process. The rationale for requiring a declaration of insolvency is to minimize abuse of the insolvency process, but this objective can be accomplished through better targeted, less harmful means, including, in particular, the critical roles

[13] For further details, see Chapter 5, Section B.4.

of creditors, and/or the judicial authority, the provision for automatic liquidation, and the potential of a denial of discharge.[14] Plans presented in bad faith, for instance, would be handled by the 'doomed-to-failure' module explained later in this chapter.

d. A creditor's application

A creditor's application for continuation proceedings would only be required if the entrepreneur has not yet come forward with such an application supported by a plan proposal. Some creditors, particularly institutional lenders or original equipment manufacturers (OEMs)[15] with a significant stake in the particular debtor, may also possess non-public information about the debtor's state and prospects that would lead them to favour a continuation instead of a liquidation. By allowing creditors to file, the Modular Approach recognizes and capitalizes on the knowledge and interest of such creditors.

After a creditor application has initiated continuation proceedings, the administrative authority would notify the entrepreneur, who would have a chance to present a competing or amended continuation plan within a short time frame. If the entrepreneur does not propose a plan, the authority would convert proceedings and initiate a liquidation unless the applying creditor files a stand-alone continuation or transfer plan.

A creditor's application would not be redundant when continuation proceedings have already been commenced to vote on a debtor plan. A creditor who still wants to present a competing plan would only need to propose such a plan ('creditor plan proposal' module).

> Stand-alone continuation proceedings can be initiated by:
> - the entrepreneur—any time, with a plan presented immediately or shortly after;
> - a creditor—any time, primarily to incentivize the entrepreneur to propose a plan.
>
> Continuation proceedings can be initiated from liquidation proceedings by:
> - the entrepreneur—any time, with a plan presented immediately or shortly after;
> - a creditor—any time, primarily to incentivize the entrepreneur to propose a plan.
>
> In commenced continuation plan proceedings, any creditor may present a competing plan.

e. Where to file

Continuation proceedings would require a platform or register where such proceedings are hosted and published. The Modular Approach does not prescribe the

[14] For a more detailed discussion, see Chapter 5.

[15] Original equipment manufacturers, such as carmakers, are companies that are very sensitive to disruptions in their supply chain and commonly insist on detailed information sharing in their contracts with suppliers. Therefore, such companies may be well-informed and well-equipped to make a decision to file.

specific venue for continuation proceedings. Options are proposed for consideration in terms of possible competent authorities in Section C.2.b. of this chapter and are further illustrated in examples of implementation in Chapter 7. The task of managing the debtor's business would remain with the entrepreneur unless an insolvency professional is appointed ('insolvency professional involvement' module).

f. Decision on continuation

The competent administrative authority would need to decide whether to confirm or dismiss a continuation plan within a short period, such as one or two weeks.

When asked to confirm a continuation plan, the administrative authority would examine whether the plan complies with legal requirements regarding plan content and plan acceptance.

- *Content*: The plan may propose ways of enabling the debtor and/or its business to trade out of distress by providing, for example, for the deferral of payment obligations, a write-down of principal and/or interest, a reasonable time limit within which the obligations undertaken pursuant to the continuation plan shall be discharged, debt for equity swaps, asset disposals or other downsizing measures, provision for new funding, etc. The plan may also provide for an auction mechanism to schedule debt payments and reductions.[16] Alternatively, the plan may simply propose a value-maximizing sale of the business, on a going-concern or piecemeal basis, or recapitalization through issuance of new shares or equity. The sale of the business as a going concern would greatly benefit from additional non-insolvency rules that allow the transfer of licences and executory contracts without requiring the express consent of the licensor/counterparty to the contract[17] or, even more efficiently, that allow the sale of the shares of the company as part of the plan's content without the consent of shareholders whenever the business is balance-sheet insolvent.
- *Classes of creditors*: Where creditors are to be treated differently, the plan must separately address and explain the definition and treatment of each class of creditors whose interests it proposes to affect, placing in separate classes creditors who have different types of claim. Such a classification cannot be arbitrary. It must reflect specific types of claims or interests and would require a similar treatment for similar rights. Examples include those creditors holding security interests on par with each other, statutory preferential creditors, general unsecured creditors, etc, as well as those creditors holding the same type of claim that the plan proposes to treat differentially *inter se*.

[16] The ACCORD scheme provides an example. See Hausch and Ramachandran (n 11).

[17] Some jurisdictions already include such rules in their insolvency law, for example, Spain, art 146bis IL, or in their Civil Code, as in Italy, art 2558 CC, which is applicable to any sale of a business as a going concern, whether inside or outside bankruptcy. This type of rule constitutes an exception to general private law rules, but a justified one. By definition, chances are that the acquirer of the business as a going concern will be more likely to satisfy the executory contract than the initial counterparty, a debtor in insolvency liquidation.

- *Equity holder treatment*: Where the debtor is a company, private information about the state of the business's prospects and its viability is not only in the hands of the entrepreneur, but may also be with the debtor's (other) equity holders. At the same time, a continuation plan may need equity-holder support because the strategy relies on the continued participation or investment of equity holders. Equity holders are often relevant stakeholders in MSME cases and should therefore presumptively be allowed to participate actively in the process. However, giving equity holders a right to vote does not necessarily mean that they are entitled to veto a plan that has gained creditors' support because, for example, it provides for a sale of the business or a dilution of shares. A 'cram-down' rule is an important feature that can also impact equity holders' ability to determine the outcome. A cram-down takes different forms in different jurisdictions, but is essentially the process by which a court can force a plan on one or more claimant classes that gives members of that class less than the face value of their claims, even where the plan has not attracted the support of the requisite majority of the members of this class, so long as sufficient other claimant classes have supported the plan and the court determines it to be fair. The use of a cram-down rule must balance conflicting creditors' and equity holders' interests.[18]
- *Accepting a plan*: The plan would be approved upon receiving actual or deemed consent by all affected creditors and equity holders in all classes (fully consensual plan).
- *Class democracy and cram-down*: Where a proposed plan faces active opposition in a class or by a class, which might not often be the case in a MSME context, judicial involvement may be required under constitutional law as well as fundamental rights if the plan seeks to bind dissenting stakeholders against their will.

Where an opposing stakeholder is part of a class that supports the plan by a majority of value (claims or shares),[19] the plan should be confirmed as long as the dissenting stakeholder receives the same return as others in that class ('equal treatment within class') *and* at least as much as they could expect in an alternative liquidation ('no creditor worse off' principle or 'best interest test'). Equal treatment is a matter of fairness and a majority in a class accepting their treatment under a plan indicates that an equally treated minority is not discriminated against. The 'no creditor worse off' principle or 'best interest test' derives from the fact that creditors and shareholders

[18] A state would be able to fashion a cram-down rule for MSMEs appropriate to its insolvency regime. The courts play an important role in safeguarding the interests of creditors in a cram-down situation. For example, in 2018 the United States Court of Appeals of the Ninth Circuit in *In re Transwest Resort Properties Inc.*, Case No. 16-16221 (9th Cir. 25 Jan. 2018) held that section 1129(a)(10) of the US *Bankruptcy Code*, which requires cram-down plans to have at least one impaired accepting class, applies on a 'per-plan' basis, rather than being assessed on a 'per-debtor' basis. Under the 'per-plan' rule, multiple debtors with a single plan of reorganization may cram down a plan on any creditor class with the support of only one impaired accepting class, even where the impaired accepting class has claims against a different debtor than the crammed-down class that has rejected the plan.

[19] The requirement of a qualified majority in value or an additional (qualified) majority would add complexity to a process where little value is at stake for most stakeholders. Still, jurisdictions may decide to set such additional thresholds if they hold them necessary.

of an insolvent debtor would be entitled to liquidate the debtor's assets in common insolvency proceedings immediately. It is the plan that would detract from this right in favour of a plan treatment. Dissenting stakeholders must thus receive at least as much under the plan as they could expect in an immediate bankruptcy liquidation. However, as 'no asset cases' are frequent in MSME insolvencies, especially in those affecting micro and small businesses, and the alternative liquidation under the Modular Approach would result in a prompt discharge of the honest entrepreneur, the guarantee of the liquidation value of a claim may often provide little protection.

Protection of a minority creditor/equity holder in a class of creditors/equity holders accepting the plan:

- No discrimination—equal treatment of all class members
- Guarantee of the economic value of the claim in the scenario of an alternative enforcement of the claim (liquidation)
- *Class cram-down*: Where the stipulated majority of members of a stakeholder class do not approve the plan, the judicial authority would have the power to apply a cram-down rule against the whole class that would allow the confirmation of the plan. Here, the authority would have to assess whether the opposing class is presenting a good reason not to confirm the plan against their consent. Commonly, they would need to demonstrate that they would be treated unfairly under the plan. There are traditional tests to demonstrate the fairness of a plan:
  1. The judicial authority should apply the 'equal treatment within class' and 'no creditor worse off' principles described above, as they ensure a minimum degree of fair treatment of all members of a dissenting class.
  2. The judicial authority would also test that the plan does not overturn the relative priorities of that class and each class junior to it. Such a test would ensure that any going concern or future value beyond the value generated in an alternative insolvent liquidation would be allocated according to the waterfall of priorities established under pre-bankruptcy entitlements, unless classes agree to a different allocation. Such relative priorities between classes of stakeholders may result from contract, secured transactions, statutory priorities, company law, or even social law. While the right to receive the value that would be distributed in an alternative liquidation is already protected by the 'no creditor worse off' test, respecting priorities beyond insolvency law is essential for the distribution of any restructuring surplus value under the plan. In case of insolvent corporations, both creditors and shareholders may be regarded as financial investors in the firm. The application of contract and company law would commonly identify shareholders as residual claimants to any value in the firm. Thus, they should not be able to receive more, if any, value under the plan than a class of dissenting creditors. In MSME insolvencies, however, two aspects may provide ground for the legislator or the judicial authority to ignore a strict rule of priorities.

The first of these aspects is that, in micro and small insolvency cases in particular, the entrepreneur is not merely or primarily a financial investor. Instead, as themselves the MSME debtor or as the owner and manager of a MSME company, their primary contributions to the business are typically their skills, business and sector experience, and relationships with the workforce, suppliers, and customers.[20] Thus, they would not become a part of the priorities cascade and would be allowed to keep the restructured business, or their shares in it, against the will of a dissenting class of creditors in order to retain their soft variables for the business. Second and for similar reasons, the harm to the entrepreneur from the closure of the business may be entirely disproportionate to the benefit the closure would bring to creditors, and entirely disproportionate also to the harm they would suffer from the business's continuation. This suggests that the insolvency process should presumptively be weighted in favour of continuation. In addition, the specific circumstances in a MSME insolvency may justify a treatment under the plan that does redistribute value if the entrepreneur is able to demonstrate additional circumstances that justify the proposed redistribution.

Protection of opposing creditors/equity holders in a class rejecting the plan:

- No discrimination—equal treatment of all class members
- Guarantee of the economic value of the claim:
  - in the scenario of an alternative enforcement of the claim (liquidation)
- Adequate distribution of value under the plan:
  - considering the treatment of classes with equal priority
  - considering relative priorities between classes
  - considering the specific circumstances of the plan

Example 1. A small family-owned grocery store (partnership). Due to a recession, the entrepreneur's plan would propose the suspension of mortgage payments for two years while paying all debt to suppliers and keeping all partners unimpaired. Here, the bank holding the mortgage would need to be placed in a separate class. If the bank remains passive and other creditors vote in favour, the plan would be confirmed as uncontested. If the bank objects, the judicial authority would have to be satisfied of the following:

- No discrimination (equal treatment of all class members)—no issue in this scenario as there is no other class member
- Guarantee of the economic value of the claim:
  - In the scenario of an alternative enforcement of the claim (liquidation under the MSME approach)
    - The judicial authority would have to be satisfied regarding the value the bank could realize in an enforcement of the mortgage in a liquidation process under the Modular Approach. The value of the underlying property and the resulting proceeds that could be claimed by the bank would need to be estimated. In a housing market hit by a recession, a bank could face a deficiency. As the plan would only provide for a suspension of payments, the bank would not be worse off under the plan if there was a deficiency. Otherwise, the plan would need to

[20] See Michelle M. Harner, 'The Value of Soft Variables in Corporate Reorganizations', (2015) *Univerity of Illinois Law Rev* 2015, 509.

guarantee the value realized in a liquidation plus interest for the time of the suspended payments.

- Adequate distribution of value under the plan
  - considering the treatment of classes with equal priority
    - There is no other class of secured credit.
  - considering relative priorities between classes
    - A secured creditor could claim the value of the collateral under property law. In principle, the plan should not distribute that value to other classes. It would require a compensating cash payment during the two years of suspension of payments under the plan if a depreciation of the value of collateral is probable. More importantly, the question here would be why only the secured lender would have to make a sacrifice while stakeholders with junior rights were left unimpaired.
  - considering the specific circumstances of the plan
    - The confirmation of the plan would, thus, depend on the fact that the entrepreneur can present specific circumstances that justify the proposed solution: guarantee of the liquidation value (see above); no surplus value as no one else would run that particular business; or the need to secure the supply of the store as well as the labour of family members.

Appeal or review—The judicial decision to approve a plan may be subject to appeal or review under local procedural law, but any appeal should not automatically stay the implementation of the plan.

Example 2. Again, a small family-owned grocery store (partnership), but under the following different circumstances. Due to a recession, the debtor's plan would propose to write off (income) tax claims from the year before the crisis while paying all suppliers and keeping all partners unimpaired. Here, the tax claim would need to be placed in a separate class if tax claims enjoy a preferential treatment under insolvency law in a liquidation. Otherwise the claim could be part of a class of general unsecured creditors.[21] If the tax authority remains passive and other creditors vote in favour, the plan would be confirmed as uncontested. If the tax authority objects, the judicial authority would have to be satisfied of the following:

- No discrimination (equal treatment of all class members)—no issue in this scenario as there is no other class member. If tax claims are general unsecured claims in a liquidation, they must receive the same treatment with all other unsecured claims in their class.
- Guarantee of the economic value of the claim:
  - In the scenario of an alternative enforcement of the claim (liquidation under the MSME approach)

[21] Note that this volume does not explicitly address the issue of ranking in an insolvency liquidation, and it favours no statutory preference for public creditors in respect of tax and similar claims, in accordance with international recommendations. See World Bank Principles 2015, C12.3; UNCITRAL *Legislative Guide* 2004, 187.

        - The judicial authority would have to be satisfied about the value the tax authority could realize in an enforcement of their claim in a liquidation process under the Modular Approach. Where such claims enjoy a preference, the plan would need to pay at least the amount payable to a preferred tax creditor, otherwise only the common pro rata share of unsecured claims.
- Adequate distribution of value under the plan
    - considering the treatment of classes with equal priority
        - Other classes of equally preferred/unsecured claims should be treated equally.
    - considering relative priorities between classes
        - Here the question would be why only the tax authority would have to make a sacrifice while stakeholders with equal rights outside insolvency law were left unimpaired.
    - considering the specific circumstances of the plan
        - The confirmation of the plan would thus depend on whether the entrepreneur can present specific circumstances that justify the proposed solution: no surplus value as no one else would run that particular business; or the need to secure the supply of the store as well as the labour of family members.

Appeal or review—The judicial decision to approve a plan may be subject to appeal or review under local procedural law, but any appeal should not automatically stay the implementation of the plan.

g. *Implementation and amendment*

The implementation of the plan basically means that the debtor fulfils the duties described in the plan. Payments are made as they fall due and as envisaged in the plan; shares are issued or transferred. Claims that are not to be paid are discharged immediately.

If the debtor is not able to meet its obligations as they fall due, plan obligations can be altered if the affected stakeholders agree to postpone or reduce the payment. Where such an agreement is not possible, the debtor may reinitiate continuation proceedings or file for liquidation.

B. The Modules

The Modular Approach describes two streamlined procedural options, including a fast-track plan procedure. The attributes of the continuation process can be altered on a case-by-case basis by implementing various modules available to certain stakeholders. This section of the book describes the various modules that may form part of the MSME insolvency regime.*

The effects and principles of continuation proceedings under the Modular Approach are rescue-oriented because they work to incentivize early action from the

*Figure 4.1 is reproduced here as Figure 4.4 for ease of reference to the discussion in this section on creditor-initiated modules and entrepreneur-initiated modules.

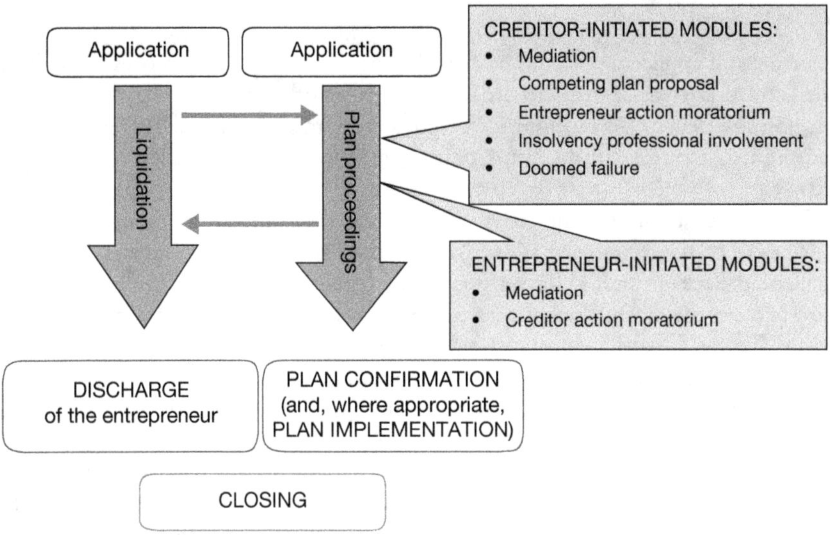

Figure 4.4 The Modular Approach—Potential creditor-initiated and entrepreneur-initiated modules—an overview.

debtor in the situation of a deteriorating business. If the debtor requires additional protection, such as a moratorium, the Modular Approach provides additional modules. The Modular Approach also reflects creditors' rights by providing for optional modules that allow creditors to increase their control over the process. The task of balancing these competing interests would be assigned to active stakeholders who may seek to invoke a different module, which could lead to an alternative or cumulative use of modules in a specific case. It goes without saying that whether independent insolvency, legal, or other expert advice becomes available in the insolvency process would, in the end, be a function of the value available in the MSME or, in some cases, some of its stakeholders.

The modules are optional for the stakeholders in a MSME continuation proceeding. In addition, they are optional for legislators as they provide for a menu of policy choices that allow for the adaptation of MSME continuation proceedings to the respective peculiarities of their constitutional and socio-economic environment. Before detailing the resulting legislative options in Section C of this chapter, all modules of the Modular Approach are explained in the next section.

1. Entrepreneur-initiated modules

These are as follows:

- Mediation
- Creditor action moratorium

a. Mediation

A mediation application would be available any time during the process and allow the administrative authority to order a suspension of a time limit for such steps as proposing a plan or collecting votes, etc, to safeguard a mediation. The order would require that the relevant disputing parties agree with the application and that the extra costs of a mediator are covered, either by the estate or by the parties.

The parties should be required to agree to forebear from any further proceedings during the course of the mediation. To avoid the risk of improper invocation of mediation, the parties should have a very limited time to agree on a mediator and on how to cover their fees. Without an agreement on costs, there can be no mediation in a MSME case. If participants reach a fee agreement, but are unable to agree quickly on a specific person, a mediator should be appointed, preferably by a professional organization of mediators, such as the International Institute for Conflict Prevention & Resolution (US), the ADR Institute of Canada Inc, or similar organization. Alternatively, the mediator could be appointed from an approved list established by the state. Many jurisdictions have credentialing agencies. The mediator should be involved in decisions regarding timing and information dissemination from the beginning of the process and should have the authority to terminate the process if, in the mediator's opinion, a party is not acting in good faith with a view to resolution.

The issue with entrepreneur-initiated mediation is that a party seeking to delay the process improperly—typically, the entrepreneur—may have nothing to lose and time to gain from an improper invocation of mediation. Thus, mediation should only be allowed as long as the conflicting parties agree to this type of structured negotiation. As with earlier entrepreneur-initiated actions, for incorporated small and medium enterprises, it would be the directors and officers initiating the module as entrepreneurs in those MSMEs.

b. Creditor action moratorium

i. Function and effects

The Modular Approach emphasizes business continuation proceedings where appropriate. It does not, however, provide for an automatic stay in such proceedings. Such a *creditor action moratorium* would only be available on the debtor's request.[22]

The creditor action moratorium could affect creditor claim enforcement as well as the operation of ipso facto clauses and set-off rights. It seeks to maintain the status quo ante, particularly the continuation of the business, until a decision about the future of the distressed business is made.

The moratorium is a critical insolvency tool that signals the transition from the individual non-insolvency to the collective insolvency process and creates a space in which rational decisions may be made about maximization of the value of the

[22] In this aspect, the approach follows the European Commission Recommendation of 12 March 2014 on a new approach to business failure and insolvency, C (2014) 1500 final, which also recommends a moratorium if requested by the debtor only; see Art. 10.

debtor's estate and about its fair distribution. In systems with an effective non-insolvency creditor claim-enforcement regime, the availability of this moratorium creates incentives for the entrepreneur to commence the insolvency process in response to initial creditor pressure, and thus early in the onset of distress.

It can be expected that most continuation cases under the Modular Approach would involve the moratorium. The moratorium does have costs, however, including the provision of an adverse signal about the debtor's status and prospects, the impairment of the debtor's relationships with stayed creditors and other counterparties, and the potential for entrepreneur abuse and thus of value destruction. The Modular Approach treats the moratorium as an option, recognizing that incurring these costs may not be necessary in all cases.

ii. Application

A creditor action moratorium would only be available if requested by the entrepreneur. Where liquidation proceedings had already provided for such a stay following a creditor's application,[23] the moratorium would only extend to business continuation proceedings on the entrepreneur's request—done simply by ticking the box on the application template with the request of a stay and indicating the extent and effects of that stay. Still, a non-automatic stay leaves the option of continuing the business with as little interruption as possible during a restructuring process where no stay is required.

iii. Implementation

The administrative authority could notify the parties of the moratorium based on the request. The moratorium should be available for a limited time only. Depending on the design of continuation proceedings, the stay would only last for the period required to cast votes and sanction the plan, or, in addition, cover the short period granted to the debtor to come up with a plan. The authority could lift the stay as soon as the plan fails (doomed failure module or decision not to sanction the plan). In addition, the stay could be fully or partially lifted on request if an affected creditor proves that its rights are insufficiently protected, such as when there are perishable goods or there is insufficient compensation for the continued use of collateral.

2. Creditor-initiated modules

These are as follows:

- Mediation
- Competing plan proposal
- Debtor action moratorium
- Insolvency professional involvement
- Doomed-to-failure

[23] See Section A.1.a.

The creditor-initiated modules recognize the reality that the role of creditors is critical. Apart from the entrepreneur or, for a small and medium enterprise, the directors and officers, creditors possess the best information about the MSME and its prospects. Where the debtor is distressed, its creditors, rather than equity holders, stand to gain or lose in line with the fortunes of that business. As a group, they therefore also have the best incentives to choose the appropriate liquidation or restructuring decision. Finally, and importantly, creditors have legal claims that the distressed debtor is presumptively unable to satisfy. In recognition of these facts, the Modular Approach accords them a critical role in the insolvency process. Creditors using their modules, by stipulated value, may extend control over the continuation process or even cause conversion back to a liquidation.

a. Mediation

The *mediation module* is the least intrusive module a creditor and entrepreneur[24] can use. Resources permitting, a stipulated proportion of creditors—such as 20% by value of creditors affected by the plan—may seek mediation concerning the admissibility or quantum of claims, the formulation of a plan, the treatment of guarantees, or any other issue in dispute between the parties. In general, the failure of mediation should not have adverse consequences for any party, so as not to discourage their participation in the process.

b. Competing plans

The *competing plan proposal module* is simply the right of a single creditor, or a stipulated proportion of creditors, to propose a competing plan. Any creditor dissatisfied with the credibility or viability of an entrepreneur-proposed plan may put forward its own alternative using the same forms and format. In order to offer a sustainable alternative and compete with a debtor plan, a competing plan must be proposed within a specified short period of time after the debtor has presented its plan. In case of a creditor motion initiating the continuation process, the plan may already be presented with that motion. It could also work as a stand-alone plan if the debtor fails to present a plan.

An important scenario would involve a creditor putting forward a transfer plan in competition with an entrepreneur's proposal for continuation of the business in their hands.

Both plans may be put to the relevant creditors for a vote. Where both plans are accepted, the sanctioning authority would need to decide which plan to confirm. There are a number of relevant aspects to consider—for example, which plan obtains greater support in terms of less objections in number or value, which plan offers a higher return to creditors overall, or which plan is retaining more employment. As

[24] See Section B.1.a. of this chapter.

the adoption of a plan is a process governed by stakeholders, indicators of stakeholder support should be favoured.

c. *Debtor action moratorium*

i. Function and effects

The *debtor action moratorium module* affects the right of the entrepreneur retaining control of the business ('entrepreneur in control' or 'EiCon') to administer the estate without the risk of replacement. Where this module is available, a stipulated proportion of the creditors would be able to suspend the EiCon's power to commit the debtor to the disposal of specific assets or the assumption of specific liabilities. The module would limit the entrepreneur's powers without fully replacing the entrepreneur or involving the costs of an insolvency professional.

This module responds to the risk of the destruction and/or misapplication of value in the debtor's estate arising from perverse entrepreneur incentives. The module may also incentivize creditors to commence insolvency proceedings as a way of disabling the entrepreneur's ability to diminish or misapply the value in the estate. The effect of the module may, however, interfere with the debtor's ability to continue the business—so it must be handled with care. Under the Modular Approach, the EiCon is restricted to carrying on business in the ordinary course.

An example of attempting to maintain the balance between having confidence in the debtor's ability to carry on the business and preventing undue diminishment or misapplication of value can be found in Canadian model interim orders[25] under the *Companies' Creditors Arrangement Act*.[26] These orders allow the debtor to pay necessary employee expenses, reasonable expenses incurred in carrying on business in the ordinary course, payments required by law such as employment insurance and income taxes, but preclude payments to pre-filing creditors except in limited circumstances and also preclude any further encumbering of assets. They prevent the debtor from disposing of assets of a value above a cap tailored to the specific day-to-day requirements of the business.

ii. Application

Given the possible indirect costs of an entrepreneur action moratorium, the application should only be available to creditors who together hold in excess of a stipulated proportion of the claims against the debtor—for example 20%—with this

[25] Alberta Template CCAA Initial Order (https://albertacourts.ca/docs/default-source/qb/ccaa-initial-order-template89b7c0391b316d6b9fc9ff00001037d2.pdf?sfvrsn=e986ad80_2):

> 10. The Applicant shall subject to such requirements as are imposed by the CCAA ... have the right to:
>
> (a) permanently or temporarily cease, downsize or shut down any of its business or operations and to dispose of redundant or non-material assets not exceeding $* in any one transaction or $* in the aggregate, provided that any sale that is either (i) in excess of the above thresholds, or (ii) in favour of a person related to the Applicant ... shall require authorization by this Court ....

[26] *Companies' Creditors Arrangement Act*, RSC 1985, c C-36, as amended (hereafter CCAA).

threshold figure explicitly specified by law or regulation. Where the threshold is reached, the stay would come into effect automatically for a short specified period. A party seeking to object can apply to the judicial authority.

iii. Implementation

The application would be made simply by ticking a box on the relevant form, made available online where practicable. Such a form could list sensitive debtor actions like encumbering assets or selling assets above a certain threshold. Where creditors holding claims worth the stipulated value tick the relevant boxes, the respective debtor action moratorium comes into effect automatically, without the need for any judicial or administrative authority decision. The terms of the stay would be specific and its duration limited in time. The stay can be lifted any time by the judicial authority, or where appropriate in the particular jurisdiction, the administrative authority, upon an application of the debtor or any creditor if it is no longer necessary to protect the interests of creditors from the specific debtor action.

Overall, such a mechanism allows for the examination of an intended, but disputed, debtor act, for example the disposal of assets arguably under value, or the entry into a contract that may harm business continuation effort.

d. Insolvency professional involvement

i. Function and effects

The insolvency professional involvement module ('*insolvency professional module*') allows for two levels of intervention over the management powers of the debtor.

- *Level 1: supervision and investigation*: Where considered to be competent and trustworthy, the entrepreneur could remain in control (the default position of the EiCon) and the insolvency professional would only control the management functions of the debtor up to the agreement on the plan and perhaps act as a supervisor of the plan's implementation thereafter. Intervention at these two different procedural stages is not necessarily bound together, in that creditors may request supervision in one or other stage only. In addition, the insolvency professional would investigate earlier wrongdoings of the entrepreneur or, in case of a company, its directors and enforce claims for damages on behalf of creditors.[27]
- *Level 2: management and investigation*: Alternatively, creditors should be able to displace the EiCon in favour of an insolvency professional, thus overturning the EiCon default rule.

The involvement of an insolvency professional is common in many jurisdictions, either instead of or in combination with an EiCon approach, but the costs of such involvement would be prohibitive in many MSME cases, especially when the debtor is a micro or a small business.

[27] For possible liabilities, see Chapter 5, Section A.4.

ii. Application

The insolvency professional's involvement may, in principle, be sought at any stage of the process by any creditor with a claim above a significant threshold or a group of creditors with claims exceeding the threshold. When setting the threshold, legislators should consider that the application must reflect the willingness of creditors to accept the extra cost inherent in the involvement of an insolvency professional. In the application, the creditor would have to specify whether the insolvency professional should supervise or replace the EiCon, again, preferably, simply by ticking the appropriate box in a template.

The setting of the thresholds should reflect the difference in costs incurred if the insolvency professional is acting either as a supervisor or manager. The higher costs of the latter would justify a higher threshold to implement the module—for example, 50% of all claims affected by the proposed plan or 25% of per capita GDP—with this threshold figure explicitly specified by law or regulation.

The application of the module may also cause the applicant to become liable for the remuneration of the insolvency professional if the estate is insufficient.[28]

iii. Implementation

The administrative authority will order a replacement or supervision of the entrepreneur by an insolvency professional only if the application is supported by a creditor or a group of creditors holding claims that exceed the threshold. The selection of the insolvency professional should follow the threshold rules described in Section C.2.b.i. of this chapter.

e. *Doomed-to-failure*

i. Function and effects

The *doomed-to-failure module* is the most intrusive because it terminates entrepreneur-initiated continuation proceedings. The use of the module must, therefore, be reserved for cases where any effort to continue business is an obvious waste of time and assets or an obvious misuse of procedural options. The module allows creditors to shut down entrepreneur-initiated plan proceedings very early to save costs and delay, based on the argument that the debtor's plan is doomed to fail.

ii. Application

The module may, in principle, be sought at any stage of the process by any creditor who is able to demonstrate that the entrepreneur's plan is doomed to fail. Such a failure is manifest if the application is supported by a number of creditors with claims large enough to veto a debtor's plan.

[28] As to the system of remuneration of insolvency professionals, especially in cases of insufficient assets, see Section C.2.a.

iii. Implementation

If the application is successful, the administrative authority provides for the continuation proceedings to convert to liquidation ones. If the liquidation is to be conducted by a different institution (e.g. secured creditors), the authority would mandate the institution to commence the liquidation process.

C. Legislative Choices

The Modular Approach provides for a procedural and legal framework that is tailor-made for the specific needs of MSMEs. At the same time, it offers a flexible structure that can be adapted to the special needs of jurisdictions and reflects the business and legal culture in handling a failing business or disputes in general, whether confrontation- or consent-oriented. The Modular Approach also gives leeway to make specific policy choices. The resulting options are explained in the following sections, which conclude with a brief *legislative guide*.

1. Procedure and modules

The insolvency and restructuring framework for MSMEs should always provide for an efficient liquidation procedure, a going-concern sale option, and a continuation option, all of which should presumptively include a discharge from remaining debt for individual debtors. An effective framework will encompass the full range of the Modular Approach tools, and modules should only be eliminated rarely and after careful consideration. However, legislators may decide that local conditions justify particular adaptations, as follows.

- Local legislators could decline to implement the mediation module if mediation is not an established practice, or too costly locally, or, with regard to its suspensive effect, too susceptible to abuse.
- They could decline to implement the insolvency professional involvement module if they decide that a guaranteed strict EiCon procedure is a preferred way to incentivize small-business owners to embrace the new procedure. Such reasoning could also lead to a limited implementation of the module, which would only allow for appointing an insolvency professional as supervisor.
- Legislators could also decide not to provide for a debtor action moratorium. Alternatively, they could pass on this module, but balance this move with a less restrictive availability of the insolvency professional involvement module.
- If legislators would like to increase creditor control in continuation proceedings, they could pass on the creditor action module or limit its stay in scope and duration. They could also facilitate the access to the insolvency professional involvement and doomed-to-failure modules.

Example 1—'strict EiCon' continuation proceedings.

- Application for continuation proceedings would not require a plan proposal immediately, but allow for a breathing space of two weeks
- The EiCon remains at the helm of the business
- Insolvency practitioner involvement module = no (costly) supervisor or administrator
- No debtor action moratorium
- High thresholds for the doomed-to-failure module
- Creditor action moratorium easily available with broad scope and duration (four weeks, extendable to allow for voting and confirmation, and which is only partially lifted upon request)

As a result, the MSME debtor could suspend a liquidation of the business for a minimum of six weeks if a plan is proposed within two weeks, unless creditors are able to collectively trigger the doomed-to-failure module.

Example 2—'creditor-friendly' continuation proceedings.

- Application for continuation proceedings would require a plan proposal immediately
- The EiCon remains at the helm of the business
- Insolvency professional involvement module available with low threshold for insolvency professional as supervisor and higher threshold for insolvency professional as manager
- Entrepreneur action moratorium available
- Lower thresholds for the doomed-to-failure module
- Creditor action moratorium available, but with limited scope and duration (two weeks; extendable to allow for voting and confirmation, and which is only partially lifted upon request)

As a result, the MSME debtor could suspend a liquidation of the business for two weeks only, unless extended. If a plan is proposed in that period, the debtor would probably be supervised (if creditors are active and costs are covered) and could be barred from disputed actions.

2. Institutions

This section analyses the various options for institutional involvement in a streamlined MSME insolvency process. Figure 4.5 summarizes the options under the Modular Approach.

The efficiency of any liquidation or continuation procedure under the Modular Approach depends on the people assigned to run it. Again, the Modular Approach does not prescribe a specific institutional framework, but rather identifies considerations relevant to legislative choice.

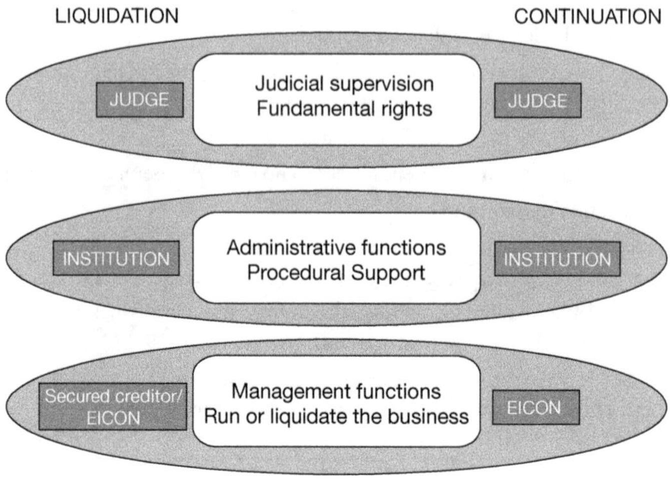

Figure 4.5 Modular Approach to management, administrative, and judicial functions.

The institutional framework is essential and must consider the following two basic principles.

- *Low-cost approach*: MSME insolvencies, especially in the case of micro and small businesses, are characterized by a lack of assets; no-asset cases are a regular phenomenon. Any involvement of additional institutions must, therefore, be given careful consideration and be duly justified.
- *Four-eyes principle for key decisions*: The Modular Approach provides for means to impair creditor claims by plan and/or discharge, as well as providing for the liquidation of debtors' assets. Any impairment of fundamental rights would usually require the right to involve a second level of authority that would review the decision if there is an appeal by an interested party. This appeal would usually require the involvement of a judge.

a. Levels of institutional tasks

Based on these principles, three tasks or functions are to be assigned to institutions under the Modular Approach.

i. Management functions

The first and most basic level is characterized by those measures that are required to manage the debtor's business through the insolvency and continuation process or to manage the liquidation of the debtor's business. Such a management function includes not only ordinary commercial decisions, but also making commercially informed choices about which of the available legal tools to deploy. It would also include the task of negotiating with creditors, investors, and other stakeholders to obtain a desirable conclusion to the insolvency process. Examples of other stakeholders include equity holders, employees, and government officials, such as tax authorities.

ii. Administrative functions

Insolvency proceedings are a legal procedure that requires oversight to ensure that applications are being considered, deadlines and formalities are being met, notices are duly provided, and disclosures duly made. Such administrative functions need not necessarily be assigned to a judge, but can often be handled by other institutions.

iii. Judicial functions

Finally, there is the judicial function of ensuring that the law has been correctly applied, reasonable findings of fact have been reached, and the parties have all been treated fairly.

Courts are a precious and scarce resource. Also, judicial processes can be lengthy, and recourse to the courts characteristically requires the involvement of sometimes expensive legal professionals. Given the significant number of possible MSME cases, the scarcity of court resources generally, and the lack of both time and value in many MSME insolvencies, the Modular Approach favours recourse to courts only if and to the extent necessary. Subject to the jurisdiction's constitutional requirements, particularly protection of property rights and due process, the Modular Approach envisages that when the liquidation or continuation process leads to an infringement of a stakeholder's legal right without their consent, access to judicial review is guaranteed.

A judge need not be involved in the supervision of proceedings, nor does it seem appropriate to impose a mandatory sanctioning hearing and order to conclude plan proceedings in such cases. Instead, a decision by a judge (following a previous hearing in some jurisdictions where constitutionally mandatory or when deemed convenient) would only and always be available where a stakeholder calls for the involvement of a court. Specifically, continuation plans that are consensually supported by active creditors and to which passive creditors are deemed to consent could thus be approved and implemented without court involvement. In addition, plans that are rejected by some stakeholders could be implemented under a majority rule without court involvement whenever the opposing stakeholder, possibly after recognizing a lack of support from other stakeholders, does not file an application to a court. As a result, the Modular Approach would only require judicial action where it is requested by affected stakeholders in a specific case or else constitutionally mandated in the particular jurisdiction.

b. Candidate institutions

At least some of the three functions could be assigned to:

- an insolvency professional, appointed by the debtor, a creditor, or a court;
- a private self-regulatory organization;
- an administrative agency;

- a court official such as a registrar; or
- a judge.

Further, the debtor or even a secured creditor could also be assigned some of these functions.

The legislative decision should consider the following factors.

i. Insolvency professionals' involvement

Insolvency professionals play a leading role in most insolvency systems. With perhaps the conspicuous exception of the US,[29] the appointment of technically qualified, independent professionals is commonplace in all kinds of insolvency proceedings. International experience shows that MSME cases are no exception. Most of the elements that define a good system of insolvency professional are common to proceedings irrespective of the size of the debtor; and yet, the smaller cases present some peculiarities that would merit a closer look.

Special tasks. On the face of it, the tasks to be performed by insolvency professionals in MSME cases will be simpler, albeit no less important, than in larger insolvencies. The liquidation of a small estate will involve the reception, analysis, treatment, and provision of information to a normally smaller group of creditors through the use of predefined templates or a technical opinion on the viability of a non-complex business plan. However, the insolvency professional's tasks will often be complicated by the lack of sufficient or of adequately drafted financial and legal information and by the lack of cooperation from the debtor and/or the management/equity holders. MSMEs are often family-run businesses where, not uncommonly, owners and directors take proud, non-collaborative positions all through the process. As a result, but also in general, mediation gains importance amongst the tasks to be performed by insolvency professionals in smaller cases. Mediation in its most strict sense—relating to the relationship between the debtor, its ownership and/or management and creditors—must be provided to the parties in a conflict. It may also need to include more persuasive and informational aspects, such as counselling from an independent specialist.

Fee restrictions. Fees have to be limited. While, as in any other profession, a market-based determination of fees would normally be preferred, the limited value of the assets, the passivity of creditors, and the lack of interest of the more sophisticated professionals justifies firm statutory or regulatory control. The law should set out factors by reference to which fees may be determined, such as the size and complexity of the debtor's activities and the nature of the assets to be realized. An alternative or complementary strategy is to define fees by reference to success criteria, such as approval of a continuation plan, sale of the business as a going concern, or the value returned to creditors. In many jurisdictions, a minimum fixed amount for the insolvency professionals is also set by regulation/law.

[29] The appointment of insolvency representatives in the US is rare in reorganization cases under Chapter 11 of the US Bankruptcy Code. However, even in this system, trustees are necessary for the liquidation of the business (Chapter 7 US Bankruptcy Code), and, in the case of individuals, the US

Qualification and integrity. The professionalization of insolvency professionals active in MSME insolvency may be highly complicated: the remuneration for the professional may be low in many economies notwithstanding the challenges of the work. Here, as in relation to other aspects, MSME insolvencies present distinctive difficulties: the work is often technically straightforward and repetitive and the remuneration may be low. These factors hamper the creation of a body of professionals sufficient in number to cater for the entire market.

Professionalization must be understood in a non-strict sense, and professionals must be allowed to perform other related professions if they so wish.[30] Good practice would be boosted by the existence and implementation of codes of conduct, and control and discipline by professional bodies. As an alternative, and in those countries where the formation of an adequate system of professional insolvency professionals is not possible or would take too much time or cost, public agencies might fill the gap in a number of ways: either by strengthening the profession via control of access requirements and implementation of correct professional standards; or by providing a body of public or publicly trained, selected, and funded professionals.

Whatever the model chosen, insolvency professionals in charge of MSME insolvencies must complement the general technical skills demanded from the profession with special knowledge of mediation, family law, and other applicable disciplines directly related to the issues that may arise in these types of cases. In countries with an already created, robust enough profession, the professional body could separate its constituents depending on the type of cases in which they specialize and are licensed to practice. The access requirements, system of fees, code of conduct, availability of insurance, and need for training would be adapted to the different circumstances of the professional practice.[31]

Supervision. In MSME insolvency, the appointment of a committee of creditors is not common, which leaves insolvency professionals without direct control by a body of creditors. Monitoring insolvency professionals in the smaller cases is a limited problem, since the tasks will be relatively straightforward and the possibility of causing damage very limited. In any case, the system ought to provide for control mechanisms. Insolvency professionals may be controlled by a public agency, or by a self-regulatory organization or, as it is the case in some jurisdictions, by an 'ombud'[32] who generates accountability within the profession.

Trustee Office plays a highly relevant role. The Russian Financial Rehabilitation process (*finansovoe ozdorovlenie*) under Chapter V of the Law on Insolvency of 2002 also leaves the debtor's pre-distress management in place for up to two years with a view to implementing a repayment plan. The management is, however, subject to supervision by an insolvency professional appointed by the creditors' committee.

[30] In some jurisdictions, the attempt to create a market of insolvency professionals has led authorities to limit severely any alternative work that the professionals included in a registry may perform.

[31] For further details see Ignacio Tirado, 'Issues Note on Insolvency Representatives', The World Bank, 2011; the EBRD Office-holder Principles; see also the International Association of Insolvency Practitioners' Principles for the Regulatory Regime for Insolvency Practitioners (forthcoming, 2018).

[32] An ombud (ombudsperson) or 'public advocate' is a professional, often appointed by government or a professional entity, with a significant degree of independence, who is charged with representing the interests of the public by investigating and addressing complaints.

Appointment. In the vast majority of systems, insolvency professionals are appointed either by a judge, or an insolvency agency, or by creditors. There are pros and cons for each of these systems, but the direct selection of an insolvency professional by creditors in MSMEs, for example, by way of a binding right to propose a person to the court,[33] gives rise to additional problems due to the common passivity of unsecured creditors in smaller cases. An appointment by a judge or an insolvency agency, or, as in some jurisdictions, by notaries or registrars, is the most common solution. Even if the decisionmaker is a judge or a public agency, the selection of candidates must be based on their technical abilities and their special suitability to a given case. An example would be their previous experience in the sector of the debtor's activity. However, in smaller cases, a system that provides for an automatic selection based on a revolving list is more acceptable, as long as the list of candidates only includes candidates generally—but sufficiently—qualified for the job.

Example—Germany

Lacking a specific MSME framework, insolvent MSMEs are subject to regular insolvency proceedings with an insolvency practitioner appointed provided that assets suffice to cover the costs of the insolvency practitioner and the court. In most cases involving micro and small businesses, assets do not suffice, which means that no insolvency proceedings take place. Instead, the entrepreneur closes the business and files for individual insolvency proceedings where the sufficiency of assets is not required because payment of costs can be suspended. The resulting no-asset case, however, requires the involvement of an insolvency practitioner even before filing, for an attempt to agree on a payment plan, even if the debtor is only able to offer a 'no-payments plan' which is, of course, rejected.

The remuneration of these insolvency practitioners is set by a court based on the value of assets and complexity of the case, and usually minimum fees are awarded. As a result, a special group of insolvency practitioners has developed who handle a huge number of these cases while doing fairly little in each case. Creditors receive no payment, and only after the case is closed may the entrepreneur enter discharge proceedings, which again may last up to five years.

In contrast, cases with some assets or even a running business often benefit from insolvency practitioner involvement, either in a quick sale or to help develop a plan solution.

Overall efficiency. Overall, however, the involvement of insolvency professionals may not add net value in many MSME cases, with particular regard to the insolvency of micro and small enterprises. Experience from systems that severely constrain the remuneration of insolvency professionals[34] indicates that an insolvency professional's involvement is, in practice, nominal only; the debtor does not receive the benefit of genuine independent expertise, and the creditors do not receive the benefit of genuine independent oversight of the debtor. By contrast, in systems where the insolvency professional has greater control over their remuneration, even when subject to challenge by a dispersed and 'apathetic' creditor group,[35] perverse incentives arise

[33] Under German insolvency law, for instance, the court must (principally) appoint the insolvency practitioner selected by unanimous vote of the preliminary creditors' committee (Germany, Insolvency Statute (Insolvenzordnung, InsO) sec 56a (2)).

[34] For example, Turkey.

[35] For example, the UK.

for the insolvency professional to inflate fees, to engage in value-destructive collusion with repeat-player institutional lenders and sometimes with the debtor itself, and to shirk on the primary responsibility of finding a value-maximizing solution to the insolvency. Either the design of a proper system of remuneration that neither pays too little nor creates perverse incentives, or the involvement of a public authority, would mitigate such incentives.

ii. Public or self-regulatory organization involvement

While the involvement of an agency is necessary for the supervision of insolvency professionals, such an agency would also be highly important in cases with no or insufficient assets to cover the costs of proceedings. This situation is very common in developing economies and in jurisdictions where there is a weak insolvency culture; for example, where the insolvency carries a strong stigma and/or the system is not perceived as a proper instrument to handle business financial distress. As a result, insolvency is declared too late, when there are hardly any assets left. This scenario is even more common in MSME cases. The problem can be tackled by the direct intervention of a public agency.

Under this Modular Approach, the agency would provide the specialists that take charge of the liquidation of the insolvent business and look into the behaviour of the debtor and its management. The UK system of official receivers could be a model of this approach. The public agency could also simply fund the execution of the limited tasks required of insolvency professionals, a solution that would prevent the jurisdiction from having to create a body of public employees. But this situation might also be solved by resorting to market mechanisms. For example, insolvency professionals appointed for these cases would be guaranteed the payment of a minimum amount out of a fund nurtured with a percentage withheld from the fees of ordinary insolvency cases or with the fees of entry to the professional body. This form of mutualization could be subsidized by the introduction of other sources to the fund, for example, a percentage of the fees paid to the register of companies for the use of the registry or a percentage of the money paid to notarize commercial documents such as loans. The payment of public money into this fund would be an alternative to the public agency directly paying the fees and would allow the costs to be fully borne by market participants.

Finally, a third option may be considered. In jurisdictions with a strong culture of public intervention in insolvency proceedings, with scarce use of the insolvency system, and with an insufficient level of formality, consideration is being given nowadays to the creation of a strong mixed private/public agency (hosted by a ministry) that plays the following roles:

- The agency receives notice of a debtor's early situation of distress from: the debtor or related parties, such as managers, or partners with a certain percentage of the capital; all public administrations, such as tax/social security/registrars, etc; and professional lenders, for example, when a debtor deposits accounts at the registrar with losses that account for three quarters of the share capital.
- It is staffed by highly qualified specialists, in the fields of both insolvency and in business valuation.

- It starts an insolvency procedure; one aimed at the continuation and rehabilitation of the business if practicable.
- It informs a court whenever asked to do so on specific topics, such as valuation of plan proposals, etc. This aim of the agency is to solve the problems of late filings, lack of information, and lack of technical independent advice to decision makers within proceedings. This solution has its drawbacks; it may be costly and is not always easy to create and staff adequately.

Example—England and Wales

The government's Insolvency Service performs two relevant roles.

First, it is the 'regulator of regulators', licensing, regulating, and monitoring the operation of self-regulatory organizations of insolvency practitioners.

Second, the Service carries out the official receiver function. Official receivers are government employees attached to the High Court and each county court exercising insolvency jurisdiction. Each official receiver by statute acts as an officer of the court and thus under the court's control. In relation both to natural person and corporate insolvency proceedings, the official receiver is the default office holder (the trustee in bankruptcy or liquidator, respectively) and has responsibility for publishing notice of the commencement of the proceedings in the official gazette. The official receiver has a duty of investigating the causes of a company's failure and may report to the court if wrongdoing is unearthed. Unless replaced by a private sector insolvency practitioner, the official receiver will assume possession and control of the insolvency estate, realize any assets, and divide proceeds amongst creditors according to the statutory distributive regime.

The official receiver system, and the Insolvency Service as a whole, operate on the principle that those stakeholders benefiting from the insolvency regime, rather than the taxpayers, should bear the costs of the regime. The Service levies a number of fees for its services, including:

- petition deposits of £550 where debtors petition for their own bankruptcy and £825 where the petition is from a creditor;
- a general official receiver fee of £6,000 charged to the case upon the court order commencing the proceeding;
- administration fees reflecting the average costs of overseeing a case, of £1,990 for a debtor-commenced bankruptcy, £2,775 for a creditor-commenced bankruptcy, and £5,000 for a company winding up;
- a trustee/liquidator fee of 15% of the assets realized by the official receiver acting as the true or liquidator; and
- a £50 fee to cover the official receiver's costs where the petition seeking commencement of the proceeding is dismissed or withdrawn.

These fees are set at a level that would enable the official receiver system to break even, including in relation to those approximately 50% of creditor-commenced cases in which no assets are recovered and the creditor's deposit is the only cover for the official receiver's costs.

Where there are sufficient asset recoveries, the fees enjoy a statutory priority over most other claims in payment from the insolvency estate. A striking consequence of the 'user pays' philosophy of the system is that some debtors, who cannot afford the £550 deposit, may be too poor to become bankrupt.

iii. Private self-regulatory organization involvement

In jurisdictions with scarce resources for strong public involvement in MSME insolvency cases or in jurisdictions with a cultural background favouring limited public activity in civil matters, the management, but also the administrative functions, in MSME insolvencies could be assigned to a self-regulatory organization of the private sector that is only supervised, and possibly co-funded, by a ministry of justice. Like a public agency, this organization would perform all tasks under the Modular Approach that require qualified, sufficiently paid personnel, and technical equipment. It could be set up on a national level, for instance by an association of insolvency professionals,[36] but also locally by local business support groups.

Example—Russia
Each insolvency practitioner must belong to a self-regulatory organization ('SRO'), which sets membership qualifications, promulgates professional standards binding on members, and operates a compensation fund against which claims might be made by those aggrieved by a member of that SRO acting in an insolvency case. Each SRO is required to be part of at least one association of SROs ('ASRO'), which in turn must set standards of each member SRO. Since 2008, ASROs have been vested with certain statutory responsibilities including that of setting standards even for non-member SROs, which come into effect once approved by the Ministry of Economic Development. The ASRO also formulates educational and training programmes for practitioners, and ensures public dissemination of information about the profession. Responsibility for overall supervision of SROs rests with the Federal Service of State Registration, Cadastral Affairs, and Cartography.

iv. Court officials and judges

Many jurisdictions principally run MSME insolvencies like any other insolvency, which traditionally leads to a full judicial process. As previously noted,[37] the Modular Approach recognizes that courts are a precious and scarce resource. It is important to use this resource for MSMEs only where a judge's involvement is required by constitutional law, or where particular actions of debtors or creditors are contested.

The involvement of court officials is a legislative option that resembles the option of involving a public agency.[38] Of course, such an agency could be independent from the judicial system, but it could as well be part of it. The point to be made is that judicial resources should not be wasted on administration but are important as the provider of procedural and substantive fairness.

Example—Canada
Canadian bankruptcy legislation provides a streamlined process for first-time or individual bankrupts. All bankrupts must involve a licensed insolvency trustee appointed by the debtor, or in the case of involuntary bankruptcies, by the court upon the request of

[36] An example would be the UK's R3.
[37] See Section C.2.a.iii. of this chapter.
[38] See Section C.2.b.ii. of this chapter.

a creditor. If the debtor has no assets to pay a trustee, a Bankruptcy Assistance Program exists, supervised by the Superintendent of Bankruptcy.

The trustee is an officer of the court whose duty is to represent the debtor and the interests of all creditors impartially.

The majority of consumer bankruptcies in Canada are commenced by assignment and result in automatic discharge. The 'consumer' bankrupty provisions include individual entrepreneurs whose business debts comprise 50% or more of their total debts, recognizing the conflation of consumer and business debt for sole proprietors that are not incorporated.

If an application for a bankruptcy order for an individual is filed, a Registrar in bankruptcy reviews the initial application, and, if there is no objection to the order, may subsequently conduct the hearing and grant the order if warranted. If the application is opposed, however, the application must be heard by a judge pursuant to section 192 of the BIA.

Court involvement is also necessary if an objection to discharge has been filed by the trustee, the Office of the Superintendent of Bankruptcy, or a creditor.

A Registrar in bankruptcy's jurisdiction is limited to the matters set out in section 192 of the BIA. In addition to opposed discharge applications, the contentious matters that a Registrar may hear include opposed taxations of costs and appeals from decisions of trustees to allow or disallow claims. A Registrar may also approve proposals where they are not opposed, and deal with any other unopposed application or procedural matter.

v. Creditors and the debtor

Finally, creditors and the debtor may assume a role in MSME proceedings under the Modular Approach. Particularly, a secured creditor or a representative of secured creditors could have a role in management, but could also perform administrative functions in a liquidation of encumbered assets. In continuation proceedings, the EiCon design under the Modular Approach[39] would entrust management tasks to the entrepreneur.

Example—Germany

The liquidation of encumbered real estate may lead to a receivership instead of an immediate judicial sale. If so, the mortgage-holding bank or credit institution is allowed to propose a qualified employee to become the appointed receiver and this proposal would be binding on the court. The receiver would not receive any remuneration. This low-cost liquidation option in section 150a of the Act on Enforced Auction and Receivership was introduced in times of war when qualified independent receivers were hard to find. It survived, however, because it offers a low-cost option in a receivership.

[39] See Section A.2.b. of this chapter.

c. *Assignment of tasks*

The legislative decision about the assignment of tasks may be different for liquidation and continuation proceedings.

i. Liquidation proceedings

Selling the debtor's assets in a quick liquidation should not be entrusted to the debtor at the management level, if possible, because the basis of the Modular Approach is an efficient liquidation where a debtor is insolvent and not willing or able to produce a continuation plan proposal. Beyond this background, debtors may not seem trustworthy to undertake the winding up of their own failed business. In a number of jurisdictions, however, trusting the debtor with the task of selling off her (business) assets may appear to be the only viable option. Here an 'entrepreneur-retaining–control' liquidation should be considered, meaning that the debtor is required to perform all relevant tasks in a liquidation in order to achieve a discharge. Creditors, in return, may challenge any requested discharge, arguing that the entrepreneur mishandled or transferred assets inappropriately, or favoured insider deals for less.

Where all or almost all assets of a MSME are subject to security interests held by a single creditor, for example, based on a floating-charge type of agreement or statutory right, the Modular Approach would allow the solution offered by some jurisdictions and permit the creditor to enforce its rights. In such a case, there is little need to involve another institution at the management level, and unnecessary transaction costs are prevented.

The secured lender solution would not be available, however, where such a secured creditor is either non-existent or not willing to act, or where there are significant assets not subject to security or subject to the security rights of different creditors. In such cases, the management function could be assigned to an insolvency professional or a public authority such as a specialized government agency, a court registrar, or even the debtor. It would be preferable for specialists (probably insolvency professionals) to be appointed in these cases because creditors are confident of their integrity. The costs for their involvement should be covered by the estate or, in the absence of sufficient assets, by public funds.

If an insolvency professional is not appointed to manage the liquidation and a stakeholder (e.g. a secured lender or even the entrepreneur) steps in, supervision would still only be necessary where a stakeholder objects to the way the auction process or any other type of liquidation action is being conducted. A secured creditor may only be interested in realizing a sale that covers its outstanding debt but does not achieve the best possible price. An application for supervision would be directed to and handled at the administration level by a public authority, such as a specialized government agency, a court registrar, or a self-regulatory organization (e.g. a professional association) that could supervise the auction or sale process but also investigate the behaviour of the managing creditor or indeed of the entrepreneur as a precondition to a discharge contested by stakeholders. Instead of acting on its own behalf, the public or self-regulatory agency could also entrust an insolvency professional with the supervision in cases where a creditor is in charge of the auction or generally the liquidation process. Any discovered wrongdoing would lead to a claim for damages against the secured creditor acting as a liquidator.

The simpler administrative tasks of giving notice, monitoring deadlines, and registering claims and objections could be done by the secured creditor or even the entrepreneur, but could also be automated by a privately or publicly hosted online platform. In that case, an individual would only be required for administrative tasks when an objection or complaint is filed.

A judge would be required only if an appeal is filed against conduct at the management or administrative level, provided that a right to access courts is guaranteed under statutory or constitutional law. In many jurisdictions, a discharge may require a judge's involvement. The Modular Approach would, however, prefer a discharge to be the automatic statutory consequence of completed liquidation proceedings.[40]

Example 1—judiciary-sparing implementation of a liquidation.

- Management functions:
  - Secured creditors' representative
- Administrative functions:
  - Secured creditors' representative—for time frame and notice
  - Online platform hosted by a public agency or private organization—for time-frame notice
  - Public agency/self-regulatory organization/court official/insolvency practitioner
- Judicial supervision:
  - Judge

As a result, MSME liquidations would be run and financed primarily by secured creditors and private stakeholders. Court fees would probably recover all of the costs of judicial involvement.

Example 2—judiciary-oriented implementation of liquidation proceedings:

- Management functions:
  - Judicial clerks
- Administrative functions:
  - Judicial clerks
- Judicial supervision:
  - Judge

As a result, MSME liquidations would be run and financed by the state through its judiciary. Court fees would probably not recover all of these costs.

[40] For a more detailed discussion, see Section A.1.e. of this chapter.

ii. Business continuation proceedings

Continuation proceedings under the Modular Approach are principally EiCon proceedings. As they would basically comprise negotiations and the casting of votes on a proposed payment plan, there is little need for additional administrative structure or costs at the management level.

The requirement of notice of the entrepreneur's application or plan proposal and disclosure of information about the debtor and its business, mostly by the entrepreneur, would suggest, however, the establishment of a supporting structure at the administration level that provides online templates for plan proposals, information on the procedure, and the available professional expertise. Such an institution could also be entrusted with verifying the completeness of the information supplied, following up where necessary to obtain further input, ensuring the provision of appropriate notices, and certifying the completion of each procedural stage. Being independent from the debtor, the institution would also receive applications to add a module and would decide whether court involvement is necessary.

The administrative tasks of a supportive institution could be assigned to a public agency, which could be part of a court organization, for example judicial clerks or registrars, an independent government agency, or, depending on the institutional environment in a jurisdiction, an independent private organization, such as a part of a Chamber of Commerce. Three considerations combine to motivate the default choice of a government entity to discharge this function.

1. There is a public interest in effective pursuit of the restructuring process, both to enable suitable investigation of the circumstances of the insolvency to ensure that any wrongdoing is detected and wrongdoers held to account, and to permit any indebted natural persons to be discharged, subject to findings of wrongdoing.
2. Many MSME insolvencies are 'no-asset' cases in the sense that their estates do not contain sufficient value to fund their own winding up. Taken together, these considerations justify the allocation of public funds to address MSME insolvency.
3. In a proportion of those MSME insolvencies where the estate can fund its winding up, there may nevertheless be insufficient value to make it worth independent insolvency professionals taking responsibility for overseeing the process. In such cases, a not-for-profit process may maximize returns to stakeholders as a group.

These considerations suggest that, as a default, a government entity may be best placed to oversee the process. This agency may be funded, explicitly or through an implicit premium in business taxes or rates, by a levy on all or a subset of solvent businesses. This approach would also more effectively cause businesses to internalize the costs imposed by them on society.

The involvement of a judge would only be required where it is actually required by law or by affected stakeholders in a specific case.

Example—Implementation of continuation plan proceedings.

- Management functions:
  - The EiCon remains at the helm of the business
- Administrative functions (including module decisions):
  - Online platform hosted by a public agency or private organization (possibly only for some tasks)
  - Public agency/self-regulatory organization/court clerk
- Judicial supervision:
  - Judge

3. Steps for implementation of the Modular Approach

Legislators who are interested in implementing a framework that follows the Modular Approach could follow a five-step guide:

1. Understanding basic procedures and available modules
2. Making a policy choice based on the actual circumstances of the jurisdiction
3. Designing an efficient liquidation and discharge process by providing user-friendly templates and forms
4. Designing a continuation plan process with fitting choice of modules and providing also supporting templates
5. Adopting and enabling a supportive legal framework (see next chapter).

Thus, the core elements of the Modular Approach provide a simple, cost-effective framework to liquidate or continue a MSME, recognizing the diversity in size and nature of micro, small, and medium enterprises. It allows flexibility for lawmakers to select modules based on local social and economic norms, values, and conditions, and to make decisions about the most appropriate institutions for oversight of liquidation or continuation proceedings. The core elements are complemented by additional modules that allow countries, and the creditors and other stakeholders working within their systems, to identify the nature and type of debtor and assets, the causes of distress, and the prospects for viability and rehabilitation of the debtor. The two basic options—automatic liquidation and continuation proceedings—meet multiple objectives; the former facilitating efficient liquidation of MSME assets and allowing entrepreneurs a fresh start, and the latter allowing the entrepreneur to continue the business while addressing the factors that caused its financial and economic distress. There are complementary tools that could be adopted by jurisdictions, as discussed in the next chapter.

5

Complementary Tools and Incentives

This chapter and the next deal with the regulatory and implementation challenges that insolvency systems may face when applying the Modular Approach, particularly concerning its use by different stakeholders. While the very design of the Modular Approach seeks to ameliorate stakeholders' perverse and conflicting incentives, additional tools are needed to ensure the proper and effective use of the regime and to give due regard to the position and role of the various types of stakeholders involved in a micro, small, or medium enterprise (MSME) insolvency process. These two chapters also identify possible barriers to the successful implementation of the regime and propose ways to overcome them. The approach to these issues is from the ground up and MSME-focused, derived from an understanding of what in fact occurs in MSME insolvency. Rather than proffering rules better suited to large entities or making ad hoc modifications to such rules, attention is directed squarely at the specific issues arising in MSME insolvencies and the tools that are appropriate in that context.

The proposed tools can be accommodated to the different forms of MSMEs, and they include options for legal systems, acknowledging that countries' legal and institutional frameworks differ. At the same time, the proposed tools draw from existing approaches of domestic regimes and from international standards. The result is a set of policy options that can fit well within the broader international infrastructure for insolvency, yet is unique to MSMEs and supportive of the modules proposed in the previous chapter.

Specifically, this chapter focuses on the roles and obligations of the MSME entrepreneur, both at times approaching insolvency and during the MSME insolvency process. The chapter also considers the possibility of contribution by certain other bodies or agencies that can assist in the performance of the entrepreneur's obligations and overcome barriers, including through provision of early warnings and information that can be channelled into the process.

A. Entrepreneur's Obligations at Times Approaching Insolvency

In many countries, the insolvency system is infrequently used, and, where it is used, cases are often limited to value-destructive piecemeal liquidation or to no-asset scenarios. This tendency understandably generates a bad reputation for the insolvency system, which is perceived by the market as inefficient and value-destructive and to be avoided if at all possible. A country with a dysfunctional market exit system sees its businesses starved of affordable credit and its economy underperforming its potential. The legislator needs to break this vicious cycle by systematically adapting and adopting mechanisms and processes found effective elsewhere and by creating incentives for market participants to start using insolvency law as medicine for sick but viable businesses, not merely as the boggy burial ground for dead ones. When it comes to MSMEs, in which individuals and sometimes families have undiversified stakes, the legislator must consider social problems, such as reputational damage or the involvement of the entire household in the entrepreneurial project. These circumstances act as an additional barrier to the use of the system.

The absence of a rescue culture and the aforementioned social constraints require a double system of positive and negative incentives to ensure the use of the insolvency framework at optimal levels. The procedures provided by the Modular Approach include measures that should incentivize debtors to use the system, but because of the potential of reputational damage and a common lack of trust in the system, these types of incentives may not be sufficient. MSME debtors may not access the Modular Approach in a timely manner, resulting in loss of value and inability to turn around viable businesses. A robust governance system is needed that provides certain concrete measures to disincentivize non-compliance (hereafter, sanctions), including compensation for damages when appropriate. This section identifies a core approach that requires early action at times approaching insolvency, akin to what is known as a 'wrongful trading' system, but unique to MSMEs. Additional options are proposed that impose more robust 'duty to file' obligations where such alternative solutions fit better with local regulatory and institutional circumstances.

The governance regime proposed here serves the double purpose of promoting the early use of the system and protecting creditors from a management that neglects their interests. While such a regime should operate alongside more stringent rules and punishment for fraudulent and criminal behaviour, it is viewed as the primary governance mechanism for behaviour less serious than fraud and specifically for incentivizing timely access to MSME insolvency solutions.

1. Improper management at times of imminent insolvency

A critical point in time to consider in the design of tools to support the Modular Approach is when the MSME is approaching, but is not necessarily already in, a state of insolvency, and has not yet entered formal insolvency proceedings of any sort. Addressing irresponsible as well as fraudulent behaviour by entrepreneurs requires that the Modular Approach is supported by a well-designed regime concerning entrepreneurs' obligations during this 'twilight zone' period of imminent insolvency.[1]

[1] The use of the term 'imminent insolvency', introduced in Chapter 1, is relatively widespread in laws across the world. Drawing from the German law that first deployed it in 1994 (*Drohende*

When insolvency is imminent, entrepreneurs should have greater regard to the interests of creditors and should attempt to address the distress situation. As the debtor progresses from full solvency to distress and possible insolvency, the interests of creditors are at greater risk. Importantly, the entrepreneur would also benefit from early consideration of the tools that a modern and properly designed insolvency regime provides. As discussed in Chapter 3, the timeliness with which the process is commenced is critical for its efficacy, and a delayed commencement may result in the depletion or destruction of value. Yet, at this time of imminent insolvency, entrepreneurs may be reluctant to access the insolvency system.

Entrepreneurs—here, managers of incorporated MSMEs, who are likely to also be the business owners—may believe that they are safe from the outcomes of insolvency by virtue of being protected by limited liability. This illusion of protection may incentivize passivity and a failure to use even well-designed insolvency processes. Entrepreneurs running small businesses are also likely to be less concerned about returning to the managerial labour market and thus more prone to take excessive risks to attempt to save their business. Furthermore, aversion to accessing the insolvency system may be exacerbated by the common practice of granting personal guarantees to the company's main lenders.[2]

There is a more widespread variant of this phenomenon. Entrepreneurs of MSMEs of all sizes and structures may be concerned about stigma, and about losing their business, which might be their only source of income. They may often be overly optimistic about the business's prospects and also be prone to adopting higher-risk strategies, attempting to avoid at all costs losing their business or the business's assets. In some circumstances, they may be inclined to collaborate with related persons or powerful creditors to hide or dispose of assets. Not infrequently, debtors will sell their assets on forced or even 'fire' sale terms,[3] just to continue another day. In certain cases, they may also deliberately conceal information or engage in other types of abusive or fraudulent behaviour, such as hiding assets from creditors or lying about their financial situation.[4]

Zahlungsunfähigkeit, literally 'threatening inability to pay'), its exact determination is usually left open to the interpretation of the stakeholders and the courts of the jurisdiction. Some systems, however, have decided to define 'immediateness' as not beyond six months (see e.g. Art. 123 of the Albania Insolvency Law, 2017) or twelve months as envisaged in Art. 5 of the Insolvency Law of Kazakhstan, 2014). Debate is ongoing as to whether the difference between imminent insolvency and actual insolvency is only a matter of time (i.e. if the passage of time should inevitably and undoubtedly lead to actual insolvency) or rather if it suffices that it is more probable than not that insolvency will occur unless measures are adopted. This latter interpretation would seem most appropriate and better aligned with the modern approaches to access to insolvency proceedings, no the proof of actual insolvency is required (for example, the approach under Chapter 11 of the US Bankruptcy Code, and indeed the one followed in the Modular Approach proposed in this volume).

[2] See Chapter 6, Section B for a discussion of the position of guarantors.

[3] A forced sale is one that the seller needs to undertake in order to meet its own obligations. A fire sale is a forced sale in a falling market. See Rizwaan J. Mokal, 'Liquidity, Systemic Risk, and the Bankruptcy Treatment of Financial Contracts', *10 Brook J Corp Fin & Com L* (2015), 27 and 30.

[4] Although, as noted in The World Bank, World Bank Group Insolvency and Creditor/Debtor Regimes Task Force, Working Group on the Treatment of the Insolvency of Natural Persons, Report on

A regime that focuses on the period of imminent insolvency is particularly important for encouraging action at an early stage and for the continuation of viable businesses, incentives that are critical to the Modular Approach. Therefore, a regime for pre-insolvency duties can complement that approach and enhance it. It can also provide an educational tool for MSMEs with regard to the proper means of addressing the situation of distress and the proper use of the modules.

2. A balanced regime

The regime for MSME entrepreneurs' obligations at times approaching insolvency should carefully balance the need to protect creditors from entrepreneurs' mismanagement and irresponsible behaviour on the one hand, and the need to incentivize entrepreneurship as well as the rescue of distressed businesses on the other. As discussed in Chapter 3, while timely resolution of the distress, including through negotiation with creditors, is crucial for the efficacy of the regime, neither MSME entrepreneurs nor creditors may understand the extent of distress or the way to resolve it.

An overly draconian regime of pre-insolvency obligations would run the risk that entrepreneurs would be deterred from running businesses, or would avoid accessing the insolvency system. Alternatively though less likely, if an entrepreneur is concerned with a regime that imposes personal liability for failure to act in a timely manner, they might close down their business prematurely. A regime based on severe punishment of entrepreneurs is also likely to be less effective and to be invoked only rarely. Criminal (or quasi-criminal) liability may require a high level of proof, which creditors and insolvency professionals would rarely be able to establish. In countries like Poland, for example, where late filing for insolvency triggers criminal liability, directors are very rarely made accountable for non-compliance. What seems on its face a most stringent rule fails to meet its aims due to lack of use.[5]

Thus, the key focus of the obligation regime for addressing mismanagement at times approaching insolvency should generally be a civil sanction for wrongful behaviour. The regime for entrepreneur obligations should also match the Modular Approach. It should incentivize entrepreneurs to utilize the modular regime, as well as providing protection to entrepreneurs from any personal liability in circumstances where they attempt in good faith to use any of the modules contemplated, including informal negotiations.

the Treatment of the Insolvency of Natural Persons (hereafter The World Bank Natural Persons Report), at para. 118: '[O]ne should not overemphasize the danger that such fraud represents. Empirical observation of many existing insolvency systems has confirmed repeatedly that the instances of real fraud are vanishingly low (on the order of 1–3% of all cases)'. This report, however, focuses on consumers, while fraud as well as non-transparent practices may be more paramount in cases where debtors conducted business activities.

[5] See Ignacio Tirado, David Burdette, Martin Piatkowski, and Nina Mocheva, 'Towards a Stronger Insolvency Framework in Poland' (Washington, DC: World Bank, 2013, *passim* (hereafter Tirado et al.).

3. Wrongful trading norms in domestic legislation and in international standards

Many insolvency systems recognize that once insolvency proceedings commence, the focus of management obligations shifts to prioritizing value maximization and preservation of the estate, primarily for the benefit of the creditors as a whole. However, there is greater diversity regarding the governance regime regarding debtors that are experiencing financial distress but are not yet in insolvency proceedings.[6]

As noted previously, it is hard in the abstract to define precisely the point at which insolvency is foreseeable and creditors are at risk and may be harmed by the actions of the managers. The dilemma is whether to defer to the business judgement of an enterprise's management or to impose specific obligations to protect creditors during the period approaching insolvency. Some regimes impose a strict duty on managers to initiate insolvency proceedings within a short period of time, but only after the occurrence of an insolvency-relevant event. This duty is discussed in more detail later in this chapter. In other regimes, directors owe their duties to the company at all times, taking account of the interests of all shareholders where appropriate, and this obligation does not change as insolvency approaches.[7]

Other systems adopt wrongful trading provisions in various forms, which essentially impose a duty on directors, once they realize that insolvency proceedings might be inevitable (i.e. at times approaching but before the commencement of insolvency proceedings) to give due regard to the interests of creditors.[8] Corporate laws often require directors and officers to continue to act in the best interests of the corporation, even on the eve of insolvency, but the range of stakeholders for whom they should have regard expands. Insolvency and other laws also often provide additional remedies aimed at compensating creditors for fraudulent behaviour or at sanctioning managerial misconduct and intentional acts resulting in insolvency and harm to creditors.[9]

The approach adopted in the *Legislative Guide* is akin to the wrongful trading regimes, albeit not identical to any of the existing domestic laws.[10] The *Legislative*

[6] United Nations Commission on International Trade Law (UNCITRAL), *Legislative Guide on Insolvency Law, 2005*, United Nations Publication No.E.05.V.10 (hereafter *Legislative Guide*) (additional parts were added to the *Legislative Guide* in 2010 and 2013); World Bank, *Principles on Effective Insolvency and Creditor/Debtor Regimes* (revised May 2016, http://pubdocs.worldbank.org/en/919511468425523509/ICR-Principles-Insolvency-Creditor-Debtor-Regimes-2016.pdf). The *Legislative Guide*, together with the World Bank Principles on Creditor–Debtors Regimes 2016, form an insolvency standard.

[7] See e.g. Canadian Business Corporations Act 1985, s 241(2)(c); *Peoples Department Stores Inc v Wise* [2004] SCC 68 [43], although the Supreme Court of Canada judgment notes that creditors may have redress via oppression remedies under corporations law for particular conduct unfairly prejudicial to their interest. See also INSOL International, 'Directors in the Twilight Zone III' (2009) 706.

[8] For example, the UK, Australia, and New Zealand. See J. L. Westbrook, C. D. Booth, C. G. Paulus, and H. Rajak, *A Global View of Business Insolvency Systems* (World Bank, 2010), 54–5. See also I. Mevorach, 'Forum Shopping in Times of Crisis: A Directors' Duties Perspective' (2013) *ECR* 523, 534 (hereafter Mevorach).

[9] Mevorach (n 8). See also *Legislative Guide* (n 6) Part IV, I, para. 7.

[10] This standard is provided in Part IV of *Legislative Guide* (n 6) which was added in 2013, and in Principle B2 of the World Bank Principles on Creditor–Debtor Regimes, as amended in 2015 (n 6).

Guide states that: '[T]he rationale of such provisions is to create appropriate incentives for early action through the use of restructuring negotiations or reorganization and to stop directors from externalizing the costs of the company's financial difficulties and placing all risks of further trading on creditors.'[11]

These provisions or standards regarding prohibition on wrongful trading focus on tackling mismanagement that falls short of fraud in the period approaching insolvency, while acknowledging that legal regimes may impose additional measures to deter misconduct. They generally favour flexibility and deference to directors' judgement over more restrictive approaches.[12] They are aimed at encouraging directors to consider rescue possibilities in times of financial crisis, while providing a regime that mitigates directors' concerns about the risks that accompany attempts to rescue the business. The *Legislative Guide* further states that provisions addressing the obligations of directors and remedies for breaches of duty should be implemented in a way that does not adversely affect successful reorganization, does not discourage participation in the management of companies, and does not prevent the exercise of reasonable business judgment or the taking of reasonable commercial risk. At the same time, the recommended standard acknowledges that creditors may be at risk in the period leading up to insolvency and therefore that directors must consider creditors' interests when making decisions at this time.[13]

The *Legislative Guide* thus recommends that when insolvency is imminent or unavoidable, the legitimate interests of creditors, as well as those of other stakeholders, should be protected and that appropriate remedies for breaches of duty to consider these interests should be provided. Specifically, it is recommended that directors take reasonable steps to avoid insolvency, or minimize its extent when it is unavoidable.[14] A range of steps may be reasonable in the relevant circumstances. These steps may include the initiation of formal insolvency proceedings. However, the standard does not suggest that directors should be obligated to file for insolvency within a specific period of time. Furthermore, the time at which the obligations arise is not defined in precise terms. Rather, it generally corresponds to a state of factual insolvency, actual or imminent, before insolvency proceedings have begun. The obligation to take steps to avoid insolvency or minimize its effect arises when directors, defined broadly,[15] knew or ought reasonably to have known that insolvency was imminent or unavoidable.[16] The steps that should be taken by directors are not prescriptive but vary depending on the circumstances, though the *Legislative Guide* usefully provides a list of possible reasonable steps.[17]

Where creditors have suffered loss or damage because of a breach of the obligations, the person owing the obligation may be liable subject to possible defences,

[11] *Legislative Guide* (n 6), Part IV, Section I, para. 7. [12] See Mevorach (n 8).

[13] *Legislative Guide* (n 6) Part IV, Purpose of Legislative Provisions.

[14] Ibid, Part IV, rec. 256.

[15] Persons subject to the obligation regime include any person formally appointed as a director, and any other person exercising factual control and performing the functions of a director (*Legislative Guide* (n 6) Part IV, rec. 258).

[16] Ibid, Part IV, rec. 257. [17] Ibid, Part IV, rec. 256.

including that the director took reasonable steps to avoid or minimize the extent of insolvency. Liability should be limited to the extent to which the breach caused loss or damage.[18] However, the law may specify additional remedies to deter wrongful or fraudulent behaviour.[19]

The EU proposal for a Directive on preventive restructuring frameworks and second chance[20] states that: 'Rules on company managers' duty of care when nearing insolvency ... play an important role in developing a culture of business rescue instead of liquidation, as they encourage early restructuring and prevent misconduct and avoidable losses for creditors.' In line with the recommended international standard in the *Legislative Guide* and the World Bank Principles, the EU Directive thus suggests specifying in the law that when there is likelihood of insolvency, directors should take immediate steps to minimize loss to stakeholders, have due regard to the interests of creditors and other stakeholders, and take steps to avoid insolvency.[21]

4. The core approach: a duty akin to wrongful trading but unique to MSMEs

MSMEs also require an approach that incentivizes appropriate action at times of distress, including through informal rescue options, and not necessarily through filing. As noted previously, an effective regime for MSMEs should be based on quick actions taken by entrepreneurs. An obligations regime that incentivizes early action and rescue, even before the MSME is actually insolvent, is therefore the preferred approach.

An approach that does not include a specific governance regime for the time approaching insolvency may be particularly disadvantageous for MSMEs and their stakeholders, because at this time it is crucial to provide guidance about obligations and incentives to act early. The possibility of imposing stricter duties to file within a specific period of time has some merit, as will be discussed later in this chapter.[22] However, at first consideration, such a duty is too narrow and may not fit well with a regime that is based on the use of modules before actual insolvency.

Thus, a 'duty-to-file approach' may not inform MSME entrepreneurs about their broader obligations at times of financial distress. The risk of breaching duty-to-file rules may also drive entrepreneurs to commence insolvency proceedings prematurely, and, as discussed in Chapter 3, premature commencement of proceedings may destroy the possibility of turning around viable businesses.

[18] Ibid, Part IV, recs 259 and 260.

[19] Ibid, Part IV, rec. 266; World Bank Principle B2.3.

[20] COM(2016) 723 final ('EU proposal for a Directive on preventive restructuring frameworks and second chance'). The proposal followed the earlier recommendations on a new approach to business failure and insolvency (European Commission, Recommendation of 12 March 2014 on a new approach to business failure and insolvency, C(2014) 1500 final) (hereafter EU Directive).

[21] EU Directive (n 20) ibid at 18.

[22] It may also be carefully designed to address MSME circumstances and align the regime with a system based on the Modular Approach (see Section A.5. of this chapter).

By contrast, a regime based on an obligation to take steps at times approaching insolvency would encourage entrepreneurs to commence good faith negotiations or take other actions that actually avoid filing for formal insolvency proceedings. It certainly would not penalize debtors for taking such actions, but rather, stimulate them to consider the various options the system provides.

Existing approaches to wrongful trading and international standards regarding director obligations at times approaching insolvency have not been designed for the unique circumstances of MSMEs. Specifically, the *Legislative Guide* and World Bank international standards are intended for companies and their directors, while MSMEs may operate as unincorporated entities. Generally, the recommended standards apply to rather sophisticated regimes, too cumbersome for MSMEs.

MSMEs require a regime akin to wrongful trading, yet one that is simple and that does not require the debtor to seek sophisticated and expensive professional advice. The regime for MSMEs should not deter the start-up of small businesses by attaching burdensome legal consequences to good-faith entrepreneurial failure.

a. The obligation and the steps to discharge it

The obligation and the steps to discharge it should be simple, and should include steps that are relevant in MSME cases. The *Legislative Guide* provides useful specific details on the steps that management may take at times approaching insolvency to discharge their obligations. However, the list of steps is extensive, and includes steps such as 'holding regular board meetings to monitor the situation', 'seeking professional advice, including insolvency or legal advice', 'holding discussions with auditors', and 'calling equity holders' meetings'.[23]

In the MSME context, where the business structure is likely to be simple and resources are limited, there is often little or no actual separation between management and ownership, and such steps are too cumbersome, irrelevant, or expensive.

The MSME pre-insolvency obligations regime should provide that, at times approaching insolvency, the entrepreneur should operate in the interests of the general body of the MSME's stakeholders and actively attempt to avoid insolvency or minimize its effect. The manner of discharging the obligation would be through active consideration of the alternative solutions provided in the Modular Approach, such as mediation, commencement of liquidation proceedings, supervised continuation process, etc. The obligation would also require that the entrepreneur ensures that information about the business and its accounts is transparent and accurate and that the MSME's resources are not used in a way that is not beneficial for the general body of its stakeholders. The obligation to act in the stakeholders' interests can be justified because the MSME is self-liquidating or because the entrepreneur is devising a continuation plan, such that the role of the insolvency professional in protecting the interests of creditors

[23] *Legislative Guide* (n 6), Part IV, rec. 256.

has essentially been assumed by the entrepreneur. When the business is incorporated, the directors and officers will need to balance this obligation with the corporate law obligation to act in the interests of the corporation, or a state may choose to override that corporate law obligation upon insolvency.

The regime may specify typical examples of misuse of resources, including the use of employee wages to subsidize the running of the business at times of distress or to pay the bank or another creditor. It should also provide assurance to debtors that there is no obligation to commence a liquidation process, for example, while other routes are reasonably explored, such as mediation.

The obligations regime may also specifically refer entrepreneurs to a supportive institutional framework to access assistance in entering negotiations with creditors or producing a plan.[24]

b. Knowledge of imminent insolvency

The obligation to take steps to avoid insolvency or minimize its effect should arise when the entrepreneur knows or ought reasonably to have known about the MSME's imminent insolvency. However, the obligation regime for MSME entrepreneurs should clarify how such knowledge would be established. Often, factors such as the loss of a key customer, the refusal by a key supplier to renew a discount, the landlord's notification of revision of rent, or departure of a key employee should set alarm bells ringing, effectively putting the entrepreneur on notice of potential distress and prompting an assessment of the solvency and viability of the business. Further, small debtors should be expected to be informed about their financial situation through monitoring of their accounts, which should be properly maintained and up to date. Sophisticated knowledge or special skills of the sort expected from directors of larger enterprises would not be expected by the regime for entrepreneurs of micro and small businesses.[25] The institutional framework should support this knowledge requirement through the provision of supportive services and through proper campaigns about means to address MSMEs in distress.[26]

[24] See Section B.4. of this chapter.

[25] See e.g. how the wrongful trading regime has been applied in the UK regarding small companies, as in *Re Produce Marketing Consortium Ltd* (No 2) [1989] BCLC 520; (1989) 5 BCC 569, 594–5:

> The general knowledge, skill and experience postulated will be much less extensive in a small company in a modest way of business, with simple accounting procedures and equipment, than it will be in a large company with sophisticated procedures. Nevertheless, certain minimum standards are to be assumed to be attained. Notably there is an obligation laid on companies to cause accounting records to be kept which are such as to disclose with reasonable accuracy at any time the financial position of the company at that time....

[26] See Section B.4. of this chapter.

c. Consequences of breach

As noted previously, the emphasis of the regime for MSME entrepreneurs' obligations should be on civil sanctions and remedies. The regime should be balanced and not overly intimidating. It should encourage proper management and access to the Modular Approach while safeguarding stakeholders' rights. Thus, entrepreneurs of incorporated MSMEs that breach the duty to take steps to address the distress situation, causing harm to creditors as a result, should lose the protection of limited liability and may be required to compensate creditors for the losses they suffer. The regime should specify this primary consequence clearly, ensuring that small incorporated debtors are aware that the protection of limited liability might be removed in circumstances of breach, particularly since managers are often owners in the MSME context.

In addition, improper behaviour at times approaching insolvency, such as excessive delay in accessing the Modular Approach, may affect the ability of the entrepreneur to use those options in the regime that would allow significant control over the process. This 'stick' is important as it has a broad application to all MSMEs, whether incorporated or not. Further, it must be acknowledged that the compensation remedy—'lifting' the corporate veil and disregarding limited liability—may have limited effect in MSME cases, where often the manager/owner has limited assets personally and may not be able to compensate creditors in any event.[27] For enterprises that are medium in size, the treat of personal liability may be more efficacious.

Additional sanctions that may be imposed on the entrepreneur may include disqualification from taking directorship roles in the future, restrictions on borrowing, and inclusion of negative information by credit history agencies. In relevant circumstances of entrepreneur misconduct, the entrepreneur may remain undischarged for a longer period of time.[28]

Insolvency law could include a presumption of misconduct or a presumption that the entrepreneur's behaviour has contributed to the aggravation of insolvency in cases where accounting duties were not complied with. Such a rule would not affect all cases of insolvency, but only those in which the entrepreneur's behaviour is to be analysed with a view to establishing liability or disqualification in accordance with a jurisdiction's legislation or regulation concerning directors and/or equity holders. Consequently, this rule would not discourage entrepreneurs from filing for insolvency in those cases where there has not been misbehaviour, but, at the same time, would constitute a powerful incentive for company directors to comply with their accounting obligations. The presumption would be rebutted if the entrepreneur could establish legitimate reasons for failing to meet accounting duties.

More severe sanctions should be imposed in more serious cases of misbehaviour, holding entrepreneurs accountable for fraudulent activities, including through

[27] See Section B.3. for a discussion of issues of enforcement.

[28] See Section B.3. for a discussion of possible insolvency-related sanctions and restrictions that the system may provide for various circumstances of entrepreneur misconduct.

taking criminal actions against them.[29] Other core mechanisms for addressing actions detrimental to creditors may apply, such as reversing preference and other vulnerable transactions that were entered into by the entrepreneurs with a view to dissipating or reducing the value of the MSME's assets in the period approaching insolvency.[30]

d. *Enforcement issues*

Duties such as the obligation to avoid wrongful trading serve two related but distinct functions. The first and primary one is the 'realignment function'. By realigning the focus of directorial duties increasingly or exclusively towards the protection and promotion of creditors' interests, the imposition of the duties brings to bear upon directors' decision-making consideration of the interests of the enterprise's creditors. Second, these duties have a 'liability function': their breach may result in the imposition of personal liability on directors with a view to making good the loss suffered by creditors. Liability imposition may also deter directors as a group from engaging in the proscribed conduct on pain of legal stigmatization, whether or not they have the wherewithal to pay compensation.[31]

It is difficult to assess the efficacy with which wrongful trading duties and their ilk serve the realignment function. They can do so by altering directorial conduct in the twilight zone. Cases where the existence of the duties did encourage directors to pay due regard to creditor interests would be hard to detect since, *ex hypothesi*, there would be no breach of the duties; indeed, appropriate action by directors may have forestalled their company's entry into insolvency proceedings altogether.[32] This point holds in significant part quite independently of the duties' success in compensating creditors and in deterring wrongdoing. It is important to avoid the 'bad person's view' fallacy, which is the view that the law's subjects obey it if and only insofar as they wish to avoid coercive retaliation for disobedience.[33] In most legal systems most of the time, in fact, the law's subjects look to it for guidance that they

[29] World Bank Principles (n 6) Principle B23. See e.g. in the UK, s 213 of the UK Insolvency Act 1986, c 45, as amended (civil liability for fraudulent trading) and s 993 of the UK Companies Act, 2006, c 46 (criminal liability for fraudulent trading).

[30] See *Legislative Guide* (n 6) Part II II.F.

[31] See Rizwaan J. Mokal, *Corporate Insolvency Law* (Oxford: OUP, 2005) (hereafter Mokal), 299 (original emphasis): 'The *dominant* role of section 214 is not to make good a particular category of loss to the company's creditors [i.e. liability], but to encourage managers to do all they reasonably ought to, to minimise that loss in the first place [i.e. realignment].' Further discussion of this 'realignment function' is at Mokal, 280–4.

[32] In view of this, Mokal (n 31) 298 suggests that, in principle:

> a more accurate [empirical] test would therefore be to compare the dividends paid out in all insolvent liquidations as a percentage of the value of all unsecured claims, before and after the coming into force of the [wrongful trading] provision. This would indicate whether the section is successful in its aim of encouraging directors to minimize loss to creditors on the eve of their company's insolvency.

[33] The idea is best put by Oliver Wendell Holmes, Jr. in 'The Path of the Law', *Harvard Law Review* 10 (1896–7) 457, 459:

intend to, and do, follow; coercive enforcement and remedies for breaches play very much an ancillary role.[34]

Subject to these crucial observations, it must be noted that the liability function of wrongful trading duties has not enjoyed significant success. Enforcement has been sparse.[35] In the UK, studies have found that successful cases under the wrongful trading regime have been quite rare, although virtually all such cases concern MSMEs.[36] In Australia, even though the wrongful trading regime has had a wider reach in certain respects, for example, with regard to the persons that could bring proceedings, there is a relatively low number of reported cases.[37]

This apparently limited impact of the wrongful trading regime in the UK has led to its recent expansion, so that it can be invoked not only by liquidators but also by administrators.[38] Additional amendments are aimed at broadening funding possibilities of actions against directors by allowing insolvency professionals to assign wrongful trading claims to interested parties.[39] Further, where a person acting as a director caused loss to one or more of their company's creditors, the Secretary of State may, when seeking to disqualify that person from acting as a director, also obtain an order requiring the person to compensate the affected creditors.[40] It has been argued that even with these amendments it is unlikely that there will be a significant increase in the use of the wrongful trading provisions, including in view of the limited impact of the more relaxed procedure in Australia.[41] It has also been argued that civil recovery such as that offered by the UK wrongful trading remedy may be of little benefit to creditors because wrongdoing directors may themselves have suffered

> If you want to know the law and nothing else, you must look at it as a bad man, who cares only for the material consequences which such knowledge enables him to predict, and not as a good one, who finds his reasons for conduct, whether inside the law or outside of it, in the vaguer sanctions of conscience.

[34] H. L. A. Hart, *The Concept of Law* (Oxford: OUP, 1963), 40, provides the cannocial rebuttal to the fallacy:

> Why should not law be equally if not more concerned with the 'puzzled man' or 'ignorant man' who is willing to do what is required, if only he can be told what it is? Or with the 'man who wishes to arrange his affairs' if only he can be told how to do it? It is of course very important, if we are to understand the law, to see how the courts administer it when they come to apply its sanctions. But this should not lead us to think that all there is to understand is what happens in courts. The principal functions of the law as a means of social control are not to be seen in private litigation or prosecutions, which represent vital but still ancillary provisions for the failures of the system. It is to be seen in the diverse ways in which the law is used to control, to guide, and to plan life out of court.

[35] Ibid, Part IV, para 43.

[36] See e.g. Mokal (n 31), 289; R. Williams, 'What Can We Expect to Gain from Reforming the Insolvent Trading Remedy' (2015) 78(1) *MLR* 55 (hereafter Williams) 60.

[37] Williams (n 36) 74, referring to various studies.

[38] The amendments were introduced to the Insolvency Act in 2015 by the Small Business, Enterprise and Employment Act. See UK Insolvency Act 1986, c 45, as amended, ss 246ZA–246ZC.

[39] See s 246ZD of the UK Insolvency Act, 1986, c 45, as amended. The directors' disqualification regime has also been enhanced as part of the reform to enhance 'transparency and trust' in UK businesses.

[40] Company Directors Disqualification Act 2006, ss 15A–15C, as amended in 2015.

[41] Williams (n 36) 83.

significant financial loss as a result of business failure and are unable to compensate creditors from their personal wealth, crucial to successful recovery under the wrongful trading remedy.[42]

In MSME insolvencies, the problems of funding and a general lack of incentives to litigate are pronounced. There are often insufficient funds available in the estate to pursue the entrepreneur or other persons. Creditor passivity may also impede action, as may lack of information about the MSME's affairs, since MSMEs often operate with a significant degree of informality.[43] Insolvency professionals or creditors will also likely be concerned that litigation will at the most result in the insolvency of the entrepreneur behind the incorporated entity or in imposing sanctions on the entrepreneur that will not address the loss to the creditors.

These are real concerns. The enforcement of obligations that are quite nuanced, for instance, where they do not impose specific time frames for pursuing specific proceedings, and that require litigation with regard to debtors with a limited estate, is challenging. Yet, the alternative of a regime that does not impose specific duties on entrepreneurs at this critical time is a worse option. True, it is difficult to measure the extent of mismanagement at times of distress, and entrepreneurs may anyway be cautious at such times, particularly where they guarantee their business obligations. However, it is also likely that entrepreneurs will tend to be passive and reluctant to address their distress for a host of reasons.

A regime that is overly strict also risks non-compliance. Alternative mechanisms based on duty to file, which are less nuanced and stricter, may be simpler to navigate, yet they may not fully address the broader duty to take steps before actual insolvency, and may impose arbitrary solutions.

Thus, an obligation regime akin to wrongful trading is adequately balanced and fits with the Modular Approach's focus on early action. It is also appropriate because of what it does not require—the need to start a formal process in any event of insolvency, actual or imminent. At least to some extent, it may deter misbehaviour and encourage proper management at times of distress. It should be viewed not only as a tool to sanction behaviour after the fact, but importantly as an educational tool, complementing the general framework for MSME insolvency.

To enhance the potential use of the regime, consideration should be given to methods of addressing funding issues. The *Legislative Guide* delineates some means for obtaining alternative funding to pursue directors who breach their duties.

42 Ibid at 19. Williams also observes (at 17–18):

> [T]here is little evidence that the particular rules in s. 214 are key drivers behind low levels of litigation under the provision. Rather the principal explanation for the low impact of s. 214 may simply lie in the fact that opportunities for civil recovery for wrongful or insolvent trading are limited regardless of the particular criteria applied to the rule ....
>
> Evidence from a number of empirical studies challenges the notion that financially distressed companies necessarily engage in 'risk-shifting' and, on the creditor side, patterns of risk adjustment across classes of creditors are complex and easy assumptions of 'market failure' are likely to be misleading.

43 Though see the discussion later in this chapter concerning tools to increase the availability of information (Section B.2.).

These recommendations include implementing mechanisms similar to those introduced in the UK, namely, the assignment of claims for value to a third party.[44] The *Legislative Guide* also recommends that the law specify that the costs of an action against the person owing the obligations be paid as an administrative expense.[45] This approach, in the case of liability for wrongful trading or for the breach of a duty to file, is the solution in jurisdictions where an insolvency professional is a mandatory participant. The insolvency professional has the duty to execute their functions in the best interests of creditors. If it is in such interest that directors be made liable and contribute to the insolvency estate, the insolvency professional commences an action. The problem of the cost of pursuing these actions is part of the general cost of funding insolvency proceedings where there are few or no assets to cover the costs of pursuing these claims.[46]

To expand the possibility that the duties will be enforced, the regime may allow the provisions to be invoked in the course of processes other than formal liquidation proceedings and may also expand the right to invoke the regime to authorities other than just the insolvency professional, including, for example, an official receiver, bankruptcy department, or a court taking action on its own initiative. The regime may also permit creditors to bring such actions in their collective interest.

It is also crucial that reform of MSME insolvency regimes include training and education programmes,[47] particularly in jurisdictions less familiar with the concept of wrongful trading and the nuanced approach it entails. Finally, and to reiterate, this part of the regime is designed for 'bad apples'. Most entrepreneurs who are aware of the standards will try to comply with them. Non-compliance may also arise, not from bad faith, but from lack of knowledge or from long-standing custom that has not moved with changing standards.

5. Alternative approaches akin to a duty to file

While a core approach akin to wrongful trading is preferred where there is a sufficient level of information, a developed market, and an informed and technically prepared judiciary, other alternatives might be more suitable in jurisdictions that lack such features. However, it may be possible to conceptualize and design such alternatives in a manner that mirrors systems based on wrongful trading, again also ensuring that these systems are tailored for MSMEs.

As noted previously, certain domestic systems follow a duty-to-file approach, that is, they require that debtors address their insolvency promptly after knowing that they are in actual insolvency and within a specific (usually short) period of time.

[44] *Legislative Guide* (n 6) Part IV, para 44. [45] Ibid, rec. 264.

[46] There are different ways to tackle this problem. Some systems do not open proceedings when there do not appear to be enough assets to cover the costs. In those systems where proceedings are nevertheless opened with a view to perhaps swell the estate by means of liability/avoidance actions and ultimately expel the business from the market, funding may come from public agencies that pay a professional or appoint an official receiver or through a fund to pay the remuneration of the insolvency representative.

[47] See Section B.4. of this chapter.

This approach is common in civil law jurisdictions.[48] It has certain salient advantages, essentially where it provides explicit instructions with time frames for debtors to follow and for insolvency professionals and courts to apply.

Poor corporate governance and insufficiently trained and skilled directors—a fairly widespread phenomenon in the MSME context—requires a more clear-cut and easier to apprehend rule on which to base liability. Indeed, insufficient and inadequate accounting information, particularly common in MSMEs, makes it difficult to assess retrospectively what the correct behaviour of the entrepreneur should have been and when it should have been executed. Judges in jurisdictions with little practice of holding directors liable for misbehaviour, again a not uncommon situation, may find it difficult to conduct an assessment on the merits of the actions of the management on the eve of insolvency. While more rigid, the duty-to-file approach constitutes a somewhat clearer rule that works as a stricter corporate governance incentive, although experience in systems that subscribe to the duty-to-file regime, for example, Germany,[49] shows that uncertainty still exists with regard to the point in time when the duty arises. When opting for one system or the other, the legislator would do well to take all considerations into account.

The existence of a duty to file does not necessarily prevent early action, and it may even foster it when the entrepreneur is only on the verge of insolvency, but not yet there. The existence of a duty to file can be understood in the first instance as also serving the realignment function by bringing creditor interests to bear on the entrepreneur's decision-making. The duty would tend to incentivize entrepreneurs to seek negotiated solutions at an early stage, similar to those examples mentioned with respect to the wrongful trading system. It is thus relevant to bear in mind that the duty to file is normally linked with the law's own definition of insolvency and therefore with both cashflow and balance-sheet insolvencies. Before a debtor is balance-sheet insolvent, the mere threat of the duty to file will operate to encourage a negotiated solution. However, as previously noted, strict time frames may also lack a clear rationale and create arbitrary requirements.

However, duty-to-file systems have varying designs. Thus, in some countries, for example, in Germany and in Poland, the breach of the duty to file is treated as a criminal offence. While this approach would seem to be a very powerful incentive, practice shows that it does not always work effectively. In Germany, the necessary involvement of a district attorney in criminal proceedings introduces complexity to insolvency cases that may hinder the insolvency professional pursuing the civil liability following a breach of the duty, since relevant documents are seized by law-enforcement agencies and so are not available to the insolvency professional for a significant period of time.

In Poland and other jurisdictions, the criminal offence rule may not be implemented because it requires a more stringent test (criminal liability usually carries a higher burden of proof than civil liability), or inadequate resources exist

[48] See, for Germany, Insolvenzordnung s 15a, or, for Spain, Art 5 of the Insolvency Law (Ley Concursal).

[49] In Germany, this duty only extends to directors of limited liability companies.

for prosecutions that are perceived as low-priority. Hence, the system backfires. Ineffectiveness of criminal law-based regimes is also possibly linked with the fact that this type of offence does not usually include a duty to compensate for damage caused, and therefore there is not sufficient incentive for the parties to act.[50]

When the breach of a duty to file brings about the need to compensate and pay damages, there are again different approaches. In some jurisdictions, for example, in Germany,[51] the debtor or the directors in breach may be made accountable only for the damage caused by the delay, while in other cases[52] defaulting parties may be made liable to compensate creditors for the amount the latter did not receive following the liquidation of the business.[53]

Systems also vary with respect to the legal effect of breaching the obligations. While in some jurisdictions the mere breach of the duty to file is sufficient to trigger liability or sanctions, in other systems[54] the breach only creates a presumption of 'negligence' that the debtor or directors may rebut if they prove that their behaviour was objectively geared towards minimizing damage to creditors.[55]

This solution is thus very close to the wrongful trading system. The main difference lies with the onus of proof. In the case of the creation of a presumption, the debtor or its directors would need to prove that they displayed diligent behaviour towards creditors and that therefore they should not be blamed for not filing for insolvency on time. Diligent behaviour is interpreted as taking reasonable steps to minimize damage to creditors and searching for a solution to the insolvency of the debtor.

This approach may also be used to foster adequate corporate governance by linking the presumption to specific misbehaviour, such as the failure to comply with accounting duties or any other corporate law rule aimed at protecting the market and market participants. In these systems, the party in default may also prove that the delay caused no damage to creditors or to the value of the business. This approach, while more balanced, may be difficult for courts and stakeholders to interpret and again would require sophisticated legal professionals and an effective legal system.

Certain systems that follow the duty-to-file approach at the same time explicitly refer to the possible use of preventive pre-insolvency mechanisms and provide 'safe harbours' from the duty in circumstances where such mechanisms are used. The reformed Romanian insolvency law,[56] for example, in addition to imposing liability on directors and other persons for various intentional acts causing insolvency, such as using assets for personal purposes,[57] obligates the debtor to commence insolvency proceedings within thirty days of the occurrence of insolvency.

[50] See Tirado et al. (n 5) p. 20 et seq.

[51] GmbH-Gesetz s 64, but also BGB s 823(2) in connection with InsO s 15a.

[52] This situation was the case of Spain's regulation of the duty to file (Arts 5 and 172bis IL). The law was amended in 2015 to introduce a duty to compensate only the damages caused due to the delay.

[53] There is also no duty to file in Canada.

[54] GmbH-Gesetz s 64, but also BGB s 823(2) in connection with InsO s 15a.

[55] Articles 164 and 172 of Spain's Insolvency Act.

[56] Romania Law on Pre-insolvency and Insolvency Proceedings 2014.

[57] Ibid, s 169.

Yet, the duty is suspended if at that time the debtor is involved in out-of-court, good faith restructuring negotiations. If the negotiations fail, the debtor must commence full proceedings within five days. Similarly, if the debtor becomes insolvent during what is called 'ad hoc mandate' or 'preventive concordat' proceedings, but there are indications that it may be possible to reach an out-of-court settlement, the obligation becomes an obligation to file within five days in case of failure. The law also imposes liability on the debtor for premature, bad faith insolvency filing. It allows, but does not obligate, the debtor to commence insolvency proceedings in circumstances of imminent insolvency.[58]

The Romanian regime, therefore, is quite balanced where it restricts the duty to file and protects debtors that are engaged in negotiations and in out-of-court processes. It tells debtors not to file for insolvency in just any circumstances, as they may be liable for premature filing, but to do so when to do so would benefit the stakeholders as a whole, though without specifying this in so many words. It also allows debtors to access the system early, when in imminent insolvency, yet it does not explicitly require taking steps to address the distress situation.

Drawing from these experiences, an adequate alternative option for MSMEs that is closer to a duty to file, but that incorporates some of the advantages of a regime akin to wrongful trading, would impose specific time frames after actual insolvency for invoking the process of insolvency available in the system. Liability for the breach of this duty would be limited to the harm caused, and other sanctions may be contemplated, as previously discussed. The approach would also include defence presumptions or safe harbours to excuse entrepreneurs from liability where they took action to minimize harm to creditors, negotiated in good faith, or took proper advantage of other tools, such as those proposed in the Modular Approach. Such a regime may also include an explicit requirement that entrepreneurs must take active steps to minimize harm when in imminent insolvency.

Thus, at least in some jurisdictions, the two approaches of wrongful trading and duty to file are converging in terms of their policy goals and mechanisms, creating a duty on entrepreneurs to act in a timely manner with due regard to creditor interests when insolvency is imminent. In considering how best to create incentives for entrepreneurs to share knowledge of distress and to act in a timely manner, legislatures should consider the level of information available to creditors about the debtors' distress; the level of expertise of the judiciary; and the ability or capacity of insolvency professionals, creditors, or public agencies to lodge complaints about the conduct of entrepreneurs in the period prior to commencing a liquidation or continuation proceeding. Accordingly, legislators may adopt the core option akin to wrongful trading, emphasizing early use of the Modular Approach; or they may design an obligation regime by imposing a duty to file or otherwise act appropriately, restricting it to avoid unintended consequences.

[58] Ibid, s 66.

6. Early warning mechanisms

Identifying a situation of financial distress at an early stage can be the key to solving many of the problems posed by MSME insolvency. Often, national corporate laws, particularly in civil law jurisdictions, include capital thresholds that force legal entities of any size to take action to remedy capital deficiency issues in a timely manner. These mechanisms are not based on cash flow tensions, but rather on the loss of the capital buffer, in a manner similar to the early warning signs of bank recovery and resolution systems. For example, those company laws that have adapted to the EU's Directive 2012/30/EU on Company Law must take action to restore capital adequacy when losses have reduced the value of equity by 50%, either by providing new capital, by reducing the capital figure, or by dissolving the company.[59] Naturally, the effectiveness of these mechanisms for MSMEs is limited. On one hand, they only apply to limited liability companies and many MSMEs do not use a corporate form. On the other, they are of limited effectiveness because the availability of additional funds to increase equity levels will not exist and the owners of the business will not have access to new financing. These early warning systems are thus, in many cases, the beginning of the end of a business, rather than a mechanism to save viable businesses.

There are, however, more efficient early warning tools that incentivize debtors to take prompt action when they start to experience financial problems. Apart from accounting and monitoring duties imposed on entrepreneurs,[60] mandatory reporting duties under bank loan agreements may be helpful if the financial authority ensures that banks take action when the trouble is detected. In some countries, third parties with relevant information, such as accountants, trade unions, or tax or social security authorities, have been incentivized or obligated under national law to flag a negative development.[61] This type of rule has also been suggested by the EU Directive.[62]

In the case of MSMEs, at least in countries with a sufficient level of technology use, online templates that can be filed at a corporate registry or a chamber of commerce, or even hard copies of available simplified accounting templates to be delivered at local sites designated to that effect (chambers of commerce, courts, etc), could be made mandatory, and a failure to comply could trigger early action. Solutions for addressing information barriers are discussed later in this chapter.[63]

[59] See e.g. the German Stock Companies Act (Aktiengesetz), s 92.

[60] See Section B.2.

[61] Within the EU, Denmark has been a pioneer in establishing early warning systems (see Denmark's Small Business Act and related legislation). The Danish strategy is focused on the creation of a publicly funded 'platform' (i.e. a network) of specialized advisers across the country, which provide early action advice to small businesses locally and which advise on symptoms that should trigger action by the entrepreneurs. Generally, early warning systems have been considered a key part of the EU's SME strategy for a number of years. For more information, see http://ec.europa.eu/DocsRoom/documents/6761?locale=en. See also Europe Small Business Act recommendations, 2011, http://ec.europa.eu/growth/smes/business-friendly-environment/small-business-act/.

[62] EU Directive (n 20) art 3.

[63] See Section B.2.d.

B. Effective Governance of the Entrepreneur's Choices and Conduct during the Insolvency Process

The problems of entrepreneur misconduct, however, do not rest only with the lack of use of the insolvency system and behaviour in the course of business when the MSME experiences distress. To the extent that the lack of a rescue culture, social stigma, and poor market perceptions are overcome, problems may nonetheless persist concerning the *manner* in which entrepreneurs utilize the Modular Approach procedures. Thus, the governance system should consider the obligation of entrepreneurs from the early stages where they experience distress, to their choice of solution, and throughout the insolvency process. If not properly designed and implemented, a specifically MSME-tailored insolvency system may be prone to abuse, particularly where a Modular Approach is implemented that allows for a significant degree of choice and flexibility. Thus, entrepreneurs may be incentivized to opt for modules that protect their own interests to the detriment of creditors or of the long-term health of the enterprise. Further, in the realm of MSMEs, inadequacy of information on the MSME's affairs and financial situation and a low level of interest from creditors may pave the way for misbehaviour. This section considers ways to ensure the proper use of modules by entrepreneurs and ways to tackle moral hazard issues, without undermining the benefits of the Modular Approach.

1. Control of the debtor's choices

The Modular Approach provides tools for entrepreneurs to address their distress at an early stage. In the usual case, the entrepreneur may be able to remain in control ('EiCon') of the process and resolve the distress situation with minimal or no involvement of insolvency professionals and minimal or no court or agency intervention. In this default position, costs are minimized, entrepreneur expertise and valuable private information remain in play, and the MSME is able to recover from the distress situation more smoothly.[64] Further, the EiCon approach provides an important incentive that can encourage entrepreneurs to utilize the MSME framework and possibly rescue the business if it is still viable. Most MSMEs are run by individuals or are family businesses, and the prospect of keeping control throughout the process constitutes, on its face, a major incentive to use the system. For natural persons, the framework also offers a discharge releasing the individual from debts and from insolvency restrictions. The discharge also incentivizes entrepreneurs to utilize the system and provides an opportunity for a fresh start.

[64] The *Legislative Guide* (n 6) considers in commentary a range of important advantages in the debtor's continued involvement in the process, in particular noting the debtor's immediate and intimate knowledge of the business, especially in the case of sole traders and small partnerships (see Part II, III, A, para. 5).

However, because of its open and voluntary nature, there is some risk that the system will be abused, allowing entrepreneurs to act irresponsibly with respect to obligations and obligees alike. In particular, entrepreneurs may be overly incentivized to access a 'friendly' regime, at the expense of the creditors. They may opt for a continuation process that allows them to stay in control even where they lack the skill to address the business's distress. Although, in the usual MSME case, the small business will be managed by an individual or a handful of individual owner/managers whose expertise is crucial for the business, these individuals may not have the means to address the situation of distress. Small businesses may not be able to afford the services of professional advisers to assist in making appropriate decisions at times of financial difficulty.

Not uncommonly, 'wishful thinking' (even Freudian denial) may drive entrepreneurs to attempt a reorganization in which they will remain in possession, even if it is not a viable solution in the circumstances, and where it may merely prolong an inevitable liquidation outcome. In other circumstances, entrepreneurs may have a close relationship with one creditor, likely the main lender, and may seek a process that is to that creditor's benefit, neglecting the interests of the creditors as a group. MSME entrepreneurs may also attempt to exploit the benefits of the insolvency framework—the discharge in particular—without providing sufficient information with respect to the MSME's affairs and activities.

Under the Modular Approach, creditors are given the instruments, such as the doomed-to-failure tool, to stop any useless attempts at a reorganization at an early stage. Early action is likely easier if an insolvency professional of any sort is appointed. Indeed, inherent to the Modular Approach is the fact that it contains a range of tools to achieve full or partial continuation of the business through a plan or through a going-concern liquidation in the relevant circumstances. The choice among the procedures is primarily in the hands of the entrepreneur, yet it is intended to be monitored by the creditors. Even where, as contemplated by the modular framework, entrepreneurs have the option of staying in control, the regime would allow the creditors to object.

Creditors should be able to require that the continuation process is monitored or supervised either by an insolvency professional or by a committee of one or more representatives of creditors; seek the involvement of the court or the relevant agency in the process; and require that the debtor be displaced.

Further, if the module selected is evidently and objectively inadequate, and the debtor uses it in an improper manner to the detriment of creditors, both the pre-insolvency obligation regime (either a wrongful trading system or the duty to file) and the two levels of insolvency professional mode discussed previously may act as deterrents. Thus, the behaviour expected from the entrepreneur at times approaching insolvency would influence the type of module selected, reducing the chances of misuse of the Modular Approach as a consequence.[65]

The law, or in some jurisdictions, a court or administrative decision, should limit the entrepreneur's scope of administration of the business for the period for

[65] An obligation regime akin to a duty to file may not be regarded as complied with when the module is objectively inadequate given the financial situation and the subjective abilities of the debtor.

which the procedure is ongoing and until a decision is to be adopted on the final exit from the business crisis. Typically, this limitation restricts or invalidates transactions outside the ordinary course of business. In other words, until the destiny of the business is decided, the entrepreneur must maintain a low risk profile in its activity. In cases where an extraordinary act of disposition is necessary, it should only be carried out under the authorization of the court or the relevant insolvency agency.

Thus, the Modular Approach provides four lines of defence to the problem of misuse or abuse of the system by entrepreneurs in their initial choice of modules:

(1) the doomed-to-failure module;[66]
(2) the insolvency professional involvement module replacing the EiCon;[67]
(3) the insolvency professional involvement module supervising the EiCon,[68] with (2) and (3) both implementing the pre-insolvency wrongful trading or duty-to-file governance regime;[69] and
(4) the denial of a discharge due to misconduct.[70]

2. Addressing information deficiencies

One of the main obstacles to the proper implementation of the Modular Approach, and a major contributing cause of entrepreneur misbehaviour, is the absence of adequate information in the MSME insolvency process. The MSME insolvency system would be substantially more effective if entrepreneurs collated and provided the necessary information and were willing and available to collaborate throughout the entire procedure. However, in some cases, and in some jurisdictions, particularly in the less-developed economies, the very existence of the information cannot be taken for granted. This section discusses both the issues of the entrepreneur's obligations to cooperate and provide information and the absence of such information, suggesting means to enhance the availability of information, including through the involvement of third parties in information gathering.

a. *Information and collaboration duties of the debtor*

The Modular Approach should clearly prescribe the obligations of MSME entrepreneurs with respect to information and collaboration and properly match these obligations to the different types of procedures contemplated by the Modular Approach. Importantly, the regime should be premised on cooperation in good faith between the entrepreneur and creditors, the insolvency professional, or the court, depending on the type of process taking place, and the provision of complete and correct

[66] See Chapter 4, Section B.1.e. [67] See Chapter 4, Section B.1.d. [68] Ibid.
[69] See Sections A.4. and A.5. of this chapter. [70] See Section A.4.c. of this chapter.

information regarding the debtor's finances and activities to the extent and in the measures provided for in the jurisdiction.

Standard obligations should include assisting the insolvency professional to perform its duties; providing accurate, reliable, and complete information regarding the debtor's financial position and business affairs; cooperating to enable the insolvency professional to take effective control of the estate, and facilitating or cooperating in the recovery of assets; and notifying the court about any intention to leave an habitual residence or move the debtor's headquarters.[71] Needless to say, if, as is the case under the relevant modular procedure, no insolvency professional has been appointed, the information and collaboration duties still apply. The information should be provided to creditors through the court or the relevant agency, or in any other manner that ensures its ready, low-cost access by creditors.

Furthermore, a continuation option should be conditioned on the continuing obligation to provide adequate information about the debtor's business and affairs.[72] If and to the extent that the MSME debtor lacks the means or the knowledge to comply with this obligation, it should seek the appointment of an adviser to assist in the process. The institutional framework for MSME insolvency should support and complement this obligation through the establishment of debt counselling services and through requirements imposed on relevant agencies to provide information about troubled businesses.[73]

Finally, requirements concerning transparency, good faith, and full disclosure should be embedded in all the procedures in the Modular Approach, including business-continuation proceedings, and significant non-compliance should be linked (as explained in Section B.3, below) to the entrepreneur being refused discharge.

b. Financial information limitations in MSME insolvency

Financial information is a key element in the mechanics of a market economy. Without proper, reliable, comparable financial statements, stakeholders cannot make investment decisions and after-the-fact control of the behaviour of market agents is not possible. This risk exists for all market participants, including, and in no less degree, MSMEs.

Experience shows that the smaller the business, the greater the information problems. Particularly but not only in developing economies, the level of informality is high: sometimes entrepreneurs and small entities do not have a legal duty to file proper accounts or the duty is rarely enforced; owners and managers have little or no knowledge of account drafting; and public training courses and awareness campaigns are rare.[74] Even in developed countries, income tax filing is often the only time micro business financial records are brought up to date. MSMEs conduct their

[71] These obligations are delineated in the *Legislative Guide* (n 6) Part II, rec. 110.

[72] Ibid, Part II (III A, 24). Under the US Chapter 11 *Bankruptcy Code* process for SMEs, the small business debtor must file periodic financial and other reports regarding its cashflow and its profitability.

[73] See further Section B.2.f.

[74] A good indication of the level of informality in developing economies can be found in the database of the Accounting and Auditing Report on the Observance of Standards and Codes of the World Bank, available at http://www.worldbank.org/en/programs/rosc.

activity 'the way it's always been', characteristically on the back of rough-and-ready accounting practices. This situation is incompatible with the proper development of the MSME sector, and, hence, of the economy in question. An adequate level of formality and, more precisely, sufficient financial information are key to a workable system to tackle MSME insolvency. Without it, access to finance is limited, there is higher perceived risk, and financing is thus more expensive. In case of financial difficulties, out-of-court agreements are hindered, many insolvency tools become useless (such as liability of directors and avoidance actions), and there are perverse incentives for MSME entrepreneurs in distress situations to destroy value. The entire system to tackle business distress may be thwarted. Even in those countries where there is a proper system of debt discharge, the fresh start of the entrepreneur is hampered by the impossibility of making a proper assessment of the discharge test given the lack of information, at least in those systems where the discharge is based on an ad hoc analysis of the entrepreneur's behaviour.

c. The need to strike a balance when imposing accounting duties

Despite its importance, there is a downside to the implementation of a fully fledged system of accounting and financial information: it is expensive. The smaller the business, the less reasonable it is to impose excessive accounting duties. These duties can act as barriers to access and demand an investment of time and training that smaller economic units may not be able to afford. Excessive accounting duties may be counterproductive, placing an unbearable burden on some MSMEs. It is necessary to design a system of financial information that maximizes the amount of information while minimizing additional costs; identifies key information to be provided, makes such provision compulsory, and leaves other information as optional; and is able to properly segment the spectrum of businesses into different groups with duties of diverse intensity.

This approach is well consolidated in the accounting profession. The International Financial Reporting Standards (IFRS) take into consideration the size and complexity of the business to gauge accounting needs,[75] and most countries with well-developed systems include lower information standards for smaller market participants. However, the differences reflected in IFRS and international practice do not always cover the specifics of smaller businesses and, in any case, implementation is often weak. In addition, problems do not always come from the type of information that needs to be included, but from the costs that are incurred in generating and sustaining the documentation of this information.

[75] The International Accounting Standards Board has published a specific document for the accounting of SMEs: *IFRS for Small and Medium-Sized Enterprises*, IASB 2009, (http://www.iasplus.com/en/standards/other/ifrs-for-smes). Some of the simplifications of the IFRS for SMEs are as follows: the elements of the full IFRS that are not relevant to typical SMEs are removed; some accounting policy options are not available to the smaller businesses; many of the recognition and measurement principles are simplified; there are substantially fewer disclosures required; and redrafting duties are reduced.

d. *Possible solutions to the problem of insufficient information*

The solution to this widespread problem concerning lack of information in MSME cases may come from a combination of measures that involve the entrepreneur, the creditors, and the institutional framework generally. Furthermore, the measures may not only stem from the insolvency or pre-insolvency framework, but also involve a number of general corporate and commercial laws and the institutions in charge of implementing them.

In particular, the information-enhancing system needs to be cheap, efficient, and capable of offering bespoke solutions to different businesses, depending on size and level of complexity. Certain concrete solutions that can be adopted in the system supporting MSME insolvency are set out as follows.

i. Templates and online solutions

Specific templates may be prepared by the agency in charge of the implementation of the insolvency system. Preferably, such templates would be provided as predefined information models prepared for the general accounting requirements of businesses, not just for the preparation of an insolvency petition. Templates should be free of cost and openly available, downloadable from the relevant website. Digitalization and online solutions, even for delivery of the accounts, would also reduce costs and increase the flow of information.[76] While implementation may pose difficulties in the short to mid term for most developing nations, it is also true that assistance from donors in this regard is easier to channel and implement. In order to bridge the gap between online technology and the reality of certain jurisdictions, specialized agencies or government bodies could provide physical copies of the templates and assist in their compilation. In those jurisdictions where access to the Internet is not widespread, hard copies of the templates should be readily available in relevant government agencies: the business or companies' registrar is a clear candidate for the provision of templates, although the different branches of the tax agency could also be an adequate and inexpensive solution, especially in jurisdictions with extensive rural areas. The utilization of templates could also be enhanced by the creation of a duty to inform of their existence and the need to utilize them at the time banks and financial institutions grant credit, or at the start-up stage of the business through a business register.

[76] A number of associations of the UK's banking and financial services industry have developed an interesting model called the *Common Financial Statement* (CFS), which provides standardized, simplified accounting and budgeting models. The organization collects information about spending patterns and average living expenditures that helps debtors plan and creditors assess and negotiate. The CFS has two parts. The first part is a detailed budget sheet that includes details of a client's income, assets, spending, and debts; the second is a summary financial statement containing a condensed overview of the client's financial situation. This system is aimed primarily at advice agencies, debt management companies, creditors, and debt collection agencies. Although it is conceived for household and consumer activity, the model could be emulated to cover the ordinary activities of the smaller businesses in the market. It also includes codes of good practice that affect creditors. See www.cfs.moneyadvicetrust.org/

ii. Bespoke rules concerning financial information

Legal requirements of financial information may be subdivided into groups of businesses based on their size and complexity. Instead of having just two types of legal requirements, as is the case in many jurisdictions where general and abbreviated financial accounting duties depend on size, having more divisions would allow for a more bespoke solution and could help maximize usefulness. This granulation would be especially relevant for the smallest part of the business spectrum. In order to mirror banking practice with non-performing loans, segmentation of debtors would also favour restructuring options and bespoke solutions.[77]

iii. Accessibility of information

Accessibility of financial information is a critically important feature of the MSME Modular Approach. There are at least three circumstances in which information on the financial status of the debtor should be available. First, debtors should have a duty to keep internal financial records. Such records would be disclosable on accessing the MSME insolvency regime, and an inference may be drawn by creditors, insolvency professionals, or the judicial authority from failure to have kept these records. Second, a quid pro quo of the advantages of the limited liability regime should be the obligation to file annual financial results or statements publicly, so that creditors and others can assess creditworthiness. Third, where a MSME does not have public disclosure obligations, when entrepreneurs seek access to the benefits of the Modular Approach they should be required to make the financial information about the MSME available to creditors, any involved insolvency professionals, and the competent judicial authorities.

e. *The involvement of third parties in information gathering*

The responsibility to provide evidence of the existence of adequate financial information should not only rest on the shoulders of entrepreneurs. The active participation of other stakeholders directly involved with the business life of MSMEs is paramount in this regard. Information on troubled businesses needs to flow from the places where it will normally exist, in particular from the following bodies.

i. Financial institutions

Banks and other lending institutions are responsible for the inception of a good portion of MSME credit. When an entrepreneur approaches its bank or financial institution, the risk assessment should be based on the provision of sufficient information concerning the MSME. Further, financial institutions have the ability to contractually impose even burdensome information duties on entrepreneurs during

[77] The minimum amount of information available should be the financial results in the yearly annual accounts, even in a very simple format, as it is often required by tax authorities in developing jurisdictions. The MSME model should thus avail itself of the mandatory information generated by tax authorities (see Section B.2.e.iii. of this chapter).

the life of the loan or financing instrument. They can also track performance and lower entrepreneur moral hazard using financing instruments that are periodically renewed against good business behaviour, or by the use of banks' current accounts and other financial products that allow for the ongoing monitoring of financial positions. The inclusion of early warning signs in their tracking of an MSME's performance constitutes a very useful tool to avoid value destruction and late insolvency filings. The risk-management practices of banks and financial institutions could, if properly designed and implemented, contribute greatly to enhancing the financial information concerning the debtor. Therefore, banking supervisors are key to contributing to the market system by ensuring adequate risk-management and monitoring practices.

Often banks, especially in the MSME and retail sectors, have granular information about the debtor's assets and additional liabilities, but this information is privately kept and there are no mechanisms for sharing it with the appropriate insolvency institutions. Further, bank secrecy can be invoked as a reason to deny collaboration with insolvency professionals, public agencies, other creditors, or even insolvency courts. The establishment of appropriate exceptions to bank secrecy, in certain cases and under adequate controls, should be explored.

ii. Financial information systems

Credit history contained in credit information systems is not only important at the moment of credit origination.[78] It can constitute a key informational tool when the business reaches a state of distress, either allowing for its restructuring or for the retroactive assessment of malpractice. A comprehensive credit report would include trading references, public record filings such as court actions, banking and other financing references, and/or significant elements that may have impacted the performance of the business. It is not uncommon that the information recorded in credit information systems is kept within the circle of financial institutions. The information, or some of it, could benefit other credit providers, including suppliers and other operational creditors. The creation of information registers could include information on utilities and other liabilities in addition to financial liabilities. They would greatly enhance the amount of information in the system.

iii. Tax authorities

Tax agencies can have material information about the MSME business. Goods and services, and value-added and corporate taxes, should provide indications and warning signs of the state of the business.[79] Even the lack of information, due, for instance, to delays in filing tax returns, is in itself a very useful warning sign of trouble.

[78] On credit information systems, see the World Bank's *General Principles for Credit Reporting* (2011) and, especially, the more recent and SME referenced *Facilitating SME financing through improved Credit Reporting*, available at http://www.worldbank.org/en/topic/financialsector/publication/facilitating-sme-financing-through-improved-credit-reporting

[79] See also the discussion concerning early warning mechanisms in B.2.e.

In some countries, yearly declarations of the value of certain assets is required, and even from time to time a mandatory universal declaration of goods. The existence of investigations concerning misbehaviour, such as untaxed services rendered or untaxed payments made or received, is also relevant information for the insolvency of the debtor and the assessment of the behaviour of its directors or controlling equity holders.

iv. Other entities

In those countries where there is a public system of social security, information concerning compliance with the debtor's duties in this regard can be relevant. It can also serve as an early warning sign of business trouble. Other entities that hold relevant information are public registries where security rights over assets of the debtor are registered.

f. Flow of information

Thus, even in the most extreme cases where it seems that no financial information exists for the relevant MSME, it is likely that through various channels, some important information can be obtained. The main problem is locating the information, collating it, and centralizing it in the right institution. There is a need to devise a system that allows for the relevant information to flow and be shared. Mechanisms should be designed to ensure that information from public agencies, such as tax authorities, registries, credit information systems, and the banking sector, are collated and made available, through the authority assuming the administrative function or the insolvency professional, to the insolvency court and stakeholders, or even, under adequate control, to parties in out-of-court solutions. These mechanisms will require the development of exceptions to bank secrecy and personal data-sharing rules that protect personal privacy but make available information relevant to the MSME's creditors.

Adequate financial information ought to be available throughout the business life of the MSME. However, the inclusion of strict information requirements to access insolvency or hybrid pre-insolvency proceedings may have counterproductive effects. If the entrepreneur has not been producing financial accounts concerning the MSME on a regular basis, having to reconstruct the accounting profile dating years back may constitute an obstacle that could have the perverse effect of delaying the opening of insolvency proceedings and thus causing destruction of the business. Further, during formal insolvency proceedings, the entrepreneur's effort to produce adequate financial information could arguably be less necessary where there is an insolvency professional whose task is, precisely, to work on the MSME inventory, and creditor and business history.

3. Sanctions for misconduct

In addition to addressing misconduct at times approaching insolvency, the system should be equipped with mechanisms to tackle other forms of misuse of the insolvency process. A regime based on a Modular Approach should prescribe strict time frames, duties to cooperate and to provide information, and opportunities for creditors to object to the process proposed by the entrepreneur or to the manner in which the process is administered. Through the enforcement of deadlines and other conditions, and through creditor monitoring, the entrepreneur should not be able to prolong the procedures, and creditors should be able to address problems of mismanagement.

The system should also include sanctions that may be imposed on the entrepreneur to ensure compliance with the prescribed duties, to address instances of misuse of the framework, deter certain types of misconduct, and protect the public from repeat abuse.[80] Sanctions may be imposed on the individual entrepreneurs controlling an incorporated MSME. In cases of unincorporated MSMEs or MSMEs not operating through a legal entity, sanctions should be imposed on the sole trader or partner entrepreneurs in a partnership.[81]

Sanctions imposed on entrepreneurs should not be overly draconian and should be tailored to the type of misconduct and circumstances of the case to ensure that they achieve their aims and that they do not prevent entrepreneurship and asset maximization in insolvency. For example, a failure of the entrepreneur to deliver on projections concerning a rescue plan or lack of cooperation during the process may result in conversion to liquidation. Yet, in relevant circumstances, creditors may prefer to proceed with a reorganization to extract more value from the business, notwithstanding the breach of duties, though creditors may require that the process is administered by a professional and that the entrepreneur is displaced.[82]

In cases of misconduct and abuse of the system, additional sanctions may be imposed in the form of restrictions, personal liabilities, or even criminal penalties. In particular, forging and concealing information should be punished with severity, given the consequential difficulties of accessing reliable information.[83]

As a general rule, though, the system should strive to provide a fresh start to entrepreneurs. The focus of the MSME insolvency regime should be on rehabilitation, rather than on punishment for failure.[84] The regime should encourage entrepreneurial activity and risk-taking and combat the stigma associated with insolvency.

[80] The inclusion of sanctions for breach of debtors' obligations is consistent with the UNCITRAL *Legislative Guide*'s general insolvency standard, which recommends that: 'The insolvency law should permit the imposition of sanctions for the debtor's failure to comply with its obligations under the insolvency law.' see *Legislative Guide* (n 6), Recommendation 114 Part II (III, A, para. 33).

[81] Ibid. [82] *Legislative Guide* (n 6) Part II (VI, A, para. 1).

[83] Sanctions may seek different goals. On one hand, by sanctioning non-compliance with mandatory rules of the system or an abuse of the process, the sanction is deploying an *ex ante* effect and improving corporate governance practices. On the other hand, sanctions for fraudulent behaviour or for repeatedly breaching rules imposed in the process may seek to expel unfit subjects from the market. Examples include a system of disqualification of directors, or of the classic rules included in old European Codes of Commerce that ban misbehaving insolvent debtors from engaging in commercial activities. Both sets of objectives are indeed applicable to the MSME framework, where malpractice is at times almost a custom in certain jurisdictions, and a problem that needs to be tackled.

[84] *Legislative Guide* (n 6) Part II (III, A, para. 32). See also The World Bank Natural Persons Report (n 4) 25–40 delineating the host of benefits to debtors and to society from providing relief to honest but unfortunate debtors.

At the same time, the sanctions included in the regime should be imposed in a robust manner in the appropriate circumstances and should not be mere 'dead letter' law. The court should be able to compel the entrepreneurs to meet their obligations and effectively address circumstances of negligent, reckless, or dishonest behaviour.

One of the key incentives of the MSME procedural framework as it applies to individuals is the provision of a discharge. However, the availability of the discharge should be restricted in circumstances of misconduct, as also contemplated in the standards recommended in the *Legislative Guide*.[85] Thus, the discharge may be refused or suspended in circumstances of breach of accounting duties, for example.[86] Furthermore, certain categories of debts may not be released on discharge.[87] The two most common ones relate to egregious misconduct, such as fraud, and those arising in the family law context.[88]

Where the entrepreneur does not comply with the requirements of the MSME framework and breaches the duties that the system imposes during the process, the discharge may be suspended and the entrepreneur may remain undischarged for a longer period of time. Such sanction may be appropriate in circumstances where the entrepreneur's conduct adversely affects the proceedings—as, for example, where the entrepreneur fails to deliver property or provide information—and the discharge may be suspended for an undefined period, although not indefinitely, until the entrepreneur fulfils certain conditions. Regard may be given to circumstances where it is clear that the entrepreneur is not in a position to provide the information or property, or where it is not cost efficient to further delay the discharge.[89] Further restrictions may be imposed on the entrepreneur during the process, as well as post-discharge, for a certain period of time, where the entrepreneur acted dishonestly or is

85 *Legislative Guide* (n 6) Part VI, para 9. Recommendation 194 specifies:

> Where natural persons are eligible as debtors under the insolvency law, the issue of discharge of those debtors from liability for pre-commencement debts should be addressed. The insolvency law may specify that the discharge may not apply until after the expiration of a specified period of time following commencement, during which period the debtor is expected to cooperate with the insolvency representative. Upon the expiration of such time period, the debtor may be discharged where the debtor has not acted fraudulently and has cooperated with the insolvency representative in performing its obligations under the insolvency law. The insolvency law may specify that the discharge is to be revoked where it was obtained fraudulently.

86 In this regard, legal regimes may consider different policy options, depending on the extent to which good accounting practices have become the norm in the system. Thus, for example, where an entrepreneur seeks a discharge for the first time with inadequate or no accounts, the system may allow granting the discharge if there are no allegations of fraud or bad faith and subject to the condition that a second discharge would be suspended or refused where the accounts were non-existent or clearly inadequate, even in the absence of fraud or bad faith. In this way, the MSME insolvency regime can incentivize good behaviour and educate entrepreneurs, albeit on the basis of threatened sanctions. At the same time, such an approach can avoid a blanket sanction that might result, at least in certain systems, in denying discharges to most entrepreneurs.

87 See the *Legislative Guide* (n 6) Part II (IV, A, para. 7) listing: debts arising from tort claims; maintenance agreements; fraud; penalties; and taxes.

88 Ibid.

89 See also the World Bank Natural Persons Report (n 4), which notes that: '[A]n overarching goal of any insolvency system is striking a careful balance between two competing considerations: first,

blameworthy in some other way.[90] Described in what follows are possible sanctions and restrictions that systems may include:[91]

a. *Restrictions on obtaining new credit*

Sanctioned entrepreneurs may not obtain credit of more than a prescribed amount without disclosing their status as persons subject to insolvency restrictions to the credit providers, or without obtaining the approval of the court or of another designated authority.[92]

b. *Restrictions on taking part in company management*

Entrepreneurs may be restricted or disqualified from acting as directors of companies or from taking part in company promotion, formation, or management for a specified period of time.[93] As noted in the insolvency standard, it is desirable that such a restriction is not so broad as to prohibit the entrepreneur generally from engaging in business activity, since that would defeat the crucial objective of providing a fresh start.[94]

c. *Information in credit history records*

Information about the entrepreneur's insolvency may be kept in the records of credit history bureaus for a specified period of time. Credit bureaus can also have a major impact on the debtor's ability to start afresh, so the restriction should be imposed carefully.

d. *Criminal sanctions*

The system should further include, either within the MSME insolvency legislation or in criminal legislation, criminal liability for insolvency offences, for which the

demanding much of those who incur obligations; but second, not demanding more than can be reasonably borne by the victims of economic volatility and other common dangers of life' (para. 115).

[90] For example, in England and Wales, a bankruptcy restrictions order (BRO) may be imposed on debtors for a period of two to fifteen years after the order is made. Alternatively, the debtor may be subject to a bankruptcy restrictions undertaking (BRU), under which it agrees to be subject to certain restrictions until a specified date.

[91] The restrictions may be wide ranging and may also include restrictions on leaving the country, practising the debtor's profession for a period of time, etc. There may also be a limitation on the number of times a debtor can be discharged (see also *Legislative Guide* (n 6) Part II (IV, A, para. 8).

[92] Under the bankruptcy regime applicable in England and Wales, debtors may be required to disclose the fact that they are subject to bankruptcy restrictions when attempting to borrow £500 or more.

[93] See e.g. the UK company directors' disqualification regime. Under this regime, disqualifications of between two and fifteen years may be ordered where the individual is found to be 'unfit' to act as a director (including because of breach of a fiduciary duty, misapplication of moneys, making misleading financial and non-financial statements, or failure to keep proper accounts). See also the *Legislative Guide* (n 6), Part IV, paras 34–35.

[94] Ibid, Part II (VI, A, para. 10).

punishment may be a fine, or in some instances, imprisonment for up to a certain number of years. Such sanctions may be imposed in circumstances of serious offences such as falsification of documents in a material manner, serious contraventions of insolvency restrictions, and concealment of property.[95] It is important that such offences are proportionate, drafted with precision and specificity, and are limited to egregious misconduct.[96]

4. General support, education, and advice for entrepreneurs

Entrepreneurs are typically people with a certain mindset and spirit. They do not always, however, possess the education and skills to monitor the financial situation of their business and to react accordingly. With regard to the MSME framework, they would usually not be capable of designing a proper continuation plan. They might not even be aware that there is a chance to turn their business around by using mechanisms under insolvency law. In all these areas, education is a useful complement. Specific knowledge in insolvency law or accounting cannot be taught to every entrepreneur. Instead, jurisdictions should establish a method of providing affordable educational counselling and legal advice.

Government agencies can play a key role in ensuring that there is a proper system of financial education for the MSME sector, including training of entrepreneurs and company directors on good corporate governance, briefing on financial accounting duties and where and how to obtain valuable resources, awareness raising campaigns, etc. These types of education could also be administered by chambers of commerce and other collective organizations in the private sector.

Every entrepreneur must be made aware of the mechanisms available to rescue a viable business in times of crisis. Here, local business clubs or boards or, more generally, chambers of commerce are often well-suited to spreading the news by organizing presentations and courses, or by disseminating informative emails and brochures. TV and increasingly also internet advertisements may also prove effective in presenting ways to rescue a troubled business to a broad audience, as has been the case in highly developed jurisdictions like Germany. In those developing nations where there is significant mobile phone penetration social media or text campaigns may be useful.

Company law could be drafted to include minimum requirements for director qualification with respect to basic knowledge in accounting, risk management, and

[95] Under the regime of England and Wales, any person guilty of a bankruptcy offence is liable to imprisonment, a fine, or both. A sentence of up to seven years can be handed down in some instances. Under Canadian bankruptcy legislation, a person found guilty of specified bankruptcy offences on summary conviction is liable to a fine not exceeding CAD 5,000 or to imprisonment for a year; or on conviction on indictment, to a fine not exceeding CAD 10,000 and/or to imprisonment for a three years; Canada *Bankruptcy and Insolvency Act*, RSC, 1985, c B-3, s 198.

[96] Forging/concealing information should be punished with severity. Many jurisdictions have rules that punish misbehaviour, but they are often not enforced. Enforcement should be encouraged if the system is to work effectively. The duty to ensure enforcement could be assigned to the insolvency representative or, in some cases—those involving criminal liability—to the public prosecutor (notified of the case by the insolvency representative, the insolvency judge, or the insolvency agency, as the case may be).

rescue options. For sole entrepreneurs, proper financial and legal education could be incentivized by tax deductibility of the costs of educational activities.

At the same time, the educational framework should encourage entrepreneurs to seek expert advice in times of trouble. Such advice must be easily accessible and affordable to a small business owner—ideally, free at the point of access. Private business clubs and/or public agencies could provide experts or at least establish a connection to possible experts. They should also disseminate brochures and online information about available options under the framework's Modular Approach.[97]

[97] See e.g. Germany, where several local chambers of commerce and chambers of crafts provide online information and individual consultations about how to handle the insolvency of a business. There is mixed evidence about the efficacy of adult financial literacy education; see e.g. J. M. Collins and C. M. O'Rourke, 'Financial Education and Counseling—Still Holding Promise' (2010) *Journal of Consumer Affairs* 1; 44(3): 483–8; and A. Lusardi and O. S. Mitchell, 'The Economic Importance of Financial Literacy: Theory and Evidence' (2014) *Journal of Economic Literature* Mar 1; 52(1): 5–44.

6

The Role and Position of Other Key Stakeholders Interacting with or Affected by the Distressed MSME

The Modular Approach and its supplementary governance regime focus ses sharply on the position of the entrepreneur. Its success would be a function largely of its early, voluntary use by entrepreneurs themselves. However, the entrepreneurs are not the only relevant players in the market arena where MSME insolvencies must be tackled and governed. The previous chapter considered how certain bodies and agencies can contribute to the proper functioning of the Modular Approach, particularly in assisting the entrepreneur in the performance of obligations and in ensuring the flow of information into the insolvency system. In devising its panoply of suggestions and proposed solutions, the Modular Approach also considers certain other stakeholders that have an important role in the proper functioning of the MSME insolvency system and that may interact with the debtor during its distress situation in important ways.

Both the inception of and the ensuing solution for the business in distress may be heavily influenced by the behaviour of creditors, with particular regard to financial creditors, and by the involvement of tax authorities. The fair and efficient handling of the MSME insolvency process may also require dealing with the position of the entrepreneur or the entrepreneur's family members as guarantors. Finally, the MSME insolvency system must have regard to the position of MSME employees. Thus, this chapter is devoted to a discussion of the issues arising for MSMEs as a result of the interaction between the debtor and these other stakeholders. It proposes several approaches to addressing the challenges arising in this regard.

A. Creditors in the Modular Approach

The Modular Approach takes account of and aims to protect the interests of creditors through the design of its options, as discussed in Chapter 4. Yet, in addition to the operation of the modular framework, consideration should also be given to creditor behaviour and the influence of creditor practices on the ability of the MSME system to function properly.

Micro, Small, and Medium Enterprise Insolvency. First Edition. Ronald Davis, Stephan Madaus, Alberto Mazzoni, Irit Mevorach, Rizwaan J. Mokal, Barbara Romaine, Janis Sarra, & Ignacio Tirado. © Ronald Davis, Stephan Madaus, Alberto Mazzoni, Irit Mevorach, Rizwaan J. Mokal, Barbara Romaine, Janis Sarra, & Ignacio Tirado 2018. Published 2018 by Oxford University Press.

First, experience in recent crises shows that creditors, particularly financial creditors, do not always observe good risk-management practices when granting credit. Reckless lending, at one extreme, and overcollateralization, at the other, have contributed significantly to the amplification of the crisis of the non-financial economy, with severe social consequences.

Second, the behaviour of financial institutions after the fact, namely, when the debtor is already financially distressed, requires specific attention. Often, banks show little interest in getting involved in the continuation of a failing business. Indeed, creditor passivity constitutes one of the main problems of any system seeking to tackle the distress of MSMEs. One strategy to address this apathy, discussed later, is to devise new tax incentives.

Third, and also affecting creditors, albeit from a different perspective, it is often the case that MSMEs find it extremely difficult to obtain financing when they are in a situation of financial distress, be it outside or inside formal insolvency proceedings. Without the support of creditors, viable businesses are not able to survive and value is unnecessarily lost for the economy.

1. Creditor lending practices

In a standard case, a MSME will have trade creditors, statutory creditors (those creditors whose claims arise as a consequence of the law such as tax authorities and social security obligations), and one or sometimes more financial creditors.[1] Trade creditors provide credit to MSMEs by supplying goods that will be paid for within a relatively short period of time. The essence of trade credit is that it should be repaid with revenues generated by the operation of the business, so that the existence of this type of credit should be a sign of the viability of the business. At the same time, keeping this line of credit open is a precondition of the rescue of viable businesses. Because this credit is normally unsecured, or is secured with collateral linked to the operation of the business, it is directly linked to trust in the continuation of the activity and, therefore, based on reputation. Few or no recommendations in this volume relate to trade creditors. They should be allowed to operate under the ordinary rules of the market and manage their risk as they see fit. It would not be reasonable for a legislator to impose additional obligations on trade creditors as such, whose very existence may often be jeopardized by the financial distress of one of their customers.

The situation is different with respect to financial creditors. Their size, sophistication, type of activity, and often privileged legal position enable them to destroy value for the economy if they act inappropriately.

Furthermore, there is another structural aspect, which emphasizes the vital importance of actively involving financial creditors in devising a rational system of resolution of MSME insolvencies. In most cases of MSME financing, there will be only

[1] The special position of employee creditors is discussed in Section C.1.

one or two banks involved as lender(s). Unlike medium businesses, some of which may feel attracted by the prospect of seeking competing forms of financing from a plurality of banks and non-bank financial lenders, virtually all micro and small businesses will work with one bank only. In addition, even in those rare cases where a MSME is a non-sporadic customer of several banks, there will still be a privileged relationship with one of them, called to play a leading role vis-à-vis the others. It may thus be safely stated that most MSMEs fall within the scope of either the one-bank or the leading-bank relationship models. Hence, in the case of MSMEs, the sole bank or the leading bank, together with the debtor, are optimal addressees of the law reform suggestions which, it is argued in this chapter, have the best chance of minimizing the negative social impact of MSME insolvencies.

a. *The structure of lending*

Good banking practice stipulates that the decision to lend to a business ought to be based primarily on the viability of the business project. Often, this practice is not strictly observed with respect to MSMEs. Banks may lend only where the debtor provides collateral and/or personal guarantees. However, MSMEs often do not have sufficient collateral to finance their activity, both at inception and during the life of the business. Unsecured financial lending is scarce and expensive. It is not uncommon for a shortage of affordable credit to exist even for good business projects. This situation is sometimes exacerbated by policies imposed by banking supervisors.

b. *Shortage of affordable credit*

The problem of a shortage of affordable credit arises not only at the time of granting credit; it also influences the borrower's behaviour at the time of distress. The higher the proportion of the loan covered by the value of the collateral, the fewer incentives banks have to engage in a restructuring of the business. The type of security also matters: floating charges, and any other type of security where economic value is linked with the operation of the business and not with a particular asset, align the interests of lenders and the debtor, creating incentives to rescue viable businesses. However, many loans involve fixed charges. This is the only type of loan in fact used in developing jurisdictions, where security over circulating assets, including receivables, is either not a legal possibility or is disregarded by banks, and where there is a heavy practice of overcollateralization (loan-to-value ratio higher than 80%). Naturally, one way to improve this situation is by enacting a workable system of security over movable assets, increasing the types of security (an issue that is beyond the scope of this volume) and ensuring that attaining financing through receivables, inventory, and other commonly held assets by MSMEs is a possibility.

c. *The regulatory framework*

Banking regulations, especially those regulations aimed at strengthening the position of banks as debtors, may exert a strong influence on banking behaviour towards distressed loans. The provisioning rules of a country constitute the point where the two sides of banking activity, as debtors and creditors, most clearly intersect. A very strict application of provisioning rules may undermine the incentive of banks to restructure, while excessive regulatory forbearance could favour the implication of banks in restructuring operations at the cost of endangering the credibility of the banks' balance sheets. A balance needs to be struck that will necessarily involve a segmented, granular analysis of distressed loans, followed by active involvement in the restructuring of viable businesses. In line with this approach, for example, a country may include rules that allow for the reclassification of loans following the approval of a restructuring agreement, so long as it is a credible agreement and evidence has been provided, for example, by the successful implementation of the plan for a given period of time.[2]

d. Banking passivity and reckless lending/enforcement

A notable problem for distressed MSMEs is where there is a lack of interest from banks in engaging in negotiations with a view to reaching an agreement that could rescue the business where it is viable. At times, the amount of exposure or the over-collateralization of a loan will deter a bank from engaging actively in the restructuring, even where the business is viable. The next section further elaborates on the general problem of creditor behaviour at times where the MSME is in distress.

2. Creditor passivity and reckless behaviour

Limited resources in MSME insolvencies lead to very limited expectations for unsecured creditors regarding any substantial distribution in respect of their claims. Thus, unsecured creditors often have little incentive to incur further costs with regard to the insolvent MSME by participating actively in negotiations or proceedings. Overall, it is rational for a creditor not to participate unless it has a special interest in the result of the proceedings, most notably because it is personally connected to the entrepreneur by family ties, or as an employee, or where it appears that some value may be recoverable.

Secured creditors, in contrast, are interested in the enforcement of their security, which usually occurs through sale of the debtor's assets. This interest may result in the liquidation and winding up of the debtor's business. This type of enforcement often does not require any court proceedings or supervision; it could be done as well using out-of-court auctions or transactions. Aiming at avoiding the cost and delay of court hearings, it is rational for secured creditors to argue in favour of quick out-of-court auctions.

[2] For a description of the current criteria advised for reclassification of loans by the Basel Committee, see the 'Prudential Treatment of Problem Assets—Definitions of Non-Performing Exposures and Forbearance', 15 July 2016, BIS Consultative Document, pp. 10 et seq. (document available at http://www.bis.org/bcbs/publ/d367.pdf).

The Modular Approach seeks to overcome these rational obstacles by counteracting the non-existent (in the case of unsecured creditors) or negative (in the case of secured creditors) incentives to participate in insolvency proceedings, while preserving the positive incentives for the beneficiaries. The default assumption is that, absent insolvency proceedings, a secured creditor may promptly enforce its rights under the general law and as agreed between the parties. This possibility incentivizes the entrepreneur to apply for a preliminary stay of enforcement and to propose a plan. Such a set of rules would also mean that the task of designing and preparing a plan is assigned to the entrepreneur because the entrepreneur is the stakeholder best incentivized and informed for this task. Further, creditor inaction may also be tackled by the approval and monitored implementation of codes of conduct. The supervising authority should ensure that financial lenders do not contribute to the destruction of viable businesses by failing to take time and effort to consider the case.

Confronted with a plan, creditors must not be bound without a chance to be heard, for constitutional and due process reasons in most jurisdictions. The Modular Approach seeks to lower creditors' participation costs through online, postal, and proxy consultation and voting. At the same time, the Modular Approach raises the costs of non-participation through (i) 'deemed approval',[3] whereby a creditor's failure to vote is regarded as a vote in favour of the rehabilitation plan, and (ii) 'scream or die', by which the absence of timely objection, such as to the suggested amount of their claim or right, is treated as a waiver of the right to judicial review. In sum, creditors' passivity after due notification binds them finally to the legally stipulated outcome of the proceedings.

3. Lenders' duties at times approaching MSME insolvency

As noted previously, it is often the case that MSMEs have a close relationship with a single or a few major lenders. Such creditors may have perverse incentives to pressure the entrepreneur to pay the MSME debts, and the entrepreneur may have incentives to cooperate, at the expense of other creditors. Lenders may also put pressure on the entrepreneur to opt for insolvency solutions such as piecemeal liquidation, which may be effective from a lender's perspective but may not be the most beneficial solution for the general body of stakeholders.

This risk of lenders' self-serving behaviour can be mitigated to some extent by applying the earlier-discussed MSME-tailored entrepreneur obligations regime to lenders, and by specifying their obligations at times approaching the insolvency of MSMEs. Legal systems that impose obligations akin to wrongful trading often adopt broad definitions of the persons subject to the obligations. Such regimes may apply to 'directors', but directors may include de facto directors who are not formally appointed, but act as directors, as well as 'shadow directors' who may be any 'person in accordance with whose directions or instructions the directors of the company

[3] See Chapter 4, Section A.2.a.iv.

are accustomed to act ...'.[4] It is, therefore, possible that under such systems lenders will be subject to obligations in circumstances where they have exercised pervasive control over the business. However, establishing such degree of control is difficult. In the UK, for example, the court may require showing that 'the nominees are put up but in fact behind the [scene] strings are being pulled by some other persons who do not put themselves forward as appointed directors',[5] and it is not enough to show that the bank, at times approaching insolvency, was significantly involved in the business and tried 'to rescue what they could out of the company using their undoubted rights as secured creditors ...'.[6] The regime that applies to more serious misconduct, such as the fraudulent trading regime in the UK, also often applies to any persons who have been a party to the fraud.[7] Yet, such allegations require showing 'real moral blame'.[8]

Other systems, as well, provide a potential scope for lender liability. The Romanian Law on Pre-insolvency and Insolvency Proceedings (2014) creates potential lender obligations, although to date there are no decisions on this issue. Article 58 of this law allows an insolvency professional to investigate persons to whom insolvency might be attributable and the existence of premises for them to be held liable; and article 169 creates liability where a third party, which could include a lender, has intentionally committed an act 'that concurred to the insolvency of the debtor'. It has been informally observed by one court that cases of alleged lender liability have been brought, but that there is an evidentiary challenge in respect of establishing the requisite intent.

France does have substantial case law on lender liability, most of which is referable to sole proprietors and other MSME businesses. In France, lenders can be held liable for granting excessive credit to small-business owners.[9] The bank or other lending institution has a 'duty to warn' the entrepreneur and can be found guilty of a breach of that duty if the credit granted was disproportionate to the repayment capacity of the borrower. The French Court of Appeal has held that the duty to warn has three obligations: the duty to inquire, the duty to alert the borrower to the risk of non-repayment, and the duty to the contributory faculties of the borrower.[10] The duty to inquire means that before granting credit, the banker must first fulfill an obligation to learn about the borrower's financial capacities.[11] The lender is obliged to carry out investigations to ascertain the borrower's financial situation, particularly in the case

[4] See the UK Insolvency Act, s 251.

[5] *Re PFTZM Ltd* [1995] 2 BCLC 354; [1995] BCC 280, 290.

[6] Ibid, 291.

[7] See the UK Insolvency Act, s 213.

[8] *Re Patrick and Lyon Ltd* [1933] Ch 786, 790. See e.g. *Morris v State Bank of India* [2005] EWCA Civ 693, where it was held that the company's bank had 'blind-eye knowledge' of the fraudulent trading conducted by the company through one of its employees.

[9] The provisions also apply to consumer debtors, such as in the case: 1ère Civ, 12 juillet 2005, pourvoi n° 03-10.921, Cour de cassation, France.

[10] Cour d'appel, France, Pourvoi n° 05-21.104. The borrower in this case was operator of a small agri-business, who received several loans from a bank, which his mother and wife had guaranteed.

[11] Ibid. See also 1ère Civ, 12 juillet 2005, Bull, n° 327 at 271 and 1ère Civ, 2 novembre 2005, Bull, n° 397.

of an individual who is unaware of banking practices.[12] The bank or other credit institution can be held liable for a breach of duty to inquire that led to the granting of credit exceeding the ability of the borrower to repay.[13] The lender's obligations extend to learning not only about the entrepreneur's financial capacities at the time of the loan, but also about its evolution during the repayment of the credit, in order to measure the risks.[14] The duty to alert is an obligation to draw the entrepreneur's attention to the possible disproportionality of the borrowing expenses with regard to its financial situation and the risks, including insolvency.[15] The duty to alert regarding excessive credit is distinguishable from enlightening a borrower on the advantages and disadvantages of credit generally.[16] Failure to comply with the principle of proportionality may be invoked by the borrower when the loans granted are excessive in relation to the borrower's ability to repay, be it an individual or a company.[17] However, the duty to warn may be reconciled with the obligation of the lender not to interfere with the debtor's business. The Cour d'appel held that the duty to warn does not necessarily translate into an overburden for the banker, because even excessive credit may be granted on condition that the customer has been alerted and has expressly consented to take the risk.[18] For the 'informed borrower', the banker has no duty to warn.[19]

In Italy, too, a bank can be held liable for granting excessive credit to a client in situations where it ought to have realized, based on its duty of professional diligence,

[12] In terms of evidentiary onus, it is up to the borrower to demonstrate the fault of the bank by bringing proof that its financial capacity did not allow it to meet its obligations to pay the amount the bank lent; and it is for the bank to prove that it has complied with the duty to warn. The borrower is not required to demonstrate that the bank has breached its advisory obligation when making the loans. Pourvoi n° 05-21.104. Under penalty of liability, the credit grantor must demonstrate that, prior to the granting of the loan, it requested that the documents justifying the financial capacity of the borrower be disclosed. Pourvoi n° 05-21.104.

[13] Cour d'appel, France (n 10). The Cour d'appel held that it is the 'duty of discernment' that imposes on the credit institution the obligation to inform itself. The lender must investigate the borrower's financial situation and assess the credibility of the file submitted; and it must provide a loan adjusted to the borrower's repayment capacity, adapted to the needs of the enterprise and its growth prospects, the profitability of the business having to be sufficient to ensure the repayment of the loan.

[14] Pourvoi n° 05-21.104. [15] Cour d'appel, France (n 10).

[16] Ibid. Only the foreseeable development of the borrower's situation must be incorporated into the warning, and unpredictable developments in the borrower's situation cannot give rise to liability. It may be a change in the economic environment or an increase in the borrower's debt ratio after the conclusion of the credit agreement.

[17] Ibid. Exceptional circumstances may arise where the credit institution has seriously breached its duty of discernment or its duty to contract in good faith, the Cour d'appel citing Com, 23 juin 1998, pourvoi n° 95-16.117, Bull, n° 208, at 171: JCP E 1998, n° 47, at 1831.

[18] Ibid. The courts can assess the quality of the duty to warn based in part on the 'savvy' or professionalism of the borrower, but where resources are limited, the courts weighing the evidence will likely consider the borrower less sophisticated.

[19] For example, in Pourvoi n° 06-11.673, Cour de cassation, a husband and wife were granted funding to open a pizzeria, creperie, and glacier. When they defaulted on the loan, they argued that the bank had failed to inform them of the risks of the loan. The application was dismissed as the husband had previously operated a similar business, which indicated he was knowledgeable in business credit practices. On appeal, the Aix-en-Provence Cour d'appel upheld that judgment, holding that the co-borrowers were in a position to apprehend the nature and risks of the transaction in which they were engaged.

that the credit granted was disproportionate to the client's repayment capacity. However, after a few cases where it was held that the tort liability vis-à-vis the other creditors for reckless lending to the debtor was enforceable by the trustee in the debtor's bankruptcy to the benefit of the insolvency estate as a whole,[20] the Italian Supreme Court de Cassation took a much more restrictive view. The Court denied trustees standing to sue on behalf of the insolvency estate, holding that damages in tort were only recoverable by an individual creditor through an individual action if and to the extent that in such action the plaintiff creditor is able to prove specific harm as a result of the deepening-of-insolvency effect attributable to the lender's imprudent or reckless granting of credit.[21] There are also cases, however, where, although reference was made to the rule that a trustee has no independent standing to sue a reckless lender as such, recovery by a trustee from the bank was ultimately allowed on the ground that the bank was jointly and severally liable with the directors, whose pre-insolvency behaviour (wrongful trading) could be characterized as a tort of which the bank was a co-author.[22]

The *Legislative Guide's* standard on directors' obligations at times approaching insolvency, which, as discussed in Chapter 5, generally follows the wrongful trading approach, also captures within the regime persons other than the appointed directors. It applies to 'any person formally appointed as a director and any other person exercising factual control and performing the functions of a director.'[23] Lenders are not mentioned specifically in the standard, however. Establishing lenders' liability may be difficult where there is a requirement to prove a certain level of control. Legislators and courts may be reluctant to impose liabilities for management upon lenders too easily. Against this backdrop, commentary in the *Legislative Guide* notes the 'increased risk of unexpected liabilities for banks and others who might be deemed to be directors by reason of their involvement with the company, particularly at the time of the insolvency'. It also notes that: 'It is desirable that relevant legislation provide due protection for such parties when they are acting in good faith, at arm's length to the debtor and in a commercially reasonable manner.'[24]

The obligation regime applied in the MSME context should indeed be carefully balanced with regard to the position of lenders. It is important not to deter the granting

[20] See e.g. *Fallimento Italsemole Srl v. Rolo Banca Srl*, Tribunale Foggia 7 May 2002, (2002) Diritto Fallimentare, II, 510–543.

[21] See in particular *Fallimento Casillo grani v. Banca Antoniana Popolare Veneta*, Supreme Court of Cassation (United Chambers) 28 March 2006, no. 7030 (2006) Foro Italiano, I, 3417–3424; *Formenti Seleco SpA in amministrazione straordinaria v. Banca Mediocredito Friuli Venezia Giulia et al.*, Supreme Ct of Cassation, 12 May 2017, n. 11798 (2017).

[22] See eg, *Fallimento La Vitimec Srl v. BNL*, Supreme Court of Cassation, 1 June 2010, no. 13413 (2010); *Curatela del Fallimento T. v. BM SpA e MC SA*, Tribunal Prato 15 February 2017 (2017).

[23] United Nations Commission on International Trade Law (UNCITRAL), *Legislative Guide on Insolvency Law, 2005*, Part IV, Recommendation 258, United Nations Publication No.E.05.V.10 (additional parts were added to the *Legislative Guide* in 2010 and 2013) (hereafter *Legislative Guide*). See also World Bank, *Principles on Effective Insolvency and Creditor/Debtor Regimes* (revised May 2016, http://pubdocs.worldbank.org/en/919511468425523509/ICR-Principles-Insolvency-Creditor-Debtor-Regimes-2016.pdf). The *Legislative Guide*, together with the World Bank Principles on Creditor–Debtors Regimes 2016, form the insolvency standard.

[24] *Legislative Guide* (n 23) at 7.

of credit to MSMEs. At the same time, there is room in the MSME context to apply a pre-insolvency obligation regime more robustly to lenders, considering their important influence on MSME entrepreneurs. Accordingly, the regime may specify that lenders to MSMEs may be liable for losses suffered by unsecured creditors arising from their conduct relating to MSME borrowing and management at times of distress. The duty of lenders may be mentioned explicitly in the context of pre-insolvency obligations and/or liability for insolvency provisions, and may usefully include some specification of actions that may be regarded detrimental. Lenders should be made aware that, at times approaching insolvency, the obligation of the entrepreneur and other persons influencing the MSME management is to the general body of stakeholders.

With respect to the entrepreneur's obligations, this regime for reckless management and lender's influence would apply alongside measures for more serious misconduct, including where lenders were party to fraud. In that regard, too, the application of the law to lenders can be explicit.

4. Tax law incentives for lenders

The challenge of MSME insolvency can also be understood as an opportunity to explore an effective set of tools aimed at promoting responsible credit borrowing and lending, responsible credit monitoring, and responsible credit collection, including, if need be, credit restructuring.[25]

Inspiration for a possible approach to the promotion of responsible credit practices can be drawn from the legal regulation of workplace accidents. The previous unregulated situation was replaced with a system that places responsibility on employers for creating safe workplaces, and compensates workers for harms experienced in the workplace, most effectively promoting aggregate social welfare.[26] Similarly, a comprehensive approach to MSME insolvency suggests that professional lenders have some responsibility in lending practices to MSMEs, as they are relatively well-positioned to assess risk and monitor for early signs of financial distress.[27] One option under the Modular Approach is to require the observance of prudential rules in the performance of lending activities, especially designed to reduce the risk

[25] A. Mazzoni, 'The Social Aspects of MSME Insolvencies: A Global View and a New Approach for Law Reform' (2016) *Rivista di Diritto del Commercio Internazionale*, 25 (2): 361–90 at 366; published also in '*Eppur si muove:* The Age of Uniform Law (Essays in honour of Michael Joachim Bonell to celebrate his 70th birthday)', Rome, 2016, Vol. I, 715–39 (hereafter Mazzoni).

[26] The initial approach of worker occupational health and safety, whereby losses arising from such accidents should be solely and directly borne by the individual worker whenever it could be shown that the accident was imputable to his negligence or contributory negligence, was ultimately abandoned by most of the more developed legal systems, and no one today would seriously advocate the reinstatement of that old approach. The reason is clear: since society has a vital interest in encouraging people to work, risks arising from work and the consequentially occurring losses must be legally handled in a conscious social perspective, i.e. by providing rules other than the mere imputation of the loss to the author/victim of the accident on grounds of negligence or personal bad luck. Mazzoni (n 25).

[27] In this respect, professional lenders may be expected to be much better candidates than their less-structured counterparties for the purpose of becoming the object of a regulatory framework institutionally designed to prevent, whenever possible, and to efficiently administer, whenever unavoidable, the insolvency of MSMEs.

of MSME insolvencies or to govern as much as possible their occurrence. Non-compliance with such specially designed prudential rules could be sanctioned by using taxation as a leverage to discourage inappropriate conduct. Desirable conduct could be encouraged by affirmative tax benefits.

These two proposed lines of action—providing special prudential rules regarding lenders' obligations in lending decisions, and using tax leverage to induce compliance—must be seen as linked, since, unless they are taken together, their impact might fail to be significant.

Virtually all national legal systems have banking regulations whose institutional goal is to prescribe the observance of prudential, technical rules in the granting of credit, the monitoring of credit granted and still outstanding, and the collection of due and payable amounts or the measures to be taken in respect of defaults. These national regulatory and supervisory systems, however, should provide an adequate linkage to the fiscal consequences of non-observance. Briefly stated, tax deductibility of losses arising from bad claims against MSMEs should not be automatically available to professional lenders. Tax deductibility should, rather, be conditional on the individual professional lender acting responsibly in the handling of the credit relationship that originated the non-performing loan.

Lenders should not be threatened with the prospect of entering into null and void transactions or arrangements in the event of non-compliance with prudential rules. The heart of this proposal is a tax sanction or the loss of a potential tax benefit in the event of non-compliance with such rules, not the imposition of mandatory forms or conditions of credit contracts or of compulsory schemes of arrangement. Accordingly, the legal format of these rules should continue to be issued on the basis of the rule-making power entrusted to central banks or other top central regulators, permitting the much-needed technical flexibility that statutory rules cannot provide. In addition, this approach would make it easier to achieve forms of informal international cooperation among regulators.[28]

More specifically, tax deductibility of banking losses arising from credit granted to MSMEs should be made conditional on evidence provided by the bank claiming the deduction of having properly complied with prudential rules on the following: (i) the initial granting or extension of the credit; (ii) the monitoring of the credit while outstanding, including inter alia proper classification of it in cases of threatened difficulty of reimbursement; and (iii) initially, collection attempts and, subsequently, promotion of or participation in a serious workout arrangement prior to the filing of any involuntary insolvency petition and/or prior to enforcement that would result in the destruction of the business.[29]

Difficulties in application, and potential negative effects of this type of reform, should not be underestimated. In practical terms, difficulties in application might

[28] Including also the 'spontaneous' observance by them of uniform policy standards that may be recommended at the international level, e.g. by the Financial Stability Board.

[29] None of these 'conditions precedent' to deductibility of losses would directly interfere with the ordinary contract rules or the ordinary creditors' rights regime under the applicable national law. Compliance with the aforesaid prudential rules would be, as is already the case today, a duty of the bank vis-à-vis the banking supervisory system, and conduct the observance or non-observance of which

arise depending on how banks would be required to give evidence of compliance with the insolvency-related prudential rules at the time of claiming the relevant tax deduction. It would be unreasonable and impracticable to require a bank to provide a detailed history of any credit in respect of which the tax deduction is claimed. Basically, it should be enough for the bank to provide evidence, as it would have to in the case of a central bank inspection, that the credit was properly analysed, classified, and approved at the time of granting, and that it was kept under proper classification and surveillance during the subsequent stages of the credit life. Lastly, but most importantly, with reference to the insolvency or pre-insolvency stage, the bank should be required to show that it either (i) promoted one of the solutions permitted under the applicable national law to exit the situation, or (ii) participated in the attempt, promoted by others, including but not limited to the debtor, to arrive at one of such solutions.[30]

There would be certain costs and benefits inherently associated with this proposal. The introduction of a change in the traditional regulatory philosophy, with the inclusion of a proactive pursuit of a particular MSME credit policy in addition to the traditional goal of ensuring the banking system's stability, and strong linkage between prudential supervisory rules and tax deductibility, is likely to initially cause an increase of regulatory costs.[31] Such costs would be of the same nature as that which is typically associated with changes in the contents of applicable legal rules. After an initial period of cultural adaptation, the benefits of the new rules tend to exceed the weight of the initial incremental costs.

The conditional tax deductibility proposal may initially be viewed by professional lenders as a source of higher costs of doing business in that there would be the possibility of denial of expected tax relief. However, to the extent that such a threat may incentivize the restructuring of old indebtedness and the consequential reclassification of the 'rehabilitated' restructured part of 'old bad claims', it may provide a new opportunity for professional lenders to retain more value in the

would determine the entitlement to or the forfeiture of a potential future tax advantage. No actionable private right would, at least in principle, be vested in the debtor counterparty or in the latter's creditors in the event of non-compliance. The situation, again, would be no different from the one that already prevails today in most legal systems, where bank liability for abusively granting or extending credit is sometimes found to subsist, but only in exceptional circumstances and certainly not on the mere ground of non-compliance by the bank with the internal prudential rules.

30 It is difficult to articulate what should be considered bona fide promotion of or bona fide participation in a solution providing a recognized exit from the insolvency or pre-insolvency situation. For the purposes of this volume, suffice it to say that (i) a strong presumption in favour of tax deductibility should be fiscally provided whenever a plan of resolution of the insolvency or pre-insolvency, of any nature and irrespective of its judicial or extrajudicial nature, is shown to have been approved by the required creditors' consent; (ii) an outright tax deductibility should be recognized whenever any such plan is shown to have produced a recovery for the creditors in excess of certain levels, whether predetermined by insolvency law or by tax law; and (iii) in the absence of an approved plan or a certified minimum level of recovery for the creditors, tax deductibility should only be granted on the basis of a judicial finding, in the order that grants personal discharge of the entrepreneur, to the effect that the insolvency had not been caused or worsened by the bank's recklessness.

31 In particular, in as much as the regulatory and connected fiscal changes would require more robust or more sophisticated or more frequent inspections by the banking supervisory authorities and/or by the tax authorities, more or less open (or hidden) cost increases would ensue.

reclassified treatment of their original non-performing loans than the more drastically reduced value that would otherwise be assigned to such claims as a result of write-offs.

Finally, what remains to be considered is the supply of new finance, without which a rescue plan is nearly always doomed to fail, as discussed in more detail in the next section. If new finance is provided by a new bank, an affirmative tax incentive should be made automatically available by the fiscal legislation. An example is the non-taxability of the income obtained from the new finance for a specified number of years. If the new finance comes from the bank that was the sole or main pre-insolvency provider of credit to the debtor, the issue of the tax incentive might be treated differently. More specifically, an appropriate scale of tailor-made solutions should be provided to ultimately avoid inconsistencies with the objectives and the regime of the proposed non-deductibility of 'old' losses if arising from negligent or reckless lending or improper credit management.

5. Financing MSME proceedings: incentives to creditors and availability of other resources

In many jurisdictions, MSMEs have difficulties accessing sufficient levels of financing. This situation arises particularly at the inception of the business and, even more intensely, when the business suffers liquidity tensions and financial distress. The continuation of viable MSMEs may only happen if the business receives financing from existing or new creditors. Otherwise, the activity comes to a stop, and piecemeal liquidation is the only real alternative.

In most jurisdictions, but particularly where the market still needs development, the absence of a rescue culture and the stigma associated with insolvency, the lack of an enabling legal framework, the lack of real possibilities such as assets free for collateral or the ability to offer personal guarantees to lower the risk of lending for small debtors, and the passivity of creditors can thwart the continuation of an at-risk MSME's activity, frustrating chances of its recovery and value preservation. In this light, the legal and institutional frameworks of a country need to provide the mechanisms to ensure that troubled but viable businesses are able to access financing with a view to trading out of their difficulties.

Possible mechanisms to enhance access to finance at times of distress, with reference to relevant key stages of MSME insolvency and with particular consideration of the specific problems encountered in the MSME context, are discussed later in this chapter. The position of the entrepreneur after it completes the insolvency process and how the financing framework can enhance the concept of a fresh start and encouragement of new businesses is also discussed.

It should be stressed, however, that there does not appear to be a single effective strategy for the financing of MSMEs in distress, given the size and range of such businesses. The universal features to consider when designing the framework must be efficiency and affordability. Implementation should be left to national variations, based on different socio-economic contexts and a variety of legal traditions. Figure 6.1 illustrates three critically important stages at which the MSME requires

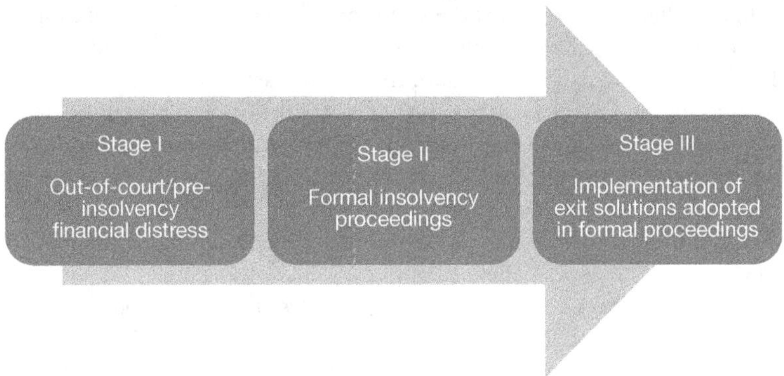

Figure 6.1 The three key stages of MSME finance.
Source: Authors.

access to financing as it moves from financial distress into formal insolvency proceedings and then as it exits the process.

a. *Stage I: finance at times approaching insolvency*

The MSME debtor often faces a number of challenges during the initial stages of financial distress, before formal insolvency proceedings have been commenced, and precisely with a view to avoiding insolvency. The debtor may face a lack of interest from financial creditors, especially creditors that enjoy fixed as opposed to floating security over valuable assets. The passivity will be even worse whenever financial creditors have securitized their SME loan portfolios. Further, MSME debtors, due to their size and the urgency of the financial distress, are placed in a very weak position vis-à-vis the financial creditor, with very limited leverage in a negotiation. This situation is particularly problematic since, often, the key to overcoming the problem of distress is to keep the business operating smoothly to retain the trust of commercial suppliers and other similar operational creditors. Generally, at this stage it is important to keep the financing of the business at the same operational level that the debtor had before the distress arose (day zero level). That would prevent suppliers and other commercial creditors from 'smelling the trouble' and would preserve the going-concern value of the business temporarily until an agreement, with an adequate restructuring, is reached.[32] The situation needs to be handled with the main creditors of the MSME: the one or, rarely, more financial creditors and the public creditor, such as the tax authority and social security.

[32] In any case, trade creditors would be unlikely to provide credit to their trade counterparties in excess of what is strictly needed to maintain the ordinary level of current transactions, thus fragmenting the aggregate indebtedness into a plurality of claims, each of which is likely relatively unimportant to the individual holder.

The first challenge will be to get the attention of the financial creditors, especially in cases where the exposure is low and sufficient collateral has already been provided.[33] In some cases, an additional problem that stems from the internal allocation of tasks within the financial institution is that the claim is sent to the recovery department; there is no longer communication with the commercial/business origination department and the new department managing the loan may no longer have an interest in keeping the business relationship alive. Its only focus will be on recovery, resulting in additional finance or even a rescheduling of the repayment terms being overlooked as a beneficial option.

These problems may be tackled by means of codes of conduct, approved and implemented for the entire MSME lending sector by banking associations, or, more effectively, by means of new regulatory prescriptions, such as new prudential rules imposed on the financial sector supervisor.[34] The code of conduct or the new regulatory prescriptions would make it compulsory for financial creditors to actively consider solutions on a case-by-case basis, basing the analysis on the viability of the business project, irrespective of whether or not the lenders have sufficient collateral pledged by the MSME. That way, viable businesses may be rescued and future business for the bank preserved.

Despite the existence of such codes of conduct or regulatory prescriptions, keeping the day zero level of financing may be a difficult task. Often debtors will have no assets to provide as collateral for fresh financing, which is why the optimization of a jurisdiction's system of secured transactions over movable assets is key. Although all tangible assets may already be attached, the debtor should be able to resort to its immaterial assets to offer creditors: security over inventory, receivables, non-intermediated non-certificated securities, etc may constitute an additional resource to keep the business running during this interim period of negotiation.[35]

Beyond additional security and soft law rules, legislation can still provide tools to foster the financing of viable, troubled but not yet insolvent businesses. Thus, the regulatory framework of banks may increase the likelihood of MSME business continuation by designing balanced provisioning rules. Experience shows that when rules are too strict and provisioning comes at a very early stage, banks lose interest in the continuation of their debtors. Perhaps more importantly, the framework ought to be lenient on the treatment of out-of-court agreements. In the case where an agreement is reached and implementation has successfully started, the system should provide for the possibility of positive reclassification of the loans. This option would constitute a relevant incentive to facilitate agreements and the financing that often comes with them. Additionally, this option should provide for an application

[33] See Section A for the discussion of creditors' involvement in the MSME insolvency process.

[34] See the discussion on new prudential rules and tax incentives for lenders in the preceding Section 4.

[35] Although this issue is generally an access-to-finance problem, and not specific to distressed financing, there exists the risk that, given the weak bargaining power of the debtor, financial institutions may demand excessive additional collateral in exchange for continued support or simply in exchange for a moratorium or a rescheduling of the debt. Over-collateralization is a banking practice that causes substantial damage in many jurisdictions, overprotecting the banking sector at the expense of the non-financial economy.

to the court to ensure the provision of new financing to distressed businesses is given high priority in subsequent formal insolvency proceedings, in case the restructuring fails. Other regulatory incentives may include protections for out-of-court agreements, and the additional financing that would come with them, from claw-back actions in case a subsequent insolvency proceeding ensues.

Naturally, both the high priority and the protection from claw-back actions in failed out-of-court rescue attempts should be subject to a number of requirements. The agreement ought to be approved by a large percentage of creditors, or it should have certain characteristics that make it objectively positive in the sense that it is not damaging to non-participating creditors. It should be subject to some sort of control by a judge or be assessed by an independent expert. These measures would be put in place to avoid, among other problems, banking malpractice, the possibility of which should not to be ruled out. The strong bargaining position of financial creditors may, in some cases, lead them to impose agreements that benefit their position at the expense of the other creditors.

Often, the other important creditor of MSMEs will be a tax authority. Legislation regulating public creditors may also pose a very serious hurdle to business restructuring and, consequently, to the provision of new financing. Thus, it is not uncommon that public creditors are, by law, not allowed to reach restructuring agreements with debtors outside formal insolvency proceedings. Tax authorities should be allowed at least to reschedule the payments of the debtor whenever the debtor has prospects of recovery and is only experiencing liquidity problems. The law should allow the reduction of guarantees generally required to postpone payments. If needed, tax authorities should also be allowed to accept write-downs of the debt. The alternative places tax creditors in the legal position of hold-out creditors, which may cause the provision of new finance by other creditors to disappear, since creditors will not want to provide fresh money that will go directly into the pockets of the public treasury.

In some jurisdictions, particularly in less-developed countries, the restructuring services of tax authorities are understaffed and unaccustomed to engaging in negotiations to reach out-of-court agreements. The improvement of this organizational element would be a key measure to facilitate business rescue of MSMEs.

Finally, agreements reached out of court should at least be treated as tax neutral. Taxing these operations often poses severe hurdles to business recovery and the provision of new finance for the debtor.

b. Stage II: finance during formal insolvency proceedings

During the stage of formal insolvency proceedings, and until a restructuring plan or a liquidation of the business as a going concern has been agreed upon, the main concern will be to keep the business alive and operating. For this objective, suppliers and trade creditors are essential. The commencement of formal proceedings brings about unavoidable reputational damage and an increase in the perception of risk by third parties. Absolute priority of all post-commencement claims, an adequate system of effects on executory contracts, and/or the presence and good management of an insolvency professional will not always be sufficient to convince suppliers and operational creditors to continue to provide commercial credit. Additional measures may be needed.

A possibility would be the creation of a public fund to support trade creditors whose claims arise after the commencement of insolvency proceedings. The fund would not provide direct financing, but rather, guarantee the provision of credit by private sector stakeholders, either directly to trade suppliers or to financial institutions that are willing to finance the operation of the business. Clearly, this type of support would only follow a careful assessment of the viability of the business. This assessment could be directly conducted by the fund, or, more likely, the fund could avail itself of the expert and independent opinion of the insolvency professional appointed to manage, or monitor the management of, the debtor during the insolvency procedure.[36] In certain areas of the economy, for example, in the rural economy, this type of support is offered by public or private cooperatives or by reciprocal guarantee schemes in which all the members of a certain community jointly guarantee the new debts incurred by one of their members.

c. *Stage III: exit finance*

This stage would commence with the approval of a plan and would last for the duration of its full implementation. During this period, the debtor's situation with regard to its creditors will be ruled mainly by the content of the plan. New financing ought to be simpler, since the business will normally have been restructured often downsized and, at least in theory, improved. Pre-existing debts will have been restructured, and therefore the financial burden will be lighter. New financing debts by trade creditors or new financial facilities will be payable as they fall due, and the insolvency law should include a provision that would allow a court to protect the preferential treatment of financing debts that arise during the implementation stage, in case of failure of the plan. In order to underpin the success of the approved plan, regulation could offer tax incentives that would be added to the restructuring of debt as regulated in the plan. A restructuring should, to the extent possible, include a reduction or a full write-off of sanctions and default interest. This type of special treatment ought to be limited in time, so as not to cause damage to other businesses competing with the previously insolvent debtor

d. *General considerations concerning new finance*

The former considerations for the third financing stage refer to the implementation stage of a plan, but the need for new financing and the enabling framework must also exist following the liquidation of assets to enable a second chance for entrepreneurs.

[36] This solution could also be helpful during the out-of-court stage. This fund, however, is not intended to substitute for banks outside insolvency proceedings, and ought to be regarded—and used—as an exceptional solution. Making it generally available to out-of-court negotiations might create moral hazard problems and end up being negative for the system.

Suitable financing solutions for restarting entrepreneurs need to be put in place. Restarting entrepreneurs need capital, cashflow, and credit, with few, if any, restrictions on future trade, without being encumbered with long repayment periods of debts captured by an insolvency proceeding.

The distinction between honest and dishonest entrepreneurs should translate into allowing non-fraudulent entrepreneurs to become beneficiaries of any supportive programmes available in the market for starting up a new business while simultaneously avoiding any preferential treatment of 'reborn' entrepreneurs, as it may lead to unfair competition and moral hazard.

Many jurisdictions impose obligations on financial institutions as principal lenders to act prudentially in lending decisions regarding MSMEs. However, for all three stages, banking law should not pose a hurdle to the restructuring of viable but troubled MSMEs. Lending to distressed businesses should remain a possibility. It is not uncommon for banking law rules on corporate governance to include limits on the bank and personal sanctions for directors of financial institutions that lend to debtors that are unlikely to repay the loan. These rules, objectively reasonable, seek to avoid excessive risk-taking and fraud. They are not aimed at prohibiting and sanctioning the financing of viable but troubled businesses. If, however, they are phrased in a very general manner, directors of banks and other financial creditors may be discouraged from financing the rescue of viable MSMEs, due to the need to avoid the risk of their own personal liability.

Similarly, consideration ought to be given to limiting securitization and scope of permissible hedging through credit default swaps and other derivatives, while still allowing financial institutions to manage risk but requiring them to retain some risk. This approach would preserve oversight and early intervention in credit relationship and create incentives to lend, but would control a speculative market.

B. The Position of Entrepreneurs and Connected Persons as Guarantors

Guarantees are taken, in large part, to hedge against the principal debtor's insolvency. Where the MSME is incorporated, very often the entrepreneur is required by the main lender to grant a personal guarantee.[37] In cases of non-incorporated MSMEs, guarantees may be obtained from connected persons, often family members.

This custom of obtaining personal guarantees can increase access to credit, inducing lenders to lend. Tampering with a category of guarantees, after the fact, in insolvency proceedings would tend to impair their value to the lender significantly

[37] This common practice is not new and has been widely documented—see e.g. J. Freedman and M. Godwin, 'Incorporating the Micro business: Perceptions and Misperceptions' in A. Hughes and D. Story, *Finance and the Small Firm* (London: Routledge, 1994); A. N. Berger and G. F. Udell, 'Relationship Lending and Lines of Credit in Small Firms Finance' (1995) 68 *J Bus* 351; J. Mann 'The Role of Secured Credit in Small-Business Lending', (1997) 86 *Geo LJ* 1 (1997).

and thus restrict the extent to which that category of guarantee would help would-be borrowers to access credit in the first place.

However, micro and small enterprises, and perhaps smaller medium-sized ones as well, raise particular issues where the guarantor is the entrepreneur herself or another natural person connected with her. Allowing guarantees to be called in without restriction might result in 'family' or 'household' insolvency, leaving an entire family destitute. While obtaining a personal guarantee from the entrepreneur can serve certain important objectives, in that it can be used as a measure to mitigate excessive risk-taking by debtors, it can also result in making entrepreneurs too risk averse.[38] Accordingly, the *ex ante* costs of restricting the utility of entrepreneur and connected-person guarantors of MSME debtors have to be carefully balanced against the *ex post* costs of allowing their entirely unrestricted enforcement.

One such balanced solution to the position of guarantors is to allow them to benefit from creditor action moratoriums.[39] Such an approach may, in some cases, be a powerful incentive to timely commencement by the debtor, and would create a space for rational decisions to be made collectively about the entirety of the debtor's obligations and affairs.

Another solution that can be included in the Modular Approach is to classify creditors holding guarantees separately for plan voting purposes. This class would be subject to the cram-down process. Thus, the treatment of guarantees would depend on an approved plan. Where a plan is approved that restructures and/or discharges the underlying liability, that does not in and of itself constitute discharge of the guarantor's liability.[40] It would, however, discharge any recourse claim of the guarantor against the debtor. In order to allow for the guarantor's discharge, the plan must explicitly provide for it and the affected creditor must either agree or a cram-down must be available against him.

To enhance fairness and efficiency of the process, the concept of 'procedural consolidation' may also be adopted in the regime for MSMEs.[41] Thus, in circumstances where invoking the guarantees would likely result in, in addition to the business insolvency, the personal insolvency of the entrepreneur and/or of his family members, the regime may provide a procedure for addressing the insolvency/guarantors' position within the same process. Subject to the same conditions envisioned by the Modular Approach, the process may provide a discharge to the individual guarantors; essentially, a reduction of the guarantee in such circumstances would constitute

[38] See D. Hahn, 'Velvet Bankruptcy' (2006) 7 *Theoretical Inq L* 523, 534 et seq. (hereafter Hahn).

[39] See Chapter 4, Section B.2.b.

[40] This approach broadly reflects the US position: *In re: Larry Ralph Gentry*, No. 14-1441 (10th Cir, 8 Dec. 2015).

[41] This concept is utilized in the field of enterprise group insolvency where the law may allow several entities to file for insolvency jointly in the same court, and where the proceedings may be administered by the same insolvency representative, thus minimizing costs and improving the ability to reach group-wide solutions. Procedural consolidation does not entail pooling of assets and debts of the entities (the corporate form is not disregarded). The entities are not consolidated, only the proceedings are (see I. Mevorach, *Insolvency Within Multinational Enterprise Groups* (Oxford: Oxford University Press, 2009) at 159; *Legislative Guide* (n 23) Part III, rec. 202 et seq.).

a de facto discharge.[42] This way, the guarantors' position can be more promptly resolved and the body overseeing the process can address the issues holistically, having at their disposal all the relevant information regarding the business, and reaching balanced and efficient results. Such procedural consolidation also reduces administrative costs for the system.[43]

Finally, legal systems may also consider whether to allow the courts to render a connected natural person guarantee unenforceable on the presumption or establishment of undue influence or unconscionability on the basis of fairness considerations, such as occurs in Germany.[44] In that regard, it may be considered whether this decision should be taken only in the principal debtor's insolvency proceedings, rather than whenever such a tainted guarantee is sought to be declared unenforceable. This latter issue is a contract law matter and requires further discussion as to whether there should be any special treatment, or not, in MSME insolvency.

C. The Role of Employees in MSME Insolvency

This section discusses the policy reasons for the need for special treatment of MSME employee claims and how this policy can be pursued within the Modular Approach. Indeed, employees are generally often the objects of specific regulation with respect to their claims during insolvency proceedings. Their position in MSMEs is even more vulnerable and thus requires specific attention.

1. Special treatment of employee claims in insolvency proceedings: country approaches

A study of the treatment of employee claims in countries that are members of the Organisation for Economic Cooperation and Development (OECD) found that most countries provide some form of preference for such claims within their insolvency regimes and many also have guarantee programmes that satisfy some part of the claims, with the guarantor pursuing the preference rights of the employees within the insolvency proceeding.[45]

Where an employer sponsors a pension plan for its employees, some jurisdictions also offer special protections in an employer's insolvency. A survey of insolvency

[42] Such discharge may be provided in the course of the company's insolvency without officially declaring the entrepreneur bankrupt, thus avoiding a bankruptcy stigma (see Hahn (n 38) 546–8).

[43] See also ibid, 550–1.

[44] German case law has developed to apply the contract law rule that any legal transaction that is contrary to public policy is void (s 138 of the Civil Code) on sureties of closely related persons with no relevant assets or income. This development was initiated by a decision of the German Constitutional Court (BVerfGE 89, 214, 231) and has since been developed by a number of decisions of the Supreme Federal Civil Court (see BGH NJW 2013, 1534 with further reference).

[45] Paul M. Secunda, 'An Analysis of the Treatment of Employee Pension and Wage Claims in Insolvency and Under Guarantee Schemes in OECD Countries: Comparative Law Lessons for the United States and Detroit', (2014) 41 *Fordham Law Journal* 867, at 875 (hereafter Secunda). See also Janis Sarra, *Employee and Pension Claims During Company Insolvency, A Comparative Study of 62 Jurisdictions*, (Toronto: Thomson Carswell, 2008).

professionals in both OECD and non-OECD countries respecting legal protections for employee pensions indicated 76% of insolvency regimes used some form of preference for unpaid pension contributions, while 29% had some form of compensation/insurance scheme to support the pension benefits owed by insolvent employers.[46] Some countries had additional provisions, with 33% using some form of director liability, and 14% assigning insolvency professionals some additional duties where pension contributions were not made.[47]

The separate treatment of employees as creditors in insolvency proceedings rests on two general justifications. The first deals with the weakness of employees relative to other creditors. Thus, commentators have pointed to the lack of evidence that a risk premium for the extension of credit is part of their compensation and to the problems of cognitive and volitional deficiencies in bargaining for such a premium or other form of insolvency protection.[48] As a result, they conclude that this lack of a risk premium for employees allows secured creditors to shift some of the insolvency risk to the employees, allows employers to obtain cheaper credit, and may result in inefficient allocation of resources to firms with a high risk of insolvency.[49] The same informational and volitional problems that lead to the lack of an employee risk premium disadvantage them in comparison with other stakeholders during corporate restructurings.[50] Employees do not bargain for the kind of control mechanisms that would allow them to constrain management from making post-contractual changes to the risks, even if they were able to establish a risk premium at the point of entering into the employment contract.[51] Finally, it has been pointed out that employees are poor risk bearers relative to other creditors, due to their lack of relevant financial information and inability to diversify the insolvency risk from their employment.[52]

The second justification for the special treatment of employees in insolvency proceedings is that individual employees are ill-equipped to effectively participate in insolvency proceedings. They lack the requisite knowledge, organization, and financially affordable access to legal expertise.[53] Individually, the amount of their claims and likely recovery would not pay the expenses entailed in effective participation. The expenses could be rendered recoverable if a mechanism to pursue such claims collectively were available.

[46] INSOL International, *Pensions and Insolvency—An International Survey*, (London: INSOL International, 2015)

[47] The twenty-one countries were: Argentina, Australia, Bermuda, Brazil, Canada, France, Germany, Hong Kong, Indonesia, Italy, Japan, Malaysia, the Netherlands, New Zealand, Poland, Russia, South Africa, Spain, Sweden, the United Kingdom, and the USA.

[48] Kevin Davis and Jacob Ziegel, 'New Priority Scheme for Unpaid Wage Earners and Suppliers of Goods and Services'. Paper prepared for Corporate Law Policy Directorate of Industry Canada (30 April 30 1998) at 13 (hereafter Davis and Ziegel).

[49] Ibid, at 14.

[50] Robert Howse and Michael Trebilcock, 'Protecting the Employment Bargain', (1993) 43 *UTLJ* 751.

[51] Ibid, at 755–6.

[52] Davis and Ziegel (n 48) 15. Gordon W. Johnson, 'Insolvency and Social Protection: Employee Entitlements in the Event of Employer Insolvency', (Paris: OECD, 2006) at 2 (hereafter Johnson).

[53] Daniel R. Korobkin, 'Employee Interests in Bankruptcy', (1996) 4 *American Bankruptcy Institute Law Review* 5 at 16–17 discusses the barriers to effective participation in Chapter 11 proceedings by non-union, non-managerial employees; see also Johnson (n 52) 2.

Table 6.1 Employees' average weekly compensation in Canada by size of enterprise.

Maximum number of employees	< 500	499	299	99	49	19
Average weekly earnings 2014	\$1,055.98	\$993.87	\$914.85	\$829.60	\$800.70	\$751.88

Source: Statistics Canada, 'Earnings, average weekly, by enterprise size' http://www.statcan.gc.ca/tables-tableaux/sum-som/l01/cst01/labr76a-eng.htm, accessed 31 January 2016.

2. The specific vulnerability of MSME employees

Employees of MSMEs seem to be in an even weaker position compared with employees of larger enterprises. In Canada, for example, employees' average weekly compensation declines as the size of the enterprise decreases, as illustrated by Table 6.1.

According to Industry Canada, only 51% of small and medium-sized enterprises survive for more than five years.[54] Thus, it would seem that employees in such businesses are subject to all of the conditions previously discussed regarding the policy justifications for specific treatment in countries' insolvency regimes. The issue is how best to ensure that the policies adopted in individual countries for the protection of employee claims are effectively applied to MSME insolvencies. These employees are likely to be lower wage employees and are unlikely to have a surplus of funds available for legal representation. The most efficient way for their claims to be pursued would be through a process that allows them to be processed collectively, rather than individually.

Many countries use a preference, a guarantee, or a hybrid of both to protect some portion of employees' unpaid wage claims when an employer is insolvent, with most using some form of the hybrid system.[55] The hybrid system has the advantage of providing earlier payment of wages, while allowing for the appropriate collectivization of wage claims in the insolvency proceeding through the subrogation process, allowing the guarantor to pursue one claim using the employees' preference. These advantages are evident in the larger insolvency context, but can be implemented within the MSME Modular Approach with some procedural alterations. The Sarra study cited earlier found that 47% of the sixty-two countries surveyed already have some form hybrid protection for employees.[56] The Modular Approach could build on these mechanisms. Further, legislation based on the Modular Approach could include the act of defaulting on payments to employees as an early warning sign (as referred to in Chapter 5). This mechanism may reduce the current widespread practice followed by many MSMEs of staying payments to employees before they default on other creditors, based on alleged loyalties, employees' low bargaining power, and employees' fear of loss of future income. Drawing on employees' good faith in their employer or their fear of loss of employment is not simply failing to pay an unpaid

[54] Industry Canada, 'Key Small Business Statistics', July 2012 https://www.ic.gc.ca/eic/site/061.nsf/vwapj/KSBS-PSRPE_July-Juillet2012_eng.pdf/$FILE/KSBS-PSRPE_July-Juillet2012_eng.pdf, accessed 31 January 2016.

[55] Secunda (n 45) 2.

[56] Sarra, *Employee and Pension Claims* (n 45).

debt as with most other creditors—it is manipulating the employees' livelihood. It is not uncommon that employees of MSMEs effectively finance the entrepreneur in times approaching insolvency and for some time thereafter. Making employee arrears an early warning sign may well have a substantive effect on the behaviour of entrepreneurs.

3. Policy implementation of employee protection in the MSME Modular Approach

The policy approaches to MSME insolvencies proposed in this volume are grounded in the premise that such insolvencies are generally low, or very low, asset enterprises where the implementation of ordinary insolvency regimes would likely result in the destruction of either the residual value or the going-concern value due to the cost and complexity of such regimes. Therefore, the Modular Approach envisioned here provides for simplified processes for either liquidation or continuation. The problem is how to incorporate existing employee protections into these processes. For example, under the usual insolvency process where the insolvency professional is a key participant, one policy option that has been implemented in Canada is that the insolvency professional in the MSME insolvency is required to: calculate the employees' claims; advise the employees of their rights under the applicable country's insolvency and/or wage-guarantee regime; and advise the relevant guarantee organization of the claim where that type of protection is offered.[57] The insolvency professional would be compensated for the work required to fulfil these obligations.

This procedure would be consistent with Convention 173 of the International Labour Organization: Protection of Workers' Claims (Employer Insolvency) 1992 (ILO Convention), which provides that countries that ratify the convention should provide protection for employee claims through a preference, a guarantee scheme, or both.[58] It would also be consistent with the EU Directive on the protection of employees in the event of the insolvency of their employer, requiring that protection be provided through a form of guarantee.[59]

However, some aspects of the Modular Approach to MSME insolvency in this volume envisage minimal involvement of insolvency professionals in the process. For the liquidation/discharge module, the debtor employer will have the most cost-efficient access to the information necessary to identify the amount and type of employee claims, as well as the information required to notify employees of their claims and rights under existing insolvency preference and guarantee legislation. The requirement to inform both employees and guarantee institutions of such calculations should be part of any standard-form MSME discharge application. Where

[57] *Wage Earner Protection Program Act*, SC 2005, c 47, ss 1, 22, 23 (Canada).

[58] ILO, C173—Protection of Workers' Claims (Employer's Insolvency) Convention, 1992 (No. 173), http://www.ilo.org/dyn/normlex/en/f?p=NORMLEXPUB:12100:0::NO::P12100_ILO_CODE:C173.

[59] EU Directive (2008/94/EC), http://eur-lex.europa.eu/LexUriServ/LexUriServ.do?uri=OJ:L:2008:283:0036:0042:EN:PDF, accessed 31 January 2016.

applicable, the collectivization of employee claims in the guarantee institution and their pursuit by a single claimant in the insolvency would provide a more efficient means of dealing with these claims than their pursuit by individual employees. A discharge conditional on the relevant institution's satisfaction that the debtor employer's calculation and notification obligations have been complied with would provide the incentive for compliance, while a denial or revocation of discharge for failure to comply would provide the negative incentive.

For the continuation module, it is reasonable that similar calculations and notification obligations would apply and be incorporated into the forms needed to initiate a MSME continuation module. Pursuit of employee participation rights, for example, voting on a plan, could be exercised by the guarantee institution or the employees themselves, and their interests in future revenue streams generated by the continued operation of the business as a result of the compromise of their current claims would be part of the assessment of any plan with respect to the distribution of its burdens and benefits.

Including such obligations in the MSME Modular Approach would overcome the informational and expertise deficits facing employees in the event that the employer enters an insolvency proceeding. Having the employer assume some of the responsibility for assembling the needed information to substantiate the claims and notify the employees of their rights would further the public policy goals of the particular country's provisions for protecting employees in the event of an employer insolvency, without dictating what those provisions should contain. At the same time, it would increase the fairness of the process by providing assistance to the most vulnerable and disadvantaged creditors, and provide a mechanism to comply with international obligations such as those in the EU Directive and ILO Convention.

If the business closes without any formal insolvency proceeding, as many MSME enterprises do, then hopefully the country's labour standards regime will provide some effective relief for those employees, but that eventuality is beyond the scope of this volume.

7

Examples for Implementing the Modular Approach beyond Specific Economic and Institutional Backgrounds

This chapter offers four examples of how the Modular Approach could be designed and implemented in specific financial, institutional, and socio-economic frameworks. The country examples are fictional, but the factual background for each example is drawn from common characteristics of jurisdictions in the region. The country examples illustrate how specific module choices could be made to create a fair, effective, and efficient MSME insolvency system. The first example is a European developed economy; the second is a newly industrialized Asia-Pacific economy. The third country example is an emerging African nation. Finally, there is an emerging European nation example, which could also apply to an emerging central Asian nation. These country examples are not proposing a specific combination of modules; rather, they are to illustrate the types of choices that could be made, given particular socio-economic, financial, and institutional circumstances.

A. European Developed Economy

1. Factual background

a. Economic background

- Developed European country
- Economy dominated by corporate groups and mid-sized businesses (by turnover)
- Nonetheless there is a large number of small/micro businesses

b. Financial MSME background

- Micro/small businesses financed by bank credit, supplier, or family and friends
- Security rights framework is well established

Micro, Small, and Medium Enterprise Insolvency. First Edition. Ronald Davis, Stephan Madaus, Alberto Mazzoni, Irit Mevorach, Rizwaan J. Mokal, Barbara Romaine, Janis Sarra, & Ignacio Tirado. Published 2018 by Oxford University Press.

- No floating charge, but similar debt instruments that place security on all the MSME's assets, referred to as encumbering all assets
- Enforcement of secured rights is efficient before and during insolvency proceedings
- Dominating role of secured credit in financial crisis and insolvency

c. *Enforcement and insolvency background*

- Efficient private enforcement of claims in legal system
- Efficient liquidation in insolvency
- Courts work relatively quickly in liquidation and enforcement at low cost
- Insolvency judges are sufficiently qualified and trustworthy
- Technical equipment of courts is still somewhat insufficient or uneven in availability
- Insolvency professionals are trustworthy, qualified, and well organized, yet there is no formal licensing procedure for consistency in professional standards
- Rescue culture is developing, but is not yet fully established (still undermined by stigma)
- Discharge for individuals only three to five years after insolvency proceedings conclude
- Debtor advice is available at low cost for discharge

2. Application of the Modular Approach

a. *Default liquidation procedure*

i. Management functions

Judiciary-oriented implementation of liquidation proceedings.

Judicial liquidation. MSME liquidations would be run and financed by the state through its judiciary. Court fees would probably not recover all of these costs. The judicial clerk can allow a secured or main creditor to manage liquidation. Discharge would require a court decision, probably issued by the supervising judge reviewing the case at the conclusion of the liquidation after (requested) hearing.

Steps:

i. Debtor/creditor make application to local designated court.
ii. Given the emergence of e-justice, online applications would also be available, to submit to designated court.
iii. Judicial clerk handles administration of liquidation; gives notice to creditors regarding filing of liquidation procedure; and can mandate main/secured creditor with managing the sales.

iv. If no creditor objects, mandated creditor or clerk proceeds to liquidate assets and pay creditors.
v. A creditor can object and can be mandated to undertake the liquidation itself. A secured lender's employee might also be used to investigate potential hidden assets.
vi. Creditor/clerk files proof of amounts received through liquidation and distribution of those amounts to creditors with designated court in order to produce discharge certificate.

ii. Administrative functions under the liquidation procedure

The administration functions can be undertaken by the judiciary (judicial clerks). Simplified forms would be developed for application and disclosure of financial situation, notice to creditors, and proposed liquidation plan, and would be available in paper form and as e-filing.

Steps:

i. Ensure that notice is given to creditors/debtor.
ii. On liquidation of the assets and payment to creditors, discharge is automatic, whether liquidation undertaken by the clerk or a creditor.
iii. The designated court issues a discharge certificate to the Entrepreneur in control (EiCon).

iii. Judicial supervision

The competent judicial authority is the local court of the judicial clerk. There is no need for judicial function where there are no objections or disputes. Where there is an objection, the supervising judge holds a hearing and resolves the dispute, including determining discharge where it is contested.

b. Continuation plan procedure

i. Management functions

Entrepreneur in control (EiCon)-initiated continuation proceedings EiCon proposes a business continuation plan.

Steps:

i. EiCon makes application to local designated court, as noted above, by paper application or e-filing.
ii. E-platform gives notice to creditors automatically regarding proposed business continuation plan. Judicial clerk is supervising or giving notice until technical requirements are in place.
iii. If no creditor objects, the plan is deemed to be approved and EiCon proceeds to implement the plan by filing the accepted continuation plan with designated court, including any distribution to creditors and terms of repayment under continuation plan.

iv. A creditor can object and propose a different continuation plan (competing plan) or seek a liquidation (doomed-to-failure).

v. EiCon files rejected continuation plan with designated court with application to confirm under majority and cram-down rules.

Creditor-proposed continuation plan Creditor proposes a business continuation plan.

Steps:

i. Creditor makes application to local designated court, as noted above, by paper application or e-filing. Business is continued by EiCon.

ii. E-platform gives notice to the debtor and other creditors regarding proposed business continuation plan. Judicial clerk is supervising (or giving notice until technical requirements are given).

iii. If neither debtor nor other creditor objects, debtor/creditor proceeds to implement the plan by filing accepted continuation plan with designated court, including any distribution to creditors and terms of repayment under continuation plan.

iv. The debtor or any other creditor can object, and propose a different continuation plan (competing plan) or a liquidation (doomed-to-failure).

v. Creditor files rejected continuation plan with designated court with application to confirm under majority and cram-down rules.

ii. Administrative functions

Simplified forms would be developed for application and disclosure of financial situation, notice to creditors, proposed business continuation plan, terms of final continuation plan, and payments to creditors, available in paper form and as e-filing.

Administrative functions can be undertaken by the local designated court acting through an online platform.

The debtor could stay enforcement actions and other enforcement acts for a stipulated short period (e.g. two weeks) by clicking a box on the form indicating which action should be stayed against which creditor; creditors could respond by requesting a lift of the stay, by requesting a debtor action moratorium, or by initiating the doomed-to-failure module.

One or more creditors could request involvement of an insolvency professional (supervising or even administrating the business) by clicking a box on the form to indicate the requested way of involvement and the willingness to bear the costs of the professional's services if the value of assets in EiCon's estate are not sufficient to cover. The involvement is useful where a creditor wishes to investigate the debtor's pre-filing behaviour.

The designated court would develop a roster of approved qualified professionals, from which parties can select or ask the designated office to select.

Where the proposed continuation plan is disputed, there would be the option for a mediation module to be applied.

iii. Judicial supervision
Objecting parties could appeal to the local court's judge to confirm a contested plan or to set aside the appointment of the insolvency professional on the basis of lack of qualification or conflict of interest.

Effect of Modular Approach in this example. The adoption of a court-oriented set of modules would allow for a timely and effective means of addressing the MSME's financial distress using public institutions, quickly returning entrepreneurs to productive activity. For the facts of this jurisdiction, the implementation of the Modular Approach would combine the self-administration of the debtor and the creditors with an accountability check by a designated court. The deemed approval mechanisms would ensure notice to creditors, the opportunity to object, and a speedy resolution where creditors do not object to the strategy.

There is an optional module to use an insolvency professional in the business continuation procedures, but such a professional is not necessary in cases of little or no assets and not possible in circumstances where there are not sufficient resources to pay for their services. The designated court (clerk) serves as an accountability check on both the EiCon and creditors assuming management functions. Disputes that cannot be resolved at that level, can be determined by the local court (judge). All modules in the Modular Approach should be available to the parties.

B. Asia-Pacific Newly Industrialized Economy

1. Factual background

a. Economic background

- Newly industrialized economy, growing production and export of software, chemicals, and pharmaceuticals, as well as agricultural and transportation equipment.
- Overwhelming number of businesses are MSMEs, both in the formal and informal sectors.
- In rural areas, men and women are primarily self-employed, mostly in agriculture. In urban areas, there are both sole proprietorships and MSMEs. There are also more medium and large enterprises, often owned by families in pyramid structure, the companies offering salaried employment.
- Recent decline in economy, placing many MSMEs at risk, but long-term prospects for the economy are healthy.
- Inefficient government bureaucracy, some corruption at the level of dealing with administrative officials.

b. Financial MSME background

- Micro/small businesses financed by bank credit, including government-owned public sector banks, foreign-owned commercial banks and cooperative banks, family-owned moneylenders, and families themselves.
- Possessory loans are a common form of security.
- Security rights framework is established, but enforcement is inefficient.

c. Enforcement and insolvency background

- Debt-recovery legislation exists, and secured creditors must apply to a debt-recovery tribunal to enforce security.
- Process is untimely in terms of filing; there are objections by creditors and a backlog of cases. Final disposition takes four to five years.
- Debtor or creditors can file for liquidation; the criterion is that the debtor cannot meet debts as they generally become due.
- Vast majority of liquidations are piecemeal liquidations.
- No rescue culture.
- No priority for post-commencement financing.
- Insolvency regime allows avoidance of transactions at undervalue.
- Uneven availability of qualified insolvency professionals.

2. Application of the Modular Approach

a. Default liquidation procedure

i. Management functions

There is a private sector-oriented approach, given the limitations of the judiciary. There is the option to enact a 'tools of trade' or 'personal residence' exemption to seizure of assets.

(EiCon) liquidation. EiCon first has the opportunity to liquidate the business. Steps:

i. The EiCon makes an application to local designated office—would use post offices, particularly in rural areas and smaller villages; and postal, tax, and other governmental offices in cities as the designated offices.
ii. Given the emergence of the software sector, online applications would also be available, to submit to designated office.
iii. The EiCon gives notice to creditors regarding filing of liquidation procedure.
iv. If no creditor objects, EiCon proceeds to liquidate assets and pay creditors.
v. The EiCon files proof of amounts received through liquidation and distribution of those amounts to creditors with designated office in order to receive discharge certificate.
vi. A creditor can object and undertake the liquidation itself.

Creditor-controlled liquidation. Creditor liquidation of debtor's assets.

Steps:

i. Creditor objects to the EiCon controlled liquidation to the local designated office and gives notice of its intention to liquidate the EiCon's assets.
ii. In rare case where there are sufficient assets, an insolvency professional may be used to liquidate assets or to seek to recover assets that may have been hidden by the EiCon. Secured lender's employee(s) might also be used to investigate potential hidden assets.
iii. After liquidation, creditor realizes value and then distributes any surplus value from the assets to other creditors.
iv. Creditor files proof of amounts received through liquidation and distribution of those amounts to creditors with designated office.

ii. Administrative functions of liquidation procedure

Administration functions can be undertaken by the secured creditor or a local designated office—post offices, etc., as described above. Simplified forms would be developed for application and disclosure of financial situation, notice to creditors, and proposed liquidation plan, and would be available in paper form and as e-filing.

Steps:

i. Ensure notice was given to creditors.
ii. On liquidation of the assets and payment to creditors, discharge is automatic, whether liquidation undertaken by the EiCon or creditor.
iii. The designated office issues a discharge certificate to the EiCon.

iii. Judicial supervision

The competent judicial authority is the local magistrate or district commissioner. There is no need for a judicial function where there have been no objections or disputes. Where there is an objection, the magistrate or district commissioner holds a hearing and resolves the dispute, including determining discharge where it is contested.

b. Business continuation plan procedure

i. Management functions

EiCon-initiated continuation proceedings. EiCon proposes a business continuation plan.

Steps:

i. The EiCon makes an application to local designated office—post office, etc., as noted above—by paper application or e-filing.
ii. The EiCon gives notice to creditors regarding proposed business continuation plan.

iii. If no creditor objects, the EiCon proceeds to implement the plan.
iv. The EiCon files continuation plan with designated office, including any distribution to creditors and terms of repayment under continuation plan.
v. A creditor can object and propose a different continuation plan (competing plan) or a liquidation (doomed-to-failure).
vi. In view of the objection, the EiCon files rejected continuation plan with designated court with application to confirm under majority and/or cram-down rules.

Creditor-proposed continuation plan
Creditor proposes a business continuation plan.
Steps:

i. Creditor makes application to local designated office—post office, etc. as noted above—by paper application or e-filing.
ii. Creditor gives notice to the debtor and other creditors regarding proposed business continuation plan.
iii. If neither debtor nor other creditor objects, creditor proceeds to implement the plan.
iv. Creditor files continuation plan with designated office, including any distribution to creditors and terms of repayment under continuation plan.
v. The debtor or a creditor can object and propose a different continuation plan (competing plan) or a liquidation (doomed-to-failure).
vi. In view of objection, the proposing creditor files rejected continuation plan with designated court with application to confirm under majority and/or cram-down rules.

ii. Administrative functions
Simplified forms would be developed for application and disclosure of financial situation, notice to creditors, proposed business continuation plan, terms of final continuation plan, and payments to creditors, available in paper form and as e-filing. Administrative function can be carried on by the secured creditor or the local designated office. Creditor could request involvement of an insolvency professional, clicking a box on the form to indicate that it will bear the costs of the professional's services if the value of assets in the EiCon's estate are not sufficient to cover. The involvement is useful where a creditor wishes to investigate the debtor's pre-filing behaviour. Designated office to develop a roster of approved qualified professionals, from which parties can select or ask the designated office to select. There is the option for a mediation module to be applied where the proposed continuation plan is disputed.

iii. Judicial supervision
Objecting parties could apply to the local magistrate or district commissioner to confirm a contested plan or to set aside appointment of the insolvency professional on the basis of a lack of qualification or conflict of interest.

Effect of Modular Approach in this example
The adoption of a private-sector-focused set of modules would allow for a timely and effective means of addressing the MSME's financial distress, quickly returning entrepreneurs to productive activity. For the facts of this jurisdiction, its focus is on self-help remedies, with an accountability check by a designated office. The deemed approval mechanisms ensure notice to creditors, the opportunity to object, and a speedy resolution where creditors do not object to the strategy. There is an optional module to use an insolvency professional in either the liquidation or the business continuation procedures, but such a professional is not necessary in cases of little or no assets and not possible in circumstances where there are insufficient resources to pay for their services. The designated office serves as an accountability check on the EiCon and creditors, and disputes that cannot be resolved at that level can be determined by the local magistrate or district commissioner. All modules in the Modular Approach would ideally be available to the relevant parties, but in this scenario, given the economic and financial background, it would be primarily the options described above would that would be used.

C. Sub-Saharan Lower Middle-Income Economy

1. Factual background

a. *Economic background*

- Small-scale agriculture accounts for a quarter of the economy and employs up to 75% of the workforce. The economy therefore is particularly exposed to drought and, to a lesser extent, to commodity and currency market fluctuations.
- Small-scale manufacturing and tourism together account for 40% of GDP. International tourism has been intermittently impaired by political violence.
- There is the potential to serve as a regional hub for financial and transport services. Previously hampered by inadequate infrastructure, this potential is now being developed through significant foreign investment.
- Very high unemployment rate of up to 40%.
- Weak governance, some political instability, and high levels of corruption are ongoing challenges.

b. *Financial MSME background*

- Banks tend to lend only to the larger corporate enterprises, and only a quarter of firms have any bank borrowing.
- Blue-chip enterprises borrow against cashflow, while larger medium ones are required to offer all-asset security.
- Smaller enterprises rely on microfinance, credit cooperatives, and pawnbrokering.

- Interest rate spreads are high even in the upper segments of the market, in part reflecting weaknesses in the debt-recovery process.
- Mobile and agency banking have in recent years taken deep and wide roots.
- The law provides for an extensive range of security interests, but registration mechanisms are slow, unreliable, and corruption-prone.

c. *Enforcement and insolvency background*

- Enforcement processes are sclerotic and wasteful. Enforcing against collateral takes several years and the secured creditor may recover no more than a third of its claim. Unsecured claim enforcement is somewhat quicker but equally wasteful, consuming up to half the value at stake.
- Insolvency legislation is a complicated and not wholly coherent mix of processes, making unhelpful distinctions between natural person and corporate insolvency.
- There is a significant disconnect between the sophisticated restructuring mechanisms provided by the 'law on the books' and their deployment in practice, the latter being exceedingly rare.
- Institutional infrastructure is weak in both the public and (to a lesser extent) private sectors.

2. Application of the Modular Approach

a. *Critical considerations*

- Minimization of discretionary decision-making, particularly by characteristically poorly remunerated public sector employees, to reduce possibilities of corruption;
- utilization of the mobile telephone network, which is secure, reliable, inexpensive, and widespread; and
- resorting to slow-moving court processes only when necessary and cost-effective.

b. *Default liquidation procedure*

i. Management functions

EiCon liquidation. EiCon first has the opportunity to liquidate the business.
Steps:

i. The EiCon commences the process via mobile telephone application or at local office. Other options include post offices (over 600 outlets across the country), bank branches (nearly 1,000), and small retailers (over 100,000) dealing with cash as part of the mobile banking network.

ii. Creditors receive notice via recorded mobile phone message and/or post.

iii. Absent creditor objection, EiCon markets and disposes of assets.

iv. EiCon deposits evidence of marketing and sale together with proceeds at one of the post office or bank branches or mobile banking network outlets.

v. Upon administrative verification, virtual and/or paper discharge certificate issued.

vi. A creditor can object and undertake the liquidation itself.

Creditor-controlled liquidation. Creditor liquidation of debtor's assets.

Steps:

i. Creditor objects electronically or at to local designated office, giving notice of intention to liquidate debtor's assets,

ii. Upon administrative verification, creditor receives virtual and/or paper authority to seize and dispose of assets.

iii. Where there is sufficient concern about the debtor's having misappropriated assets and the cost–benefit analysis permits, the creditor may deploy one of its own employees or a private sector insolvency practitioner, or apply for the intervention of a public official.

iv. After seizure, marketing, and sale, the creditor distributes any surplus value in the assets to other creditors.

v. Creditor files proof of amounts received through liquidation and distribution of those amounts to creditors with designated office.

ii. Administrative functions

Most of the administrative functions, including the provision of forms, notification, and the monitoring of process deadlines, can be automated and discharged electronically over the mobile telephone network. Basic scrutiny of information, such as the loan agreement and verification that the loan remains unpaid, could be undertaken by specialist units in the government insolvency service and the post office. Corruption opportunities would be minimized through decision maker anonymity and non-contact between them and the parties.

iii. Judicial supervision

The competent judicial authority is the local magistrate or district commissioner. There would be no judicial intervention in the absence of objection or dispute. Where there is an objection, the magistrate or district commissioner holds a hearing and resolves the dispute, including determining discharge where it is contested.

c. Business continuation plan procedure

i. Management functions

EiCon-initiated continuation proceedings. EiCon proposes a business plan.

Steps:

i. EiCon commences the process via mobile telephone application, post office, or bank branch, as discussed above.
ii. The EiCon's proposed plan is provided to creditors via the mobile network and/or in paper form, and the creditors are invited to vote in the same way.
iii. If no creditor objects or if the plan attracts sufficient creditor support, EiCon proceeds to implement the plan.
iv. EiCon implements the plan, reports electronically on progress, and pays creditors as above.
v. A creditor can object and propose a different continuation plan (competing plan) or a liquidation (doomed-to-failure).
vi. In view of objection, EiCon files rejected continuation plan with designated court with application to confirm under majority and/or cram-down rules.

Creditor-proposed continuation plan. Creditor proposes a business continuation plan.

Steps:

i. Creditor objects and other parties are notified as above.
ii. Creditor proposes a plan to the entrepreneur/debtor and other creditors.
iii. If creditor's plan attracts sufficient creditor support, including through deemed approval, then creditor receives authorization as above to implement it.
iv. Reporting and payments occur electronically.
v. The debtor or a creditor can object and propose a different continuation plan (competing plan) or a liquidation (doomed-to-failure).
vi. In view of objection, the proposing creditor files rejected continuation plan with designated court with application to confirm under majority and/or cram-down rules.

ii. Administrative functions

Simplified forms are available electronically and at the physical locations described previously, for application and disclosure of financial situation, notice to creditors, business continuation, and payments to creditors. Basic scrutiny of information could be undertaken by specialist units in the government insolvency service and the post office. One or more parties may request involvement of an insolvency practitioner and indicate that they would bear capped costs if there are insufficient recoveries. A licensed insolvency practitioner may be chosen randomly or by one or more parties, with creditor choice outweighing that of the debtor or entrepreneur.

iii. Judicial supervision

Objecting parties could appeal to the local magistrate or district commissioner on any issue in dispute, including to confirm a contested plan or to set aside appointment of the insolvency professional on the basis of lack of qualification or of conflict of interest, inadequacy of disclosed information, and/or failures in plan implementation.

D. European/Central Asian Emerging Nation

1. Factual background

a. Economic background

- Emerging 'Eastern European' or Central Asian jurisdiction.
- Former communist regime, Soviet influence.
- Economy has only recently attained lower 'middle income' in World Bank standards.
- Still large number of state-owned enterprises ('SOEs'), although with privatization process underway. Privatization process not fully transparent. Ownership of SOEs remains in part with senior officials/families from the old regime.
- Economy still has a strong rural component. Farming and agricultural sectors play a much bigger role than in Western Europe. High urban concentration in the two main cities. Part of the industry from old COMECON[1] times remains in place, although it struggles to compete with more technologically modernized economies. Oil and gas exports are relevant. The main sector is services, including some tourism.
- A few corporate groups; a small number of large and medium enterprises (in accordance with EU definition). Vast majority of businesses are MSMEs (97%).
- Microbusinesses and informal businesses (including sole entrepreneurs) are 65% of the total number of businesses.

b. Financial MSME background

- The percentage of bank credit to MSMEs is relatively low, at around 45% of all financing. The rest is trade credit, such as suppliers of raw materials and services. The smaller the size of the business, the lower the percentage of bank

[1] The Council for Mutual Economic Assistance, Soviet-led economic alliance.

financing. Entrepreneurs engaged in start-up businesses mainly work from equity investment, loans by related parties, and trade credit.

- Security rights framework is established, both for real estate and movable assets:
  - The vast majority of land is registered. The land registry works relatively well. The tenure of registered titles is reliable.
  - The registry of movable assets has been set up recently, following a system akin to UNCITRAL's Model Law (i.e. the country has departed from a classic European document-based registry). The registry is not as yet widely used. Banks rarely rely on movable collateral. Although most assets can be provided as collateral, there is no experience, and, with the exception of cars and machines, banks do not accept movable collateral.
- No floating charge is possible.

c. *Enforcement and insolvency background*

- Debt-recovery systems are slow and inefficient. Courts do not have sufficient infrastructure, judges are not specialized, and procedures are rigid. There is a backlog of cases in those courts competent to decide on commercial matters.
- Enforcement of secured rights is slow and relatively inefficient. Although extra-judicial enforcement is possible, most often it is driven to court by the debtor.
- There are no special procedural rules or courts for microbusinesses.
- There is a new hybrid out-of-court work-out procedure. Required majority vote increases with the content of the agreement; non-participating creditors may be bound; approved agreements are protected against avoidance actions.
- Formal insolvency proceedings allow for both a reorganization and a liquidation. Ninety-five percent of cases end in piecemeal liquidations. Although the law allows it, there are no cases of going-concern liquidations.
- Insolvency proceedings follow a 'German style' unified approach: a common stage followed by liquidation or reorganization.
- Insolvency proceedings are rigid and the parties have several opportunities to delay them, especially by bringing appeals against the list of creditors and inventory.
- Judges tasked with insolvency proceedings have an adequate degree of honesty and some specialization.
- Technical equipment of courts is still rather insufficient.
- Insolvency practitioners are not trustworthy. They are mostly technically unprepared and have a bad reputation in the market. There are professional bodies, but their reputation is also low.
- Rescue culture is very slowly developing, and insolvency stigma is an issue, especially in case of microbusinesses.

- Insolvency proceedings take an average of two to four years to be completed.
- According to a new law, discharge for honest individuals is possible only after five years.

2. Application of the Modular Approach

a. Default automatic liquidation procedure

i. Preliminary considerations

In this example, the vast majority of MSMEs that use insolvency proceedings are grossly insolvent, having few or no assets and no possibility of rescuing the business as a going concern. Apart from the changes to the procedure introduced by the Modular Approach, two elements would be key to the success of a renovated regime:

- Either an enhancement of the information available on the financial situation as well as on the evolution of the business is ensured through additional legislation (legal duties, templates, credit-reporting systems), or the existing information is channelled adequately to the court or agency, if and when involved, such as information existing in banks or tax authorities.
- There is the introduction or adequate implementation of a duty to file or a wrongful trading system.

ii. Management functions

As a classic civil law jurisdiction with very limited rescue culture and a widespread sense of potential fraud by debtors, and even creditors, liquidation proceedings would need some type of court/agency involvement.

iii. Administrative and liquidation functions

The liquidation would be conducted by the court or an agency, which would need to be in direct contact with the court system. No tax fee should be levied. A streamlined elimination of non-viable businesses and the allocation of existing resources to creditors in the best possible manner is in the public interest and it would thus be justified. With the information received, the judicial secretary or clerk may allow the secured and/or main creditor to conduct the liquidation, although, if the information available is insufficient or unreliable, she may have to start the process for the appointment of an insolvency representative or at least adopt measures to enhance the information available to creditors. A debtor-controlled liquidation process would also be a possibility, although, given the degree of development of insolvency practice and the constant fear of fraud existing in this jurisdiction, the debtor would need to be subject to some kind of control by the majority creditor, a secured creditor, or an officer.

Undoubtedly, for constitutional reasons, a discharge would require a court decision, probably issued by the supervising judge reviewing the case at the conclusion of the liquidation.

iv. Procedure

- The application is filed by the MSME or by one or more creditors through a template publicly available online and in public places (chambers of commerce, banking associations, etc.). The application would be received by the relevant officer at the local designated court.
- Online applications could be made available, but only as an option (not mandatorily).
- The court officer receives the documents and proceeds as follows: (i) gives notice to existing creditors; (ii) registers the petition in an online, free-access publicly accessible platform; (iii) adopts any other measure deemed necessary to ensure potential creditors are made aware (such a measure should be exceptional, limited to cases where the MSME operates in different cities, etc.); (iv) following the issuance of the notice and the registration of the petition in the registry, a short stay starts, and alternatively, no stay is in place, but the debtor or creditors may request it; (v) if no information is available or the available information appears unreliable, the officer may request additional information from the debtor as well as from banks, credit-reporting systems, and public agencies; (vi) exceptionally, an insolvency representative is deemed to be appointed when such appointment is requested alongside a confirmation that an insolvency practitioner is willing to act; alternatively, a main/secured creditor takes steps to facilitate seizure and liquidation of the assets.
- If no creditor objects, the creditor, the officer, or a professional proceeds to liquidate assets and pay creditors.
- If there is a reason to believe there exist concealed assets, measures ought to be adopted to identify them and, perhaps, start avoidance actions.
- Once the assets have been liquidated and the proceeds allocated, the officer or the creditor must render accounts in detail and deposit them in court, open to public scrutiny. Only when sufficient time has passed will the insolvent MSME entity be dissolved and struck off the registry, and the sole entrepreneur discharged.
- The supervising judge will only be involved when requested by parties who see their legitimate rights being prejudiced. If the dispute can be resolved by filing documents as proof of the allegations, no hearing should be necessary, as hearings tend to delay proceedings. Only when an oral proof is necessary should a hearing take place; otherwise basic procedural rights would be breached. The judge however, will need to declare the discharge of the debt.

Given the circumstances of the jurisdiction, its institutional limitations, and the general lack of trust in the insolvency system, the Modular Approach adopted is unlikely to be a fully simplified one. Most likely, the circumstances will require greater legal certainty than the fully simplified modules allow. However, the proposed design, which results in quick and automatic liquidation, is speedier and more efficient than a liquidation process that takes years, often to no avail. The advantages of applying a Modular Approach are evident.

b. Continuation proceedings

i. Preliminary considerations

In this country example, as is the case in a number of jurisdictions in the European/Central Asian area, the ordinary framework already includes the possibility of reaching an agreement out of court and the debtor may propose a reorganization plan within formal insolvency proceedings. However, neither of these systems works in practice. Both out-of-court and in-court solutions suffer from the passive behaviour of creditors, especially of secured creditors. The out-of-court solution was designed with majority-approval requirements that are too high and procedural requirements that are still too rigid. Courts are too easily involved and legislation prohibits tax authorities from restructuring their debt outside of formal proceedings. The in-court reorganization solution is burdened with all the problems inherent to the general insolvency system, and the business is already too damaged when the debtor seeks to approve a plan. Some of these shortcomings may be improved by the Modular Approach.

ii. Administrative and management functions

Given that the MSME will be, in the vast majority of cases, a family-run business, and the family's only source of income, retaining control is a most effective mechanism to incentivize the use of the new system. Hence, the entrepreneur in control (EiCon) option will be the solution. Although creditors may also file, only rarely will the procedure be triggered by them. Creditors will either be secured, and hence often uninterested, or tax authorities seeking alternative means of collection, or unsophisticated trade creditors. Commencement by creditors may be used in cases where there are conflicts between shareholders that block the solution. But, considering the low level of sophistication of the jurisdiction under analysis, a creditor-intiated proceeding is only ever likely to happen in the case of medium enterprises.

In contrast to the status quo, the Modular Approach does not require that the debtor be insolvent. The plan will normally be proposed by the EiCon. It will be a simple continuation plan, including both a debt restructuring and a business restructuring.

iii. Procedure

- The MSME applies to the competent local court. The application may be made on paper or, to the extent possible, online. When implementing the Modular system, the government should create an online application system, openly accessible, with clear instructions and templates. Simplified forms should also be developed with a description of the basic and specifically relevant financial information. Since in this type of jurisdiction, access to electronic means is not widespread, especially in rural areas, there should be local points scattered around the country where templates are made available. Those physical points could also provide advice as to how the templates are to be used.

- The templates should also have a section for a continuation plan. The template will be a simple one, with a clear separation between the different types of measures (debt restructuring (maturity and amount), business restructuring, payment plan, etc.). To the extent possible, the plan ought to be submitted with the application, or within a very brief period thereafter.
- The petition will be registered on an openly accessible electronic platform so that all creditors are made aware. The possibility for additional publicity measures should exist, in the same manner as described for automatic liquidation.
- The electronic platform notifies creditors of the situation and of the existence—or the immediate future filing of—a business continuation plan. The notification should also inform of the commencement of a brief period (i.e. two to four weeks) when creditors may not enforce over property of the business or file for liquidation. This system is to be managed by a court/agency officer, who will check for compliance with all the formal requirements. Since banks, tax authorities, and employees are likely creditors, ensuring that a proper notification to creditors is taking place should not be difficult for the system. Creditors could respond by requesting a lift of the stay, by requesting a debtor action moratorium, or by initiating the doomed-to-failure module. Given the very short period of time envisaged for the stay, the lift should be granted only under exceptional circumstances.
- Creditors could request the involvement of an insolvency professional to supervise the administration of the business. The jurisdiction's general rules to cover for the expenses of no-asset cases should apply here, in cases where the estate is insufficient to cover the remuneration of the professional. The involvement will be necessary when there are objective reasons to believe that there has been misbehaviour. In this regard, the court/agency officer should be able to request the appointment of an insolvency representative or to conduct a preliminary research to decide whether such an appointment is justified.
- There should be an option for a mediation module in cases where the proposed continuation plan is disputed. The same considerations made in the previous paragraph concerning costs would apply.
- Creditors may oppose, object, and propose a different continuation plan (competing plan), or directly file for liquidation (doomed-to-failure), only after the negotiation period has expired. If the plan was proposed by a creditor, the debtor may also object.
- If no creditor objects, or if the debtor does not object in case of proposal by a creditor, the MSME in control proceeds to implement the plan by filing the accepted continuation plan with the competent court, including any distribution to creditors and terms of repayment under the continuation plan.
- The court will again only be involved when strictly necessary. Court involvement to some extent would be necessary when there are dissenting creditors. The involvement may concern the content of the plan, the required majorities, or the breach of any mandatory formal requirement.

In this country example, creditors are likely to be easy to identify, and hence legislative policy actions may be properly targeted. Creditors will be financial institutions, tax authorities, or trade creditors. Since the continuation of the activity is key to continuation of the enterprise, the protection of trade creditors is essential. Post-commencement financing ought to be allowed, and all banking regulatory hindrances removed. Ensuring early use of the procedure is paramount. In line with this objective, the entrepreneur retaining control is key; and allowing access for solvent debtors to encourage early action is a substantive improvement on existing insolvency regimes.

E. Conclusion

The four examples of how the Modular Approach could be designed and implemented in specific financial, institutional, and socio-economic frameworks illustrate the types of choices that can be made under the Modular Approach, tailored carefully to the particular country. While fictionalized, the examples closely track some of the structural and financial characteristics of the region, offering insights into how various modules could be designed and implemented.

The Modular Approach may help overcome some of the main impediments to business restructuring across a range of jurisdictions. The 'scream or die' and the 'deemed approval' principles should create timely and effective resolution to MSME financial distress and should help ensure due participation by creditors. The range of management, administrative, and judicial approaches illustrate how the Modular Approach offers consistent principles and objectives of rehabilitation, and fresh start, and effective and timely liquidation where appropriate. While the principles remain consistent throughout, the Modular Approach offers a diversity of options that can be tailored to the specific needs of the countries, recognizing the different challenges presented in different regions and legal frameworks.

8
Conclusion

An effectively functioning insolvency regime is an essential part of any economy. The Financial Stability Board, which monitors the global financial system, recognizes insolvency and creditors' rights as one of fourteen policy domains that are key to sound financial systems and notes that internationally recognized best practice standards are 'deserving of priority implementation depending on country circumstances'.[1] MSMEs dominate virtually all of the world's economies by number, are critical in terms of innovation and entrepreneurial dynamism, and have higher failure rates than larger businesses. Yet it is the latter minority that has been the primary focus of existing insolvency regimes. This lack of fit between what insolvency systems provide and what the vast majority of their subjects need is harmful, and this harm is increasingly noticed.

Against this background, our author group of seven scholars and a judge decided to seize the gauntlet of appropriately addressing MSME insolvency resolution. We have designed the Modular Approach from the ground up, starting with the unique challenges faced by MSMEs as they begin to experience financial distress and then working to craft solutions that are responsive. We have sought to provide an approach that can fit in any legal system or economy. However, we have refrained from attempting to provide a one-size-fits-all definition of MSMEs; instead, the volume focuses on entities that are 'micro', 'small', or 'medium', while we remain aware that what is regarded as such may depend on a country's broader economic circumstances.

The subject matter of the MSME insolvency regime that we propose may take different forms and may include companies as well as sole traders, simple partnerships, and other unincorporated businesses. We recognize that small businesses, even if incorporated, usually need to secure loans with the personal assets or personal guarantees of the principals, thus blurring the line between personal and business liability. Therefore, the approach that we advocate has a broad application and, at the same time, a clear focus on MSMEs. It transcends the typical distinctions between regimes that apply to companies or entrepreneurs and regimes for natural persons or consumers.

[1] Financial Stability Board, Key Standards for Sound Financial Systems, available at: www.fsb.org/what-we-do/about-the-compendium-of-standards/key_standards.

Micro, Small, and Medium Enterprise Insolvency. First Edition. Ronald Davis, Stephan Madaus, Alberto Mazzoni, Irit Mevorach, Rizwaan J. Mokal, Barbara Romaine, Janis Sarra, & Ignacio Tirado. Published 2018 by Oxford University Press.

For MSMEs of any form, operating in any country, the volume proposes unique solutions. In this work, we break with the bias towards the large entity in the design of insolvency laws and with the legal path dependency of recent decades; both of these take existing procedures for granted. We have created modules and accompanying procedures that are responsive to the needs of MSMEs. Much recent development relevant to MSME insolvency has been through the enhancement of rescue procedures and preventive measures, including, on the regional level, the ongoing development of an EU Directive on preventive restructuring frameworks and second chance, and the (?) consideration of the application of consumer bankruptcy laws to MSMEs. Most reform efforts have focused less on creating procedures specific to MSMEs. Often, the approach was to make ad hoc changes to standard insolvency regimes in relation to MSMEs by, for example, removing some requirements, shortening statutory timelines, or dispensing with certain types of stakeholder engagement. Yet, arbitrary boundaries between MSMEs and standard regimes persist, leaving many issues unresolved, such as the problem of rigid preconditions for availability of processes and the generally clumsy application of procedures not designed to address MSMEs. In addition, the broader regulatory and institutional framework in many countries often lacks the means and incentives for effective deployment and use of tools for MSMEs and for controlling moral hazard for entrepreneurs and creditors alike.

We were conscious that international standards for insolvency, drawing on the procedures and experiences of domestic legal systems, have also tended to focus on larger businesses, and, in that regard, on standardizing policies, objectives, and mechanisms to ensure that legal systems meet best practice standards. While MSMEs are not excluded from the scope of international standards, most notably including the UNCITRAL *Legislative Guide* and the World Bank Principles, MSMEs have not so far benefited from a dedicated consideration of their specific circumstances at times of financial distress, and the design of solutions for these entities. That path is taking a new turn, however, as these international organizations, which have led international policy development in the insolvency arena, have begun to prioritize the issue of MSME insolvency more comprehensively. The result of our analysis in this volume is that when taking that path internationally as well as regionally and domestically, it is important to commit to a 'think small first' approach[2] to fully

[2] Borrowing from the principle employed by the European Commission to seek to make the EU regulatory framework more supportive of small businesses. 'The "Think Small First" principle ... was intended to ensure that SME specific issues and concerns were mainstreamed into Community and national policies' (see European Commission, Evaluation of the application of the Think Small First principle in EU legislation and programmes, Final Report, 11). The Commission has explained the principle's rationale in terms highly relevant to this volume's concerns:

> When proposing new legislation, the legislator should have full knowledge of the impact the regulation will have on businesses in terms of compliance costs and administrative burdens. Business-impact assessments and cost–benefit analyses, where appropriate, should be carried out in close cooperation with the business community. In doing so, the legislator should give special attention to the compliance requirements for SMEs. If SMEs can comply with the regulation at a reasonable cost, then so too can large firms, whereas the reverse is not necessarily true. This 'think small first' principle should act as a litmus test.

See Recital 6 of 97/344/EC: Commission Recommendation of 22 April 1997 on improving and simplifying the business environment for business start-ups.

achieve the universal insolvency objective of creating a fair system where all relevant parties receive equal concern and where processes are efficient and transparent.

A system for MSME insolvency should be designed from the ground up. We were not required to reinvent the wheel, and we started from the premise that there should be due recognition of existing mechanisms and widely recognized procedures for workouts, liquidations, and reorganizations. But instead of tinkering with and modifying these procedures to accommodate MSMEs, we suggest that these procedures should be unpacked and the elements and aspects of such procedures should be used to rebuild a process tailored for MSMEs, where tools must be provided in a maximally flexible way.

MSMEs are not only abundant, thus most deserving of insolvency policy attention; they also demand a specific approach. Whether they operate as sole traders or companies, they tend to lack the types of physical assets that are acceptable to financial lenders as collateral; they tend to be relatively undiversified; and most of their creditors are disinterested in the insolvency process as there is little or no value available for distribution. The circumstances of larger entities are different, where there is an extensive estate of significant value; stakeholders are engaged; and the involvement of insolvency professionals, lawyers, and courts is cost-justified. MSME insolvency law must take the unique circumstances of small businesses into account. It should start with the presumption that the entrepreneur is usually central to the insolvency process of the MSME, that there are likely limited resources, and that creditors are likely rationally passive. It should also acknowledge that the parties to any insolvency case are best placed to select the tools appropriate to that case.

The volume proposes an approach that is premised on these assumptions. The objectives of the Modular Approach for MSME insolvency are to preserve and maximize value, to distribute that value fairly, to ensure accountability for wrongdoing, and to enable discharge of over-indebted natural persons. The modularity of the approach entails two dimensions. First, it provides a core default process and additional modules for the parties—the debtor and the creditors—to choose from, so that the process can best fit the circumstances and interests of the key stakeholders. Second, it provides existing legal systems with certain options; in particular, in terms of the level of supervisory intervention and court involvement in the different processes.

We recognize that there are a variety of different cultural, social, and economic norms, and we have attempted neither to transplant any system into others nor the full harmonization of MSME insolvency law. Countries considering reform should design their MSME regime in a way that respects their constitutional requirements, and with full consideration of the policy choices involved and their respective costs and benefits. Legal systems should provide a regime capable of being responsive to the challenges of MSMEs and should allow the flexible distribution of not only insolvency tools but also process functions. Specifically, countries should identify the main category of function for each step in the insolvency process: management, administrative, and judicial. Countries should then make critical policy choices as to who is allowed or required to perform these various functions, including a consideration of the necessary level of involvement of insolvency practitioners, government agencies, court officials, and judges.

In view of these assumptions and considerations, the Modular Approach proposes a process accessible to and initiated by the entrepreneur, who does not need to declare or demonstrate insolvency. The entrepreneur may decide to shut down or sell the business and to be discharged from all debt and start anew. Automatic liquidation and discharge proceedings would offer a quick and low-cost solution. The entrepreneur may also decide to attempt a business turnaround. The Modular Approach offers a continuation process in which the entrepreneur remains in control and proposes a way to resolve the distress by either continuing or transferring the business, subject only to administrative oversight. This core process includes mechanisms to facilitate the acceptance of a plan even when creditors are passive, through the mechanisms of 'deemed approval' and 'scream or die', in turn providing a fresh start to the entrepreneur. It capitalizes on private information and preserves idiosyncratic investments. It also lowers costs by not requiring the involvement of courts or professionals in most cases.

Modules may be chosen by local policymakers to allow parties to the continuation process to limit the rights of stakeholders or to involve third parties. Thus, the Modular Approach includes processes that can be initiated by the entrepreneur, to request a mediation or to limit creditor rights of enforcement, and by creditors for the purpose of limiting the rights of the entrepreneur to administer the estate, for example, by involving an insolvency practitioner, proposing a competing plan, or insisting on a liquidation.

In this volume, we stress that an effective framework will encompass the full range of the Modular Approach's tools, and that modules should only rarely be eliminated by lawmakers and only after careful consideration. However, lawmakers may decide that local conditions justify particular adaptations; for example, declining to implement the mediation module if mediation is not an established practice, or the insolvency professional involvement module if they decide that a guaranteed strict entrepreneur-in-control procedure is a preferred way to incentivize small business owners to embrace the new procedure.

In addition to designing the procedures for MSME insolvency, we highlight the need for a supportive regulatory and institutional framework. Thus, the modular framework is complemented by additional tools designed to address barriers and obstacles in the implementation of the modular regime. These tools are designed specifically for MSMEs and provide options for countries to accommodate different legal cultures and institutional frameworks. That supportive framework includes suggestions for taxation measures that would address typical problems arising with respect to MSME financial distress, early warning mechanisms, methods of addressing funding obstacles, bank supervision rules and other measures to encourage responsible lending, and methods of addressing the role of credit histories and the treatment of guarantees.

We also make suggestions that specifically focus on the duties and obligations of the entrepreneur, who has a central role in the Modular Approach. The suggestions aim to ensure that the entrepreneur does not delay the liquidation of a non-viable MSME or avoid taking actions that would assist the rescue of viable businesses, because, for instance, of concerns about stigma or because of lack of knowledge and resources. Providing proper incentives and oversight mechanisms requires consideration of duties during, but also before the initiation of, insolvency proceedings. MSME financial distress can arise from a lack of management skills or corporate governance mechanisms to deal with business viability and downturns in the economy. In turn, this lack of skill or effective governance can result in untimely filing of insolvency proceedings, failure to prevent further downward spiraling of finances, failure to deal with operational and financial failures, and a lack of resources to hire effective expertise to deal with the insolvency. The volume proposes in this respect a core (default) governance rule that is based on a simplified and tailored wrongful trading regime applied to MSMEs. We also suggest alternative modules and hybrid regimes that may fit better in certain jurisdictions or circumstances.

We hope that the Modular Approach developed in this volume will assist in the design of new international and regional standards tailored for MSME insolvencies and in their implementation in domestic laws globally. We acknowledge that our vision requires that international organizations, as well as domestic policymakers and regulators, are committed to such focus on the needs of MSMEs and are prepared to systematically rethink the treatment of MSME insolvency, departing from previous paths as necessary. Certain countries may be more receptive than others to embarking on such a mission. We hope, however, that, with the greater acknowledgement of the role of MSMEs as primary drivers of economic growth, more effective systems for them to address financial distress will gradually be developed. Such a paradigmatic shift can occur, with the aid of international organizations that regularly provide technical assistance in reform and capacity-building in developing and emerging economies. It is an opportune time for reform.

9

Annex 1

Introduction of the Modular Approach for MSMEs: A Basic Toolkit for Legal Reform

This annex offers a basic checklist of steps that should be completed to implement reform that incorporates the Modular Approach. Although its content, in part, draws from the experience of the authors in legal reform, it offers a bespoke toolkit for the reform of micro-businesses and takes the perspective of a would-be law reformer in a given jurisdiction.[1] Naturally, which laws are to be amended, how this reform ought to be designed, and which institutions should be involved in the process will depend very much on the specific circumstances of each country. This annex is merely a simplified attempt to offer a general solution and, as such, it is not meant to be prescriptive. We are indeed aware of the limitations of such an attempt.

In summary, the process should have three stages, all of them complementary, each of them with less value if considered individually. They should follow a predefined order. The first part of the sequence would be to conduct an assessment. Second, and based on the results of the assessment, a drafting stage would be initiated. Third, following approval of the reform (and, in some cases, even earlier), an implementation stage would be commenced. Each part of the process is equally important, and, surprising as it might be, the seemingly more ancillary stages (assessment and implementation) usually take longer and require the most resources.

[1] Legal reform in the field of insolvency and pre-insolvency has been common over the past two decades, affecting fully developed markets as well as developing and middle-income countries. Legal reform has been mainly an internal issue in developed economies (with the exception of some regional country alliances, such as the European Union or, to a lesser extent, ASEAN) while jurisdictions with less developed markets have not infrequently resorted to international financial institutions. Undoubtedly the champion in assisting insolvency law reform has been the World Bank. The Bretton Woods institution has often used a two-tiered road map when assisting countries in legal reform: first, a thorough assessment of the country's insolvency system is conducted through instruments like the Report on the Observance of Standards and Codes (ICR ROSC) or the Financial Sector Assessment Program (run together with the IMF). After the assessment has been completed, the World Bank would provide technical assistance in the reform process, whenever requested by the country (for more information on these activities, see http://www.worldbank.org/en/programs/rosc. Although this annex draws inspiration from the approach and the practical experience of World Bank programmes, it adopts a substantially different perspective: we focus on the steps that ought to be followed by a legislator, were it to attempt to introduce the Modular Approach for MSMEs without necessarily resorting to the assistance of outsiders.

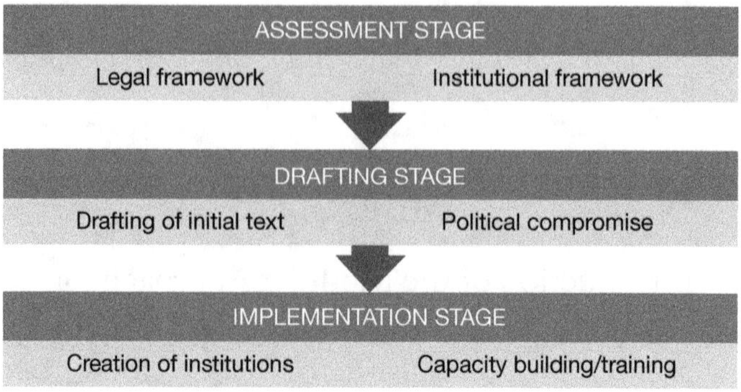

Figure 9.1 Stages to development of the Modular Approach.

A summary of the process is offered in Figure 9.1, followed by a brief description of each of these stages.

A. The Assessment Stage

The first stage of the reform process, or any reform process, is to provide as accurate a diagnosis as possible. We anticipate an internal reform process and therefore assume the reformer knows the applicable insolvency legislation (law and regulations). A proper assessment of the situation ought to proceed, therefore, with quantitative data collection.[2] In order to get a sufficiently detailed picture of a country's insolvency system, as applicable to MSMEs, the following data, at least, should be available:

(i) total number of cases, ordered by size (overall number, micro-businesses, small, medium, and large);
(ii) number of cases segregated by type of exit (reorganization plan vs liquidation);
(iii) average time from start to finish of each of the different types of proceedings and sizes;
(iv) percentage of return to creditors for each of the types of proceeding and size;

[2] The amount of data available on a country's insolvency system varies greatly from jurisdiction to jurisdiction. Even in the more developed economies, data are often fractional and incomplete. Having good quantitative information is vital. In some countries, data on insolvency law are gathered and published by the existing insolvency agency; in other cases, especially countries without a specialized agency/entity tasked with the implementation of the insolvency system, the data may have originated in different institutions, depending on the type of proceedings (central bank/association of financial institutions in the case of out-of-court workouts, and the courts/ministry of justice for in-court processes). In some jurisdictions, data are generated by a centralized statistics department. Not infrequently, concerned stakeholders, such as chambers of commerce or corporate registries, collect relevant information.

(v) average cost of each of the types of proceeding; and

(vi) where a plan has been agreed, how many cases have ended with full implementation of the plan, and how many in a subsequent liquidation.

Experience shows that in the less developed markets or those with a less effective system (e.g. low figures in number (iv)), it may, given the fewer cases, be easier to collect the relevant data. Naturally, if a system is seldom used, that may be a reflection of the absence of an insolvency culture or the reputational cost of using it, or of the negative perception that stakeholders have of the system. In order to make an appropriate analysis of the data, the reformer ought to compare the figures with the number of businesses created annually, the overall number of businesses existing at the moment of the assessment, and the number of inactive businesses. An inactive business, for instance, could be a business with no known activity for at least three months. These numbers can typically be obtained from the taxation or social security authorities or from the court system (for example, using as an indication the unusual number of uncontested suits against a given debtor). This comparison will provide the picture of how many businesses, often micro-businesses, simply disappear without conducting insolvency proceedings or, at an earlier stage, a mandatory company law liquidation. The data may then reflect the gaps in the system, exposing the jurisdiction's needs.

The data should be complimented by a thorough analysis of the situation. If it is established that the system does not work, it is necessary to identify the reasons. A revision of the country's system would benefit from a comparative analysis: reformers will do well to check not only international standards and best practice (UNCITRAL, World Bank, etc.), but also the laws of countries with effective insolvency systems and those jurisdictions with similar characteristics, with particular regard to countries that have recently modernized their system. The reformer's review of laws should also consider other laws within the jurisdiction: it is essential to put the insolvency system in the context of other legislation with which it interacts or that may bear an influence on the implementation of the new approach. This assessment of the country-specific context and relationship of insolvency law with the rest of the legal framework will, at the very least, include the following:

(i) the general framework that enables restructuring and liquidation operations (i.e. those branches of the law that are needed to negotiate, restructure, or liquidate a business, including contract law, company law, business-related legislation, procedural legislation, etc.);

(ii) tax law, and the regulation of public creditors, with special regard to their ability to compromise or write down debt and the existence of any procedural and material priorities;

(iii) banking law, in particular, the part of banking regulation that influences the behaviour of banks in cases of debtor distress by, for example, provisioning rules, assignments of debt, etc.; and/or

(iv) the applicable procedural legislation.

This last legal branch is of special importance, especially, although not only,[3] with respect to in-court proceedings. In some jurisdictions, formal insolvency proceedings are a special or extraordinary type of procedure, sometimes involving ad hoc tenets and rules in order to offer a streamlined solution to a specific factual situation. In other jurisdictions, insolvency proceedings include no special rules and ordinary procedural rules apply to insolvent debtors. This latter type of model tends to be rigid and excessively open to internal litigation (i.e. challenges to decisions adopted within insolvency proceedings, even if referred to merely functional matters such as appointment of appraisers, partial rendering of accounts of the insolvency representative, etc), with the consequence that insolvency proceedings last too long and value is destroyed, to the detriment of all the stakeholders involved. Overly strict and formal procedures are not fit for this type of collective action, and, as we have attempted to show, they are particularly nonsensical in the case of micro and small businesses.

The quantitative data collection and the desk review of the system and its related legal framework need to be accompanied by a qualitative assessment by the stakeholders that are, one way or another, involved in the implementation of the insolvency system. This assessment can be done by means of a widespread circulation of questionnaires and by in-depth interviews. Questionnaires, if adequately designed, can be a good source of information. Stakeholders should be invited to elaborate on their responses and to answer openly and freely. Experience shows that questionnaires have their disadvantages: completing them properly takes time and effort, and therefore it is often difficult to reach people with the necessary level of experience and seniority; and questionnaires sent by a government authority may drive respondents to be soft and politically correct, an occurrence more frequent in less developed jurisdictions. Oral in-depth interviews share this last trend, but it is easier to find knowledgeable people within each organization for oral interviews, and, if well conducted, they can provide highly valuable information. The experience of some of this volume's authors shows that long, personal interviews (approximately one and a half to two hours long) can be productive if the interviewer meets two requirements: the questions are neither basic nor obvious, but require a high degree of expertise to answer, and answers are treated anonymously. Deep questions allow high-profile experts to express their opinions and, not infrequently, they are happy to be heard. The application of the Chatham House rule, to be made clear at the beginning of the interview, is no doubt key to the success of a qualitative interview.[4]

[3] The intervention of the court system and hence the application of some sort of procedure often happens in proceedings designed to take place mainly out of court (sometimes labelled 'hybrid' proceedings). It can occur because the final agreement is taken to court for confirmation, because a professional is at some stage appointed by the court, or because some or part of these agreements may be subject to avoidance transactions, to mention only a few possibilities.

[4] By the Chatham House rule, we mean the following: 'When a meeting, or part thereof, is held under the Chatham House Rule, participants are free to use the information received, but neither the identity nor the affiliation of the speaker(s), nor that of any other participant, may be revealed.' Source: https://www.chathamhouse.org/about/chatham-house-rule.

Interviews and surveys or questionnaires ought to inquire about both the adequacy of the black letter laws on insolvency and about the practical on-the-ground implementation of the system. They should include questions about alternatives to the insolvency system. If the stakeholder expresses negative views, the questionnaire or interviewer should try to obtain an understanding of what alternative paths the stakeholder can recommend to tackle the distress of a MSME. This approach will provide a more complete picture of the application of the system and indicate other parts of the legal framework that may need adjustments.

Although the degree of their importance will vary from country to country, the following stakeholders are relevant for the reform of the system of MSME insolvency in any jurisdiction:

(i) chambers of commerce and associations of entrepreneurs, including any association of sole proprietors and micro-businesses;
(ii) commercial banks individually considered, credit cooperatives, non-deposit-taking financial institutions (including microfinance entities), and any relevant association of banks and financial institutions, including those that provide consumer credit and finance the retail financial sector;
(iii) the central bank and the regulator and supervisor of the financial system, if they are different;
(iv) tax authorities or agencies;
(v) notaries and registrars (registry of companies, business registry, main secured-transactions registries);
(vi) associations of trade creditors, if possible covering different types and sizes of creditors, and to the extent these are different from the chambers of commerce;
(vii) lawyers operating in the area of micro-businesses, advising both debtors, banks, and trade creditors; and
(viii) judges and generally the stakeholders involved in the functioning of the court system.

These stakeholders should be surveyed or interviewed, but their participation should not be limited to the preparatory stage of the reform. Given their key role in the implementation of the system, they ought to be involved in the formulation of the reform. Interim documents should be shared with them to receive feedback. But the legislator must not forget that most of the stakeholders have their own interests and agenda. Ensuring they have a say in the reform process does not mean that they should dictate the final text and its implementing measures. The reformer must be aware of this self-interest and resist lobbying. The ultimate objective of the reform should be to provide a jurisdiction with a functional and efficient system to tackle the financial and economic distress of MSMEs. Other considerations ought to be irrelevant.

The assessment stage should also focus on the jurisdiction's institutional framework. By that we mean all the institutions that, directly or indirectly, have oversight or responsibility for the MSME insolvency system. Data collection and the surveys and interviews will allow the reformer to identify a number of institutional shortcomings. All too often, the institutional framework is to blame for the poor results of a system. Experience shows that, even with the best possible law in place, a poor institutional setting will inevitably result in failure. These deficiencies in the institutional framework can negatively affect the move to an effective MSME system, since institutional change is always more difficult than legal reform. The analysis should concentrate, at least, on the following:

- *The court system*—A realistic analysis of the court system is paramount; perhaps the most important part of the assessment stage.[5] In the vast majority of jurisdictions, courts are understaffed and lack adequate infrastructure. This lack of resources and support results in long delays, with insolvency cases lingering for months in the best of cases, and years in the more ordinary situation. In the case of MSMEs, with a small number of creditors, a simple business structure, and small amounts of debt involved, failure of the court system to deliver a quick and efficient solution renders the whole system useless. Precisely because of this reality, our Modular Approach restricts court intervention to the minimum necessary for due process. Another element that needs to be looked at is the level of specialization of courts: in countries where judges are specialized in insolvency or, at least, in commercial matters, the results of court proceedings are more reliable and predictable, and therefore the courts are able to provide a better service to the users. Judges ought also to be asked for their opinion on the procedural system (for instance, whether it is too prone to delays due to unnecessary challenges within proceedings), as well as where, in their view, the main delays occur and the reasons for such delays. The reformer should also attempt to identify other elements that may be the underlying cause for the slow progress of insolvency cases (e.g. the absence of a sufficient number of clerks and support staff to assist judges, the case-management and case-allocation system, or the level of digitalization of files). Unfortunately, corruption of judicial and court staff may also be a problem in some jurisdictions.
- *The insolvency agency*—In some countries, the insolvency and pre-insolvency system is partially managed and implemented by a public agency, often a subdepartment of the ministry of justice or the ministry of finance or economy. As with the court system, the reformer must be satisfied that the agency is capable of performing its duties: it should be adequately staffed (both in terms of number of employees and of their technical level of expertise), and it should have sufficient resources. In those jurisdictions where the court system has

[5] Not infrequently, conducting an honest and thorough assessment of the court system is also the most difficult part of the reform process. In some jurisdictions (especially in African and ex-Soviet Union countries), the judiciary has enormous respect and is almost feared. It is all but politically untouchable, and legal reformers are very reluctant to take any action or make any criticism. Self-criticism of the judiciary can be absent, as is the willingness to recognise mistakes or make important changes. Aware as we are, that often the main problem lies with the shortcomings of the court system in effectively resolving MSME insolvency, reform is sentenced to failure if this element is left untouched.

severe problems regarding, for example, its technical capacity and efficiency, this agency may be in a position to play a very significant role. It could be very useful in the implementation of the Modular Approach for MSMEs, as described in this volume. Where an insolvency agency exists, the reformer should pay attention to the relationship between the agency and its competencies, and the court system. Not infrequently, there are frictions between both implementing institutions that provide an indication of the efficacy of the system. Overlaps and the capacity of one to interfere with the other should be avoided.

- *Insolvency representatives*—Insolvency professionals are usually key players in the implementation of insolvency proceedings. In light of this involvement, the success of the system itself largely depends on their performance. Unfortunately, international experience shows that many countries count on a poor network of insolvency representatives; one that lacks good organization, has insufficient technical capacity, and is often poorly regarded by the main stakeholders. These organizational problems are a reflection, or perhaps a cause, of a system's failure. The reformer would do well to pay particular attention to these professionals and to ensure that efforts to improve the court system are coupled with measures to raise the level of knowledge and skills of insolvency professionals.[6] In the case of MSMEs, if the Modular Approach is implemented, the participation of insolvency professionals will be limited. Their appointment is an optional module, only requested when the parties deem it necessary. However, given the poor practice of MSME insolvency in most jurisdictions, it is foreseeable that, at least in the first years of implementation, parties will trigger the appointment of a professional in a large number of cases. Hence the need to focus attention on these professionals, even when the reform is limited to MSMEs. As we explained in the institutional part of the volume, insolvency professionals practising in the MSME world (particularly in the case of micro-businesses) will not require high technical standards in financial accounting but would need additional training in mediation techniques. In other words, the reformer should consider the aspect of a specialization of professionals.
- *Bailiffs and other officers*—The implementation of the procedural legislation often lies in the hands of bailiffs and officers of the court. As stated, the application of such laws directly influences the implementation of the insolvency framework. Although it is by no means a priority, reformers will do well to analyse the situation and the performance of such professionals.

[6] Arguably, the reformer will face a 'chicken and egg' problem: insolvency systems work poorly because insolvency professionals are not capable, but good professionals will never be attracted to a system that does not work and is basically limited to piecemeal liquidations where there is little to do and little remuneration. We are persuaded, however, that it is in the hands of the reformer to improve the legal framework and to create a proper market of professionals. Actions on this front are required, alongside legal reform and other improvements to the institutional framework.

- *Private parties*—Finally, technical capacity, honesty, and professional good practice of lawyers and other participants in insolvency proceedings may also influence the development of the system. The behaviour of banks and other financial institutions when granting and monitoring loans to MSMEs, as well as when assessing the manner in which to approach their financial distress, is a weighty factor in the final outcome of cases. The reformer ought to pay attention to these issues.

The gathering of quantitative and qualitative data, and the subsequent analysis of the legal and institutional frameworks, should enable a country's reformer to start a well-grounded drafting of the necessary reforms.

B. The Drafting Stage

The drafting of the reform is the legislator's most solitary job; it is also very country-specific, since the identity of the person or persons who are tasked with the draft and how the drafting is done will very much depend on the internal distribution of competencies. In some countries, the drafting will be done by a law commission (or by a special committee of the law commission). In the majority, the ministry or agency that is championing the reform will do the drafting, and the law commission (should one exist) will be merely an after-the-fact consultation body. Experience shows that drafting works better when a smaller number of people are in charge, avoiding political interference at an early stage and usually resulting in a more systematic and consistent text.

The drafting team will first need to decide whether a separate insolvency law for MSMEs is the best option, or simply the inclusion of a separate chapter in the existing general insolvency law, together with specific amendments to concrete rules that will also apply, albeit in a different manner, to non-MSMEs. There is no best practice in this regard, and the decision will normally be based on the number of changes to be introduced as well as on the country's own legislative techniques. For example, in some countries, amendments to more than a given percentage of an existing law require a separate piece of legislation. As stated previously, the introduction of the Modular Approach may require a thorough and comprehensive approach to reform, including changes to other laws. The drafting team will need to be in frequent dialogue with the parts of the government and the legislative body competent in the related matters (labour, banking, procedure, etc) and be able to achieve consensus, before the final draft, on the scope and main tenets of the reform. It is not uncommon to find that the relevant ministry or agency tasked with the legal reform has acted alone, isolated from the rest of the government. This approach increases the chances that the reform will be thwarted at a later stage.

To avoid this situation, it is advisable to set up a steering committee that should be in permanent dialogue with the drafting team. This prudent step, and the team's willingness to compromise when advisable, may save time and increase chances of success. Alternatively, the drafting team may present to the steering committee an

Figure 9.2 Consultation and decision-making process in MSME reform.

already finalized draft for comments and discussion. The result of the discussion may then be incorporated in the text in the form of a second draft, or successive ones.[7] Figure 9.2 illustrates how the consultation and decision process could work effectively.

Once the draft is complete and negotiated with the relevant ministries or agencies, and it has incorporated, if applicable, the comments and suggestions from the members of the steering committee, it is usually sent directly to the legislature. Experience shows that this stage can be very complicated. Lobbying and political action occur in the legislative debate and an initially well-reasoned draft may be damaged. But, there is no alternative. Early compromise and consultation will maximize the likelihood of achieving meaningful reform.[8]

[7] Certain jurisdictions operate in a very open manner, incorporating stakeholders and anyone with an interest in the reform process. A famous and somewhat extreme example can be found in Germany's 1994 insolvency law reform: two reports were made public in the mid 1980s and widely debated in academia as well as in the industry; the final version of the law was approved in 1994, but only entered into force five years later, in 1999. While such a level of transparency is to be commended, most jurisdictions will need a reform more urgently, and, in any case, the introduction of a Modular Approach to MSME insolvency does not, to be sure, require such a level of debate. After all, the German Insolvenzordung of 1994 reformed a system that had been in place since the nineteenth century.

[8] This stage is also where a reform such as the Modular Approach will have to fight its more difficult battle. Countries with non-functional insolvency systems tend to adopt a very conservative approach, being particularly concerned with the avoidance of fraud. It is difficult to convince them that the possibility of widespread fraud in their national practice is precisely linked with the absence of insolvency

C. The Implementation Stage

Once the law introducing the Modular Approach has been passed, the new system needs to be implemented. The less developed the reformed system, the more advisable it would be to allow for a relatively long period of time to prepare the institutions and the stakeholders that are to apply the law.

Judges and insolvency professionals need to acquire appropriate knowledge of the new system. It is paramount to organize detailed, well-designed training. Usually, it is the insolvency agency, the relevant ministry, or the national judicial training organization that must take on this task to ensure a thorough capacity-building programme is put in place before the law is in force. This initial programme should be complemented with subsequent ones, to be provided periodically. Training should be a durable commitment of the implementing agency.

Finally, a dissemination strategy ought to be put in place. Given the unsophisticated nature of many persons who operate in or as MSMEs, the dissemination should have a wide scope, and be aimed at the general business community. Workshops, courses, conferences, and advisory services in public institutions, chambers of commerce, etc are all in order. Accessible online training modules should be developed where possible. Knowledge of the existence of the reform and a sufficient understanding of what it entails are no doubt necessary for the success of a reform that will bring new concepts and ideas to a world resistant to change.

A final word for the reformers: the implementation of insolvency law reform is particularly slow; more so than for other laws with less technical and less intense social features. It takes time to be assimilated by the market and its stakeholders. So, our last piece of advice would be to exercise patience!

culture, which itself derives from an inadequate system (amongst other social factors, more difficult to control, such as stigma); that there is no reason to believe that their country is more prone to fraud than the rest. As a result, politicians with no knowledge of insolvency (beyond their own country's practice) may be reluctant to endorse a system that is, ultimately, based on the free choice of the parties involved. We are aware of this risk. The solution lies with good preparation and political persuasion by the members of the drafting team.

10

Annex 2

Lessons from One Jurisdiction on How to Identify Policy Needs of MSME Insolvency

Legislators and policymakers may finish reading this volume and wonder how they can start a process to adopt the Modular Approach to MSME insolvency. This annex offers an example of how one jurisdiction identified the policy needs for reform of the treatment of the insolvency of MSMEs by working with individuals on the ground to develop ideas for a fairer and more effective system.[1] In Canada, it is generally acknowledged that the insolvency system works relatively well, particularly for consumer debtors and large enterprises. However, as in other jurisdictions, regulators have had questions concerning whether the system adequately serves MSMEs.

A study commissioned by the Industry Canada Marketplace Policy Branch of the Canadian Government resulted in Janis Sarra conducting a study on MSME insolvency in Canada in 2015–16, with the goal of identifying challenges that MSMEs face within the existing Canadian insolvency regime.[2] Part of Sarra's methodology was to undertake a survey of more than sixty practitioners who deal on a daily basis with MSME insolvency, including insolvency professionals and loan officers. This annex contains a summary of the methodology of the Sarra study and its findings, followed by some questions that policymakers could commence with in identifying how best to design and adopt a Modular Approach to MSME insolvency.

[1] The findings reported in this annex are taken directly from the study undertaken by Janis Sarra, *Micro, Small and Medium Enterprise (MSME) Insolvency in Canada*, http://ssrn.com/abstract=2862039 ('Sarra study'). See also Janis Sarra, 'An Opportune Moment—Retooling the Bankruptcy and Insolvency Act to Address Micro, Small and Medium Enterprise (MSME) Insolvency in Canada', in Janis Sarra and Barbara Romaine (eds), *Annual Review of Insolvency Law 2016* (Toronto: Carswell, 2017) at 1193–303.

[2] Specifically, the Marketplace Policy Branch of Industry Canada requested that the report: examine access to and utilization by Canadian small and medium enterprises of the formal insolvency process, including trying to ascertain the reasons for the decline in filings; undertake a qualitative study of data from the Office of the Superintendent of Bankruptcy ('OSB') on the reasons for SME insolvency and types of debt; survey a representative sample of trustees and five to ten loan officers, to identify the perceived barriers to accessing and utilizing BIA proceedings; and generate policy questions and considerations on the issue of SME insolvency proceedings. For the full report, see the Sarra study (n 1).

Micro, Small, and Medium Enterprise Insolvency. First Edition. Ronald Davis, Stephan Madaus, Alberto Mazzoni, Irit Mevorach, Rizwaan J. Mokal, Barbara Romaine, Janis Sarra, & Ignacio Tirado. Published 2018 by Oxford University Press.

A. Canadian Survey of Trustees

The Sarra study on MSME insolvency was a qualitative empirical examination of MSME filings under the Canadian Bankruptcy and Insolvency Act (BIA), including a survey of fifty-three licensed insolvency trustees and ten distressed-loans officers. It sought to identify the challenges that face Canadian MSMEs as they slide into financial distress. What is clear from the data is that the current system has significant barriers, in terms of both cost and administration, to effectively allowing insolvent MSMEs, particularly micro and small incorporated enterprises, to carry on business where there is potential for a turnaround.

1. Methodology of the trustee survey

In commissioning the study, Industry Canada was interested in the views of licensed insolvency trustees in terms of the particular challenges facing SMEs, and it made sense to also collect views on sole proprietorships and micro enterprises. Sarra convened three focus groups involving fifteen licensed insolvency trustees in total, who helped identify the issues that should be canvassed in the survey. The survey consisted of ten questions.[3] The participation of trustees was sought through a global email sent to all licensed insolvency trustees in Canada, seeking their involvement. The professional association of licensed trustees, the Canadian Association of Insolvency and Restructuring Professionals (CAIRP), also helped to identify trustees working across a range of settings: urban and rural, small communities and large, micro, and small enterprises, and in different sectors of the economy. An email request to participate was also sent to trustees who had attended the Annual Review of Insolvency Law conference in the prior five years. Although trustees self-selected to respond, the response rate of fifty-three is significant. There are 217 licensed insolvency trustee firms with 1,046 individual licensed insolvency trustees in Canada,[4] many of whom do not deal with MSMEs. Surveys were conducted in English and French, and trustees had the opportunity to respond in writing or by telephone interview. Twenty-four trustees of the fifty-three who were surveyed opted for a telephone interview, which lasted from 30 to 60 minutes. The surveys were conducted from November 2015 to February 2016.

In terms of surveying lenders to MSMEs, the goal had been to speak to a small number of loan officers (five to ten). Here, it was much harder to get participation. Aside from general approaches to lenders in the MSME market, trustees surveyed were asked to recommend small loan officers and other lenders who might participate. Thirty-nine refusals to be interviewed were received before ten loan officers willing to participate were found, four by written survey, four by telephone interview, and two by a combination of both.

[3] The questions can be found in the Sarra study (n 1).

[4] Office of the Superintendent of Bankruptcy, March 2016.

The survey used the parameters set out by Industry Canada for defining MSMEs, based on the number of employees, and, for purposes of the survey, 'medium' enterprises were further divided into smaller medium and medium enterprises. The majority of trustees responding to the survey deal with small businesses, micro businesses, and sole proprietorships. The percentage of the responding trustees' practice that consists of MSMEs was quite high, meaning that their insights are were particularly relevant. The loan officers interviewed deal with all MSME sizes, typically with loans ranging from 250,000 CAD to five million CAD.

The primary limitation of the survey was that there were no resources to canvass entrepreneurs who had been through the Canadian process or who had avoided the Canadian process due to prohibitive costs; or to undertake a survey of a broader set of stakeholders, such as trade suppliers, to canvas their experience with the system. The result is that the data gathered, and the recommendations made, are viewed very much through the lens of insolvency professionals and loan professionals, and so a number of aspects of the Modular Approach that do not require the use of insolvency professionals are not evident in the study. Many other issues, such as cost-effective notice, deemed approval where creditors do not object, and reduced use of court resources, resonate with the various aspects of the Modular Approach.

2. Survey results

This section summarizes the results of the survey, with explanatory texts for many of the observations and insights. It also discusses the responses of the loan officers interviewed.[5] Of note is that, while the trustees have a direct personal economic interest in any legislative reform and loan officers have their principal's interests to consider, the survey responses indicated a sincere effort had been made by these practitioners to use their professional expertise and experience to assess the efficacy of the system.

Generally, the vast majority of trustees expressed the view that there should be amendments to Canadian legislation to ensure that the treatment of insolvent MSMEs gives viable businesses a chance for rehabilitation where possible and at the same time ensures timely bankruptcy where the business should be sold or liquidated. Several trustees discussed the problems of 'midnight moves' by debtors of company assets to avoid landlords, and shuttered businesses or orphaned companies not being wound up through formal processes because of the costs of bankruptcy proceedings. One trustee suggested considering a 'deemed bankruptcy' right away, in that sometimes there is delay and value lost to creditors even though it is clear that a proposal is not possible.

All ten loan officers surveyed agreed that some legislative reform to make the process more timely and more cost-effective would be helpful. Two loan officers noted, however, that there is still considerable stigma associated with the idea of 'bankruptcy' and there is frequently a lack of understanding by debtors of the options available under legislation.

[5] For a more detailed discussion, see Sarra 'Retooling' (n 1).

Eighty-five percent of surveyed trustees believe that existing statutory provisions could be enhanced to improve effectiveness and timeliness; and 73%, believe that the statutory provisions could be enhanced to make the process less costly.

Survey participants were asked for specific ways in which the statutory scheme for MSME insolvency could be improved. The most frequent suggestion was to reduce the number of decisions that require court approval and to provide greater flexibility in time limits under the BIA. Other suggestions included greater flexibility in the process, streamlining the claims process, redefining access to proposals, greater clarification in the process, and revising methods of trustee remuneration for MSME files.

a. A streamlined process for micro and small businesses

Many trustees pointed out that the objective of the provisions in the BIA is to encourage proposals for businesses that are viable, and to allow for a timely decision as to when bankruptcy is more appropriate. Many trustees recommended allowing MSMEs a process similar to the option that exists for unincorporated consumers, where the number of MSME creditors is limited and levels of debt are small and straightforward. Trustees observed that often in these cases a stay is required to determine if a proposal can be made, but the process of presenting and voting on the proposal could be considerably streamlined. Numerous trustees suggested that all sole proprietors should have access to the expedited proposal restructuring provisions without restriction on debt levels.

More than two thirds of the trustees and all of the loan officers interviewed by Sarra reported that the BIA provisions are far too costly for the majority of micro and small businesses, and they often cannot come within the definition of the streamlined consumer provisions. One trustee observed that of every ten micro businesses they work with, nine cannot access the insolvency process because the cost is prohibitive. With respect to bankruptcy, it is difficult to file if there are no unencumbered assets because of the high minimum cost. The fees for the service must be paid up front or there is the risk of non-payment. The requirements on a small corporate bankruptcy are cost prohibitive, including a creditors' meeting with no creditors in attendance, sales package/process for assets with minimal realizable value, taxation, etc. Thus, the loan officer or the trustee will often forward secured asset files to an auctioneer to sell and pay out the bank or taxation authorities. The difficulty is that these business owners have little protection from general creditors in that instance.

The proposed solutions to the cost of micro and small bankruptcy were mixed. Loan officers suggested that there should be a service that does a quick 'look-see' on viability, such that the bank can act quickly to determine whether or not a business is viable. Some suggested trustees could perform this preliminary assessment, while others proposed a trustee-type service, but supplied by the federal government. Trustees suggested that there needs to be a mechanism to pay the insolvency professional's fees on liquidation, as bankruptcy is a public service, and where there are no assets to pay for the service and a secured creditor is unwilling to pay, the debtor often simply does not file. Loan officers reported that they simply avoid the BIA bankruptcy process because of the expense, when they can realize directly on their security.

With respect to the existing provisions under the BIA, the majority of both trustees and loan officers interviewed suggested that the existing consumer proposal process could be streamlined for micro and small businesses. A streamlined proposal could redefine access to proposals, modernize notice provisions, reduce numbers of creditor meetings, and create a deemed approval mechanism.

One helpful streamlining measure would be the ability of the debtor to cure defaults such as delays in meeting payment terms under the proposal without the necessity of filing an amended proposal. The terms could allow inspectors or creditors at a creditors' meeting to extend the payment terms on recommendation of the trustee. Such an extension should not require court approval, payment of filing fees, or additional cashflow reports. Only if it is proposed that the quantum of dividends to be paid under the proposal be reduced would the debtor have to file an amended proposal and recommence the process.

The loan officers surveyed also supported the implementation of a streamlined process. They observed that MSMEs are typically 'less sophisticated' in their finances; they may only have a bookkeeper in-house and often do not understand the benefits of engaging the services of a financial adviser or trustee. A streamlined process where the costs of the process are clear up front may assist in overcoming this barrier to filing.

Figure 10.1 summarizes some of the most frequent recommendations on how to streamline the process. Within these broad categories there was a range of views, but 83% of surveyed trustees and 80% of surveyed loan officers supported creating

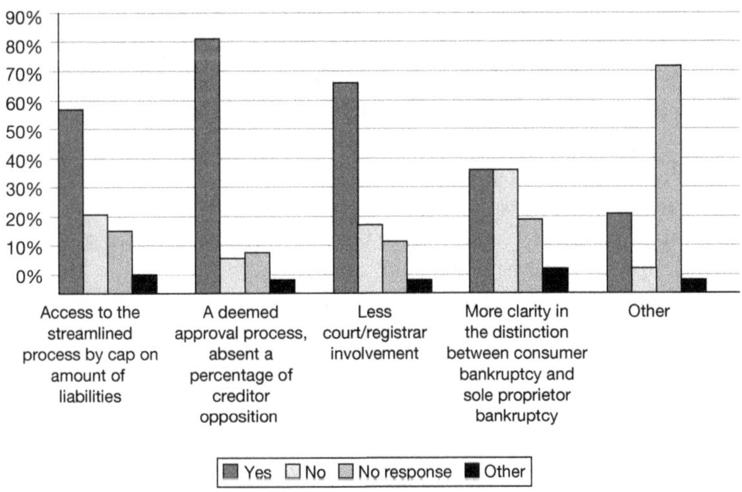

Figure 10.1 Trustee recommendations on streamlining the process.

Source: Sarra study (n 1).

a deemed approval process for at least micro and small businesses. The following is a summary of some of the recommendations made by the trustees and loan officers. The Sarra study contains greater detail.[6]

i. Redefine access to proposals

There were numerous suggestions as to how to improve access to proposals, with the objective that the small business person comes out of the process with a viable business, where possible. There was broad support for a new specific set of provisions designed for MSMEs and a recommendation to change the liability cap to increase access to the process for incorporated micro and small businesses, including sole proprietorships.

The majority recommended allowing inclusion of personal debts of principals of the company in a proposal, inclusive of personal guarantees provided to third parties on MSME debts, corporate or otherwise. Where there is a blending of corporate and personal debt, there is need to consider both at the same time, as business loans have to be secured with personal assets and personal credit cards are frequently used to support the business. One trustee observed that many business people transfer assets into a limited company to protect themselves, but on incorporation, tools of the trade are no longer exempt from seizure under Canadian bankruptcy law. Access to rehabilitation requires protecting tools of the trade in all circumstances so the business person can earn income. Trustees recommended creating an ability to compromise personal guarantees in a MSME corporate proposal, which would save using two separate filings.

ii. Notice

Almost all of the trustees and loan officers interviewed emphasized the importance of effective notice in both bankruptcies and proposals—an issue that becomes even more important for a streamlined process. One trustee suggested that bankruptcy is often the most effective way to transition a business, and that sometimes trustees pursue proposals for sole proprietors where the likelihood of success is very low, simply to have a deemed bankruptcy in order to avoid a bankruptcy notice in the newspaper. Yet filing proposals to avoid the notice requirements adds unnecessary cost for creditors in other parts of the process.

The majority of trustees responding to the survey believe that the notice provisions under the BIA are outdated and need to be improved. One trustee observed: 'the public bankruptcy notice is archaic and adds unnecessary costs to the process'. Newspaper advertisements are often prohibitively expensive. Another trustee observed that sometimes trustees refuse to do small business proposals because of the cost of notices. Print ads are viewed as ineffective, as many people no longer read the newspaper, unless they are in a small community. One trustee suggested that few creditors are missed in the initial filing, so the requirement of public notice to creditors is unnecessary. Others noted that if public notices are not required in

[6] Sarra study (n 1); see also Sarra, 'Retooling' (n 1).

consumer proposals and summary bankruptcies, it is difficult to understand the logic for requiring them in ordinary bankruptcies.

Numerous trustees recommended eliminating sending out notices by registered mail or ordinary mail, suggesting that most creditors just throw out all the information mailed to them, wasting time and paper. Trustees observed that registered mail is very costly where there are numerous creditors. However, another trustee observed that there are few creditors that need to be sent registered mail and where it is required—such as for resiliation of contracts, disallowing claims, and lease disclaimers—it is very important that there is certainty the notice is received. Others suggested that it should be sufficient for the trustee to swear an affidavit of mailing to confirm that the notice was sent to the last known address, although there was disagreement among trustees in this respect, with several trustees observing that the cost of writing the affidavit, finding a commissioner for oaths, and swearing the affidavit is not any more cost-effective than registered mail or a delivery service.

Many trustees recommended that notice should be allowed to be sent by electronic means—such as email or fax, or through a link to a website—with new standards created for assessing sufficiency of notice. Several suggested that the first letter to creditors could be sent by mail, with an electronic link for information, which would serve as notice for the rest of the process. Another recommendation was to create a public noticeboard on the OSB website, which could replace newspaper public notice, where creditors could check at any time to see if the business is bankrupt or in receivership. Such a service would be highly accessible and cost-effective. The question is how to ensure creditors receive effective notice of the proceedings and of any proposed treatment or compromise of their claims.

Another recommendation was to make the level of information required to be published and disseminated more summary regarding the initial filing of the notice of intention to file a proposal. Trustees recommended providing stakeholders with *pro forma* information on what steps the debtor needs to take in order to resolve the causes of the insolvency.

In sum, almost all the trustees surveyed suggested that it is time to explore technologies to modernize notice under the BIA, in turn making the processes more transparent, timely, and cost-effective.

iii. Initial stay period and extension of stay periods

There were many and diverse views about the initial stay period and extensions of stay among the fifty-three trustees surveyed. In terms of the initial stay, the majority believe that an initial stay should be automatic for all MSME, sole-proprietor, and consumer proposal filings. Many observed that there is insufficient information available to formulate a proposal at the time of filing and it is necessary to have preliminary discussions with significant creditors before formulating a proposal. The 'breathing space' of the initial stay is critically important, with trustees observing that, in the face of impending garnishments or asset seizures, trustees are forced to use more complicated options when a consumer proposal with an initial stay of proceedings would be far more efficient and cost-effective. Trustees observed that the first thirty days after filing a notice of intention that creates a stay are often used to stabilize the company's situation with its creditors, suppliers, etc; and that MSMEs often manage emergencies during this period and do not have the time to work out the terms of an eventual proposal.

Most trustees and loan officers suggested a stay period of sixty days, on the basis that it is rare for a company to be able to make a proposal within the current initial stay period of thirty days. The majority of trustees recommended that the trustee should be allowed to extend the initial stay unless creditors object. The recommended periods of extension ranged from thirty to ninety additional days. Trustees observed that the granting of the first extension is often a 'rubber stamp' by the courts and the real work on the proposal occurs or is finalized during the following forty-five-day period. One trustee recommended that extensions of the stay could be given if there are positive cashflows as determined by the debtor and reviewed by the trustee; the time for the extension would be at the discretion of the trustee, after disclosure to creditors and an opportunity to object. Another suggestion was to give thirty to sixty days to prepare a cashflow statement rather than ten days, perhaps requiring an update once a month to keep creditors informed. Trustees suggested that they should have an obligation to report accrued charges to the primed creditors on a biweekly basis and the primed creditors, if appropriate, could proceed to court to set limits or other constraints on the priority charge. That safeguard could facilitate a more streamlined approval process.

Notwithstanding that the majority of trustees responding to the survey would like a more streamlined process, the vast majority expressed the view that the current six-month limit on proposal proceedings under the BIA worked well in the majority of cases, but that the court should be given authority to extend that period. The loan officers interviewed also preferred a six-month cap on proposal proceedings as a general rule, but supported the idea of giving the court the authority to extend that period in some circumstances. They were generally supportive of giving the trustee the authority to extend the stay period at least once or twice, but noted that notice to creditors and the ability to object to the extension were very important protections against debtors that were using the process merely to delay inevitable liquidation.

iv. Clarify the distinction between consumers and sole-proprietor debtors

The surveyed trustees were equally divided as to whether there needs to be a better distinction made between consumer debtors and sole proprietors, 48% expressing the view 'yes' and 48% expressing the view 'no', with the remainder having no opinion. Many trustees expressed the view that it is not problematic, because the personal and business liabilities of the micro and small business person are so intermingled it is difficult to separate them. Others, however, believe that there should be a separate mechanism that offers businesses a streamlined process.

Many trustees suggested that there needs to be a clearer mechanism to address the blending of corporate and personal debt of micro and small businesses, as business loans are usually required to be secured with personal assets, and debtors frequently use personal credit cards to support the business. The current system masks this confluence of personal and business debt. It was recommended that the proposal provisions should allow inclusion of personal debts of principals of companies with no limitation, inclusive of personal guarantees provided to third parties on MSME debts, corporate or otherwise.

v. Reduce types of decisions requiring court approval

Many trustees observed that proposals are essentially a new contract between the debtor and the creditors, and that if the creditors approve, the amount of court involvement necessary should be limited. The majority of responding trustees believe that courts add costs due to the administrative burden, and that reducing the amount of court time for unopposed filings would have a meaningful impact. A deemed approval approach to MSME proposals should still allow for court hearings where a creditor requests it. One trustee observed that the biggest barrier is where a MSME knows it will need an extension, but cannot afford the cost of the court process to obtain it; for example, the success of a proposal or viability depends on a future event, expected to take place more than thirty days in the future, but requiring the protection of a stay of proceedings. If one were to eliminate the requirement for court approval for an extension if unopposed, it would allow that business a chance to survive.

Numerous trustees recommended reducing the need for additional court orders, although one trustee observed that the court and registrar's involvement should be maintained as they assist with monitoring and serve as final arbiters of issues. Another observation was that registrars keep trustees honest and give trustees peace of mind that they are acting appropriately and 'getting it right'.

Small corporations are often highly dependent on a principal shareholder, with the business not easily saleable to a third party. The BIA currently requires court approval for the sale of assets to related parties, including the principal shareholder, and trustees observed that if the creditors approve a sale to a related party, it should be sufficient, assuming the proper disclosures have been made regarding relationships. It would save unnecessary costs and reduce the burden on the court. Trustees also recommended that court ratification of a proposal should only be required if a creditor opposes the ratification or if the trustee presents a report recommending the refusal of the proposal. What is important is to ensure that the court is available to preserve the integrity of the insolvency system, to protect the public interest and public trust.

Trustees noted that the cost of the multiple court applications for extensions are prohibitive and are a barrier to filing, trustees reporting that each court appearance to extend time costs between 5,000 and 10,000 CAD.

vi. Improve the claims process

The vast majority of survey responses in respect of improving the claims process were directed at issues related to the taxation authorities and to claims with respect to the statutory wage-protection programme. The most frequent suggestion was finding a way to have greater flexibility *vis-à-vis* government claims. There were a few additional suggestions made, but trustees generally expressed the view that the claims process is quite effective. One recommendation was that there should be an ability to compromise personal guarantees in a MSME proposal.

Trustees recommended that if an arm's-length creditor does not dispute the company's declared amount of debt, there should be a simplified claim form or no form at all, to expedite the process. There should be a standardized form or electronic communication, by which the creditor could acknowledge that it agrees with the claim amount disclosed by the debtor. Creditors should be allowed to be paid electronically instead of by cheques as a way to expedite and streamline the claims process.

vii. A mechanism for deemed approval of proposals

Trustees recommended that a streamlined proposal process for MSMEs in the BIA should require holding a meeting only if requested by the creditors. Many recommended that for micro and small businesses there should be no statutory requirement for a meeting of creditors where proper notice is given, unless a requisite number of creditors, such as 25%, request a meeting. The majority of surveyed trustees and loan officers expressed the view that if the goal is speed and ease of restructuring micro and small businesses, then a deemed approval mechanism makes sense, because creditors would still be able to object and seek a court hearing.

Many suggested that trustees should be given authority to proceed to canvass creditors, and where a requisite number support, or are not opposed to, a proposal, it should be deemed approved. Recommendations for the amount of opposition that would be required to defeat a proposal ranged from 25% to 50% of the proven dollar value of debt, with a 'headcount' of creditors opposing also recommended as between 25% and 50%.

If not a deemed approval process, there were many recommendations to change the voting threshold for approval of proposals to a simple majority in value and headcount, trustees suggesting that two-thirds dollar value voting approval threshold does not seem to be logical if the objective is to rehabilitate businesses where possible, since a lower dollar threshold should improve the approval rate of proposals.

b. Is a new source of interim financing needed?

The trustees and loan officers were asked whether or not there should be a source of funding available, such as a programme to provide temporary loans or loan guarantees to MSMEs that address their financial difficulties, until the enterprise can again access other sources of capital. There was a very strong majority of 74% of trustees who were opposed to this idea.

A majority of trustees responded that there are capital market providers who are already available to fill this need in Canada, including the availability of further secured debt from primary lenders, credit unions, the Business Development Bank of Canada ('BDBC'), high-yield and high-risk lenders, and companies that do factoring. Thus, in their view, there is no need for a programme to provide temporary loans or loan guarantees to MSMEs that address their financial difficulties until the enterprise can gain access to other sources of capital. B lenders exist, and their interest rates reflect the additional risk they take in providing these loans.

None of the loan officers interviewed thought that a new financing mechanism is needed. They believe that there continues to be sufficient liquidity in the market to finance viable businesses; and that the issue really is that the debtor waits too long before trying to access the financing (e.g. attempting to seek financing only the night before a payroll is due that they cannot meet). Loan officers reported that often, by the time the debtor discloses the financial distress, there is no longer a viable business to save. Many trustees and loan officers were concerned with the moral hazard of creating such a programme, and others were concerned with priority issues and problems of monitoring and accountability.

c. *Would mediation assist the proposal process for MSMEs?*

Trustees were asked if mediation would assist in better identifying whether or not and how a MSME business could be rehabilitated. Seventy-eight percent of the trustees surveyed responded 'no'. The surveyed trustees overwhelmingly expressed the view that mediation would not assist, and that creditors were unlikely to participate in a mediation to identify whether or not and how a MSME business could be rehabilitated. In part, this lack of participation reflects a 'rational choice' or 'rational creditor apathy', in that creditors' claims may not be worth the costs of participating in the mediation process. However, this response was likely affected by the perception that trustees in Canada already play a mediation role in circumstances where there is potential rehabilitation of the business and parties have an interest in a going-forward relationship.

d. *Taxation authority as creditor*

The trustees and loan officers surveyed in the Sarra study were also asked whether there were any issues with Canadian taxation authorities in the insolvency of MSMEs that may hinder the basic objectives of the legislation relating to rehabilitation, fresh start, and promoting restructuring over liquidation. While many of the responses are specific to the Canadian taxation system, some have broader application:

- Trustees expressed concern about the failure of taxation authorities to respond in a timely manner to important decision points during insolvency proceedings as MSME businesses often cannot survive the wait for a decision, and premature liquidation results in loss of value, including to the taxation authorities.
- The majority of trustees surveyed reported a general unwillingness by taxation authorities to negotiate: what they referred to as an 'arrogance' in staff using their priority position to extract more from the debtor than it is capable of paying, creating conditions for failure of the proposal. Several trustees suggested that dealings with taxation authorities need to be improved, in that trustees and the authorities seem engaged in a constant and unproductive set of differences, where taxation staff treat both insolvency professionals and debtors with a lack of respect.

- There was concern expressed that the staff of taxation authorities seem incapable of making business decisions, and when staff just follow bureaucratic rules, assets are left to waste. Several trustees observed that there is poor understanding of the public policy underlying proposals or their practical value and that intensive training should be undertaken with all taxation authority staff.

e. Additional data from the survey

There were a number of additional observations and recommendations as to how to improve the treatment of insolvent MSMEs under Canadian law that did not fit neatly into one of the topics above. Many trustees expressed the view that as MSMEs comprise a majority of businesses in Canada, there should be better information and education to help new businesses commence and be successful. Others expressed concern about ethics in business today, which may also speak to the need for greater education.

Trustees observed that MSMEs are increasingly being tied to the financial affairs of the company's principals. There is a general piercing of the corporate veil with little protection for company owners from creditors. In turn, both the company and the entrepreneur personally need to file under the BIA, and this duplication in process adds to the overall insolvency administration cost and can lower creditor recovery.

Several trustees suggested having banks held more accountable for their decision-making processes and involvement in insolvency proceedings. One factor detrimental to the insolvency process is the inability of most major banks to move at the same speed in decision-making as the insolvency professional and the debtor companies. Trustees suggested a need to find a way to involve secured creditors more in the proposal process without giving them a complete power of veto: their ability to refuse to negotiate with creditors often destroys any chance for recovery for other creditors.

The Sarra study also found broad support for a better and clearer process for dealing with the principals/managers/employees of insolvent companies who fail to cooperate with the trustee or receiver or actively interfere with or sabotage the bankruptcy or receivership proceedings. The trustees noted that, in a consumer bankruptcy, these matters are principally dealt with at the bankrupt's discharge hearing, but there is no similar process for the non-bankrupt principals of an insolvent company. Special investigations of fraudulent activity by the OSB on the part of debtors can take years, with little benefit to the creditors. The trustee or receiver may end up having to hold the file open for years, and testify in court, with no benefit to the estate. The party funding the insolvency proceeding may have no interest in funding the trustee to testify in a fraud hearing long after the business has been wound up and the assets sold. Sometimes the funding party and the target of the investigation may be the same person.

Finally, there were concerns expressed that the present regulated counselling fee of 85 CAD is too low to provide a real service to debtors and the amount should be raised to at least 200 CAD so that appropriate time can be spent with the debtor. Some trustees are outsourcing counselling, and it is not helpful in assisting debtors because there are not enough resources to pay for the time needed.

3. Recommendations coming out of the Sarra survey

There were many and diverse types of recommendation made by trustees and loan officers—the professionals that work daily within the existing statutory framework. Dr Sarra in her report referenced recommendations on which there was the greatest consensus, or where an idea was novel and warrants consideration.[7]

1. Trustees and loan officers who work directly with MSMEs agree that there is a need to consider a streamlined approach to bankruptcy of MSMEs, so that they can access formal proceedings: such a process would counter the current trend of secured creditors simply realizing their assets without regard to other creditors' interests.
2. There should be a new streamlined framework for MSMEs that is administratively simpler and eliminates the need for repeated court appearances. The MSME proposal process could include the following elements:
    - An automatic stay of forty-five or sixty days on commencing the proceeding, with the ability of the proposal trustee to extend the stay period for an additional period if notice has been given to creditors and there is no objection. Objections would be dealt with by the court.
    - The MSME proposal process should be available to sole proprietors, whether or not incorporated, as well as micro and small businesses. Consideration should be given to extending the streamlined process to medium enterprises and, if so, to the conditions under which such a streamlined process would be available.
    - Access to a MSME proposal process could be defined by a combination of numbers of employees and a cap of liabilities, the latter being much higher than the current limit.
    - Authority should be vested in the licensed insolvency trustee to undertake specified tasks in order to facilitate agreement between the debtor and creditors of proposals, eliminating the requirement to seek supplemental orders from the court on appointment.

[7] Complete recommendations can be seen in the Sarra study (n 1), and additional comments and recommendations are set out in Sarra, 'Retooling' (n 1). The arbitrary selection of recommendations in this section does not diminish the value of considering all of the insights and recommendations. Also, the Sarra study did not canvass the views of any other stakeholder groups and trade suppliers, and she noted that a process of reform should engage with a broader community regarding a range of possible options for the treatment of MSME insolvency.

- There should be the ability to make a proposal to creditors without the need to hold a meeting of creditors, unless a specified percentage of creditors, such as 25%, request it.
- Proposals in a streamlined process should provide for at least the liquidation value of creditors' claims in the proposal.
- If, after a specified period, creditors have expressed support for the proposal in terms of a specified number of creditors holding a specified percentage of the debt, the proposal should be deemed approved, without having to seek court approval. Objections can be dealt with by the court.
- Government could consider making the threshold for deemed approval of a MSME proposal a simple majority of creditors in both number and value of the claims.
- There should be limits placed on the period of time the taxation authority has to respond to the proposal, after which it is deemed to have approved the proposal.
- The proposal process would be subject to a six-month limit in the normal case, but the court should be authorized to extend the six-month limit for MSMEs in circumstances that the court considers appropriate.
- There should be a streamlined process to cure a temporary default in the terms of a MSME proposal, including deeming it cured where creditors receive notice and do not object.

3. Notice provisions should be modernized, including allowing for electronic notice.
4. A simplified standard form claims process should be created that can be expedited where there is no dispute in the amounts owed to creditors.
5. Voting processes should be modernized, including use of new technologies to allow for electronic voting by creditors.
6. There should be a review of how trustees are compensated for their professional services, including consideration of a fixed tariff for the MSME proposal process.
7. It would be advisable to increase funding for and availability of education and skills building for individuals commencing new businesses.
8. The new MSME proposal process should provide for an opportunity for counselling on debt management and should increase the fees for counselling to allow for meaningful education.

In conclusion, the Sarra study established that while existing legislation in Canada may be largely effective for medium and larger enterprises, there needs to be a mechanism that allows for a more streamlined and accessible process to deal with the financial distress of micro and small businesses without the loss of safeguards for creditors, including employees. Many of these recommendations from trustees and loan officers in Canada who work with MSMEs corroborate the need for reform, and are reflected in the proposals in this volume.

4. Some possible questions to start the inquiry into adopting a Modular Approach

The Sarra study is one resource for policymakers who wish to commence a process to consider implementing a Modular Approach, in that it gathered data from professionals working on the ground. However, Canada is a developed country, with a sophisticated insolvency law regime. Many of the insights on the need for reform were drawn from a starting premise that there is a well-developed insolvency profession and highly developed banking system, in which loan officers are repeat players in MSME insolvency. Other jurisdictions, as noted throughout this volume, do not necessarily have either, and thus a policy discussion regarding the Modular Approach needs to address a different set of questions. The list below offers only a starting suggestion of how the inquiry could be commenced.

1. What are the current barriers in your jurisdiction to dealing fairly and effectively with MSME insolvency?

   A. Cost barriers?

   Costs caused by excessive time taken. Do in-court proceedings take too long? Which parts of the existing proceedings take longer (e.g. the formation of the list of creditors, finding relevant information, asset recovery)? Is the excessive time taken caused by insufficient infrastructure? Does the court system count on a system of clerks and officers that assist judges in their work? Are the files and cases dealt with in electronic mode? Do the parties and insolvency professionals count on free, public templates? Are time delays caused by a widespread practice of challenging procedural decisions such as decisions by the court or office holders?

   B. Lack of a rescue culture?

   Does the opening of insolvency-related proceedings bring about sanctions? Do the sanctions or negative legal limitations (e.g. disqualification of ability to act as a director or as an entrepreneur, inability to act as tutor or guardian, inability to serve as civil servant, etc) stem automatically from the opening of insolvency-related proceedings? Or would they only apply following an assessment of the debtor's behaviour? Is there social/personal stigma associated with the commencement of insolvency-related proceedings? Would it be correct to state that, generally speaking, small businesses procrastinate at the moment of filing for insolvency-related proceedings? Are creditors also reluctant to begin proceedings? Would creditors be allowed to foreclose or trigger early termination or impose sanctions upon the mere filing of insolvency-related proceedings?

   C. Lack of professional expertise?

   Is there sufficient awareness amongst the MSME community regarding the benefits of using insolvency related proceedings? Are dissemination campaigns and training actions being implemented with a view to generating awareness and sufficient knowledge of the benefits? Does the effectiveness of the process for entrepreneurs in micro and smaller businesses depend on a network of professional advisers at a relatively low cost? If so, are they publicly funded or private (i.e. organised by chambers of commerce, associations of entrepreneurs, etc)? Does the country have a system of sufficiently qualified insolvency professionals? Are they self-regulated? Is there a system of licensing? Are these professionals under the supervision of a public insolvency agency? Is there professional training in place on a permanent basis? Do these organizations of professionals have codes of conduct and mechanisms to enforce the rules set out in the codes? Is there a negative perception of professionals in terms of technical capacity and honesty?

D. Barriers to effective notice to creditors?

Is there an effective system to serve notices to creditors? Does the country have an online registry where the issuance or adoption of key decisions may be posted? Is there an online public gazette where decisions may be made public without additional cost? Is the notification of decisions to creditors or to the debtor an issue? Is there a problem arising from debtors' frequent changes of address?

E. Too much creditor apathy?

Do creditors participate actively in the restructuring or liquidation proceedings of insolvent MSMEs? If not, does the country's law include any rules to encourage their active involvement in the negotiations and in the decision-making process? Is there a deemed approval mechanism that encourages creditor participation?

F. Lack of incentives for MSMEs to file in a timely manner?

Does the opening of insolvency proceedings create a social and reputational problem? Does the opening of formal proceedings entail the automatic loss of management rights? Does it also bring about personal sanctions? Does the insolvency system include duty-to-file or a wrongful trading provisions that generate personal liability in case of damage to creditors? If such provisions exist, are they applied in practice?

G. Mingling of MSME business debt and personal debt or guarantees?

Is it common for lenders to require personal guarantees from MSME borrowers, independently of or in addition to security rights? Who are the most common guarantors? In the case of legal entities, are directors and/or shareholders often required to personally guarantee the debts of the business? Do guarantees include security rights? Is it common for family members to guarantee business loans? If so, does the country have any rules to protect them from creditor abuse? Does the insolvency system have rules to coordinate insolvency proceedings of guarantors and the main debtor? Are there household insolvency rules?

H. Time barriers to resolution?

Are there time limits on negotiating a workout of a MSME's financial distress? If so, are they an accountability check or a barrier to effective restructuring? Do time limits result in premature liquidation of MSMEs? Are there problems with creditors responding to or voting on proposals for liquidation or continuing plans? Is the administrative system, including the court system, responsive to the need for effective and timely processes?

I. Barriers to discharge of the entrepreneur?

Does the jurisdiction provide for the possibility of granting honest but unfortunate debtors a fresh start in a timely manner? If discharges occur, do they undermine social norms in terms of paying one's debts? Have cases of fraud been detected? If so, what are the mechanisms in place to detect fraud? Are there any debts that are non-dischargeable, and if so, are there time or other limits on non-dischargeable debts?

2. If there is to be a more streamlined proposal process for MSMEs, what elements from the Modular Approach are best suited to your country?

   A. Under the liquidation option?

   Under the entrepreneur-initiated model?

   Under the creditor-initiated module?

   B. Under the plan continuation option?

   Under the entrepreneur-initiated model?

   Under the creditor-initiated module?

3. If there is to be a deemed approval process for liquidation or a continuation plan, what level of creditor opposition should require court or other supervisory approval of the plan?
4. Is there a mediation culture in your jurisdiction, such that mediation could be effectively deployed in a MSME insolvency?
5. Are statutory creditors a barrier to dealing with MSME insolvency? If so, would a deemed approval mechanism assist with addressing the problems?
6. Should there be a source of funding available, such as a programme to provide temporary loans or loan guarantees to MSMEs that address their financial difficulties until the enterprise can again access other sources of capital?

11

Annex 3

Questionnaire for Lawyers

This questionnaire has been used for in-depth interviews conducted under the Research Project UST/2014/JCOO/AG/CIVI/7627 of the Directorate General Justice and Consumers of the European Commission (European Union) entitled 'Contractualised distress resolution in the shadow of the law: Effective judicial review and oversight of insolvency and pre-insolvency proceedings'. The project is a multi-jurisdiction analysis of the system of pre-insolvency and in-court solutions to financial distress, with particular regard to small and medium enterprises. The lifespan of the project has, to date, been from 2015 to 2018.[1] Although the questionnaire is separated into different sets of questions depending on the type of advice provided by the lawyer being interviewed, the main bulk of the questions apply to all interviewees.

The questionnaire assumes that the interviewer knows the law of the jurisdiction in which the questionnaire is being administered. Some questions include direct enquiries about the law, but they are meant to elicit the lawyer's opinion of the regulation at issue. In other words, these questions are asked to determine whether there are controversial elements or differences of interpretation in the law.

A. The Context of the Interviewee

1. Briefly describe the clients you work with most often. In the description, refer to: (a) the type of client (debtor/creditor), (b) the size of the client (medium/large/very large), (c) the territorial scope of the client (regional/national/international), and (d) the type of client activity (sector of activity, i.e. services, industrial, financial, etc).
2. In which capacity would you normally act? In-house lawyer/seconded lawyer from a firm; general legal counselor; barrister/litigator.

[1] Rizwaan Mokal and Ignacio Tirado are two researchers on the Project, together with Lorenzo Stanghellini (University of Florence) and Christoph Paulus (Humboldt University of Berlin). Irit Mevorach is a member of the Oversight Committee of the Project, and participated actively in the debates.

3. In cases of debtor clients, do you or your firm normally also provide legal advice in areas different to business/debt restructuring? (corporate law/tax/labour, etc)
4. Experience: how long have you been advising debtors/creditors in debt/business restructuring? Please differentiate between debtors and creditors.

B. Lawyers Mainly Advising Debtors

5. At what stage of financial distress do debtors come for advice? Please specify if there is a difference depending on the type of debtor (i.e. industry, the type of debt— financial/tax/employees/suppliers—the structure of shareholding, type of management, etc). Also, have creditors already foreclosed on the debtors or started other judicial initiatives? How often have creditors already filed a petition for an involuntary bankruptcy?
6. When debtors come for advice, have they normally already started some form of negotiation or held discussions on a restructuring attempt?
7. In your opinion, who are the players within the debtor's organization most active in the process (both in the decision to take action and in the definition of the strategy) (financial directors/accounting department; executive director; board of directors; legal department; controlling shareholders, statutory auditors, etc)?
8. Are other advisers often involved (i.e. consultancy firms, experts from investment banks, experts from private equity firms)? On average, how many cases involve other advisers? Of those cases, approximately how many are hired after consultations with you?
9. Briefly describe the most common initial approach by debtors in your experience (i.e. are they fully aware of the degree of distress)? Do they convey it to you or it is apparent at a later stage that the situation was misrepresented to you? Why, in your opinion, would that happen?
10. Do debtors normally have a predefined idea of the type of strategy to pursue and even of the type of legal channel to use?
11. Typically, what are the debtor's most urgent concerns? What measures do you advise to take at the initial stage to tackle the urgent concerns (illiquidity, civil and criminal liability, asset shielding)? Why do debtors usually seek your advice (i.e. the most common triggers, such as intra-organizational conflicts, bad results, over-indebtedness, liquidity issues, foreclosures, threats or filing of involuntary petitions), and what typically are their most urgent concerns? What measures do you advise to take at the initial stage to tackle the urgent concerns (illiquidity, civil and criminal liability, asset shielding)?

12. Describe the information you request from the debtor Do you have a checklist? Would you make it available? What information do creditors normally demand from the debtor?
13. Are household or family ties an issue in restructuring operations? Please elaborate.
14. In what circumstances do you suggest rescuing the business? In what circumstances do you suggest liquidating the business on a break-up basis (piecemeal)? Do you have a preferred strategy between these options? In approximately what percentage of cases do you advise an attempt to rescue the business (e.g. 0–25%; 26–50%; 51–75%; 76–100%)?
15. If the debtor company appears rescue-worthy in principle, is it your preferred strategy to try to rescue the company out of court (i.e. through an agreement outside formal, fully in-court proceedings), or do you, in general or in particular cases, regard formal insolvency proceedings as an adequate and preferable tool? Why? Please elaborate.
16. In what circumstances do you suggest the use of formal insolvency proceedings? In what circumstances do you suggest out-of-court solutions? Do you have a preferred strategy between these options? In approximately what percentage of cases do you advise an out-of-court solution (e.g. 0–25%; 26–50%; 51–75%; 76–100%)?
17. When you pursue an out-of-court solution, is such solution regulated or unregulated (purely contractual)? How often do you suggest an unregulated out-of-court solution (e.g. 0–25%; 26–50%; 51–75%; 76–100%)?
18. What percentage of success does this option have in your experience (e.g. 0–25%; 26–50%; 51–75%; 76–100%)?
19. Are financial creditors (or indeed any other kind) reluctant to use non-regulated solutions? If so, what is their main concern?
20. If an out-of-court regulated option is chosen, which of the options existing in your jurisdiction would you most often advise? (Please differentiate by types of debtor/activity/type of creditors/size of debt, etc.) Would you consider suggesting a tool or a proceeding that is regulated by foreign legislation? If so, what are the tools/processes you would suggest using?
21. What are the main advantages of out-of-court options? What are the main disadvantages? If your jurisdiction has more than one type of out-of-court procedure, please describe each of them and their advantages and disadvantages.
22. Briefly describe the procedure (steps), in practice, to negotiate an out-of-court agreement in your jurisdiction (what do you do once you have accepted the case? who do you contact? what do you start with?). Are creditors approached on a targeted basis (i.e. only certain creditors) or all creditors at the same time? Describe the approach used to negotiate with creditors (informal or pursuant to established procedures such as mediation, ADR). How often does an attempt made without a pre-insolvency or insolvency

tool succeed? According to the debtor, what are the reasons for the failure of that attempt?

23. In which cases are steering committees used? By steering committees we are referring to meetings of the most relevant creditors out of court, not to be confused with the in-court creditors' committee. Does the debtor have a say in this regard? Does it have any influence as to the type of steering committee chosen and what would normally be your advice in this regard (a steering committee with an agent bank to negotiate binding or non-binding decision making processes, etc.)?
24. How often do you engage in negotiations with the representatives of employees when it is not mandatory to do so? Is your experience in this regard positive? Why or why not? Is there anything in the insolvency regulation that makes these negotiations particularly burdensome? Does this type of creditor, in your opinion, constitute a problem for the restructuring process?
25. How often do you engage in negotiations with the tax authorities? Is your experience in this regard positive? Why or why not? Is there anything in the insolvency regulation that makes these negotiations particularly burdensome? Does this type of creditor, in your opinion, constitute a problem for the restructuring process?
26. a. How often do you engage in negotiations with key suppliers/contractual counterparties? Is there anything in the insolvency regulation that makes these negotiations particularly burdensome?
    b. When the debtor is a company, how often do you engage in negotiations with the shareholders and/or their representatives? Do you think that the directors' interests are aligned with those of the major shareholders?
    c. How open or reluctant are shareholders generally to cooperating with restructurings or to contributing further to the restructuring effort? Is there a big hold-out potential?
27. In most jurisdictions, financial contracts with banks will include detailed and strict covenants, some of which are likely to have been breached by the time your client approaches you (insolvency/liquidity ratios, information duties, negative pledges, etc). In your opinion, is the breach of those covenants enough to trigger early termination of the financial contracts? Do banks ever rely on them to terminate contracts early? Do you ever perceive banks as using covenants opportunistically in this context? Do they use them as leverage to gain a superior bargaining position? Do these covenants, in your opinion, constitute a hurdle to business restructuring?
28. How often are financial institutions (or key suppliers, if involved in the negotiation) willing to provide additional financing? Is there any hurdle in the legal system (lack of sufficient priority, risk of avoidance, risk of criminal liability, etc)? What do financial institutions pay particular attention to when deciding whether to provide additional financing (e.g. rescue plan versus a

liquidation plan; operating revenues greater than operating costs; financial institutions or key suppliers over-exposed to the debtor)? Which quality/detail/author of the plan will financial institutions typically require?

29. a. Do avoidance actions in case of a subsequent insolvency constitute a hurdle to an agreement out of court? Why?
    b. Does the risk of civil or criminal liability in case of a subsequent insolvency constitute a hurdle to an agreement out of court? Why?

30. What are the most common aspects of the out-of-court agreements that you have participated in? Provide a brief general description of a standard agreement. For your answer, differentiate between unregulated agreements/agreements without court sanctioning and agreements that are regulated and/or have court involvement at some point.

    Question 30 may be expanded, if necessary, with a number of additional questions on content:

    a. How often is debt rescheduling part of the agreement? How long, approximately, is the rollover on average? Please elaborate. Is there any limitation to the application of debt rescheduling for any particular creditor?
    b. How often are debt write-downs part of the agreement? What percentages are accepted? Please elaborate. Is there any limitation to the application of debt write-downs for any particular creditor?
    c. How often do these agreements include a restructuring of the business (change in corporate form, closing down of activities, opening new activities, enhancing viable parts of the business, laying off workers, changing distribution channels, changing management, etc.)? Does your legislation pose any particular hurdles to business restructuring operations?
    d. How often do these agreements include a change in the structure of the shareholders (e.g. a debt-for-equity swap to the effect of diluting the 'old' shareholders; debt-for-equity swap to the effect of cancelling the interest of all the 'old' shareholders; the arrival of a new investor; etc)? Are the 'old' shareholders entitled to a pre-emption right? How often? Please elaborate. Please comment on any hurdles posed by the legal framework to conducting these operations and on whether the law adequately protects the interests of creditors vis-à-vis shareholders and minority shareholders vis-à-vis majority shareholders, and vice versa.
    e. How often do these agreements include a total or partial sale of the business? Does the legislation allow for going-concern sales? Does it include special rules that facilitate the business sales (in particular, transfer of contracts/licences without the counterparty's consent)?
    f. How often is the sale of an important asset or of part or all of the business made to a directly or indirectly related party? In these cases, how is the

sale price determined? Do you think that the interests of creditors are adequately protected under the law if these sales take place?

g. Are there clear and neutral or favourable rules regarding the taxation of these restructuring operations? If not, does taxation, in your opinion, constitute a hurdle to restructuring operations?

31. In your opinion, what are the main problems for the approval of an out-of-court restructuring plan (e.g. majorities are too high, the information duties too burdensome, expenses of mediators/auditors/etc., taxes too high, etc)?
32. Roughly what percentage of the agreements end in formal insolvency proceedings following failure to implement them (e.g. 0–25%; 26–50%; 51–75%; 76–100%)?
33. In the case of agreements negotiated out of court where there is some sort of court intervention, does the system work efficiently? (Please share your experience where the intervention of the court is merely a confirmation of the plan.) Does even minimal involvement of the court constitute a problem? (Does court intervention prove a hurdle for agreements after they are negotiated?)
34. What is your experience where the intervention of the court is merely a confirmation of the plan? Does the existence of judicial discretion create a hurdle to negotiations in advance? (This question refers to court confirmation where the judge may reject a plan based upon the merits of the plan's content as opposed to when there is no such material discretion; where the judge may act without previous opposition by a creditor; etc.)
35. Do you advise the use of pre-packaged agreements?[2] What are their main advantages and disadvantages?

C. Lawyers Mainly Advising Creditors

The previous questions should be asked, with an adapted text as necessary. The following are additional questions.

36. Provide an overview of the type of lending your clients normally have with large debtors: secured vs unsecured; types of security; types of assets covered; types of clauses (cross-default, negative pledge, etc). Are personal guarantees also included (of shareholders/managers)?
37. How does the type of lending/security influence creditors' behaviour towards restructuring agreements? In particular, when creditors have a large percentage of their debt covered by fixed security (e.g. mortgage over real estate), are they willing to enter into out-of-court agreements? Why or why not?

[2] Each jurisdiction will be more specific as to what is meant by 'pre-packaged'.

38. Do creditors accelerate loans or terminate financial contracts based merely on the breach of covenants? If yes, please state which covenants are the most important to this decision (insolvency/liquidity ratios, information duties, negative pledges, etc).
39. Are creditors normally willing to engage in the negotiation of out-of-court agreements? How long does negotiation with creditors usually last (e.g. how long does it take for creditors to formally accept what has been informally agreed with the negotiator? Do creditors tend to stand by their negotiator's decision)? Which factors are more likely to affect the length of negotiations (financial complexity, size of credit, size or nationality of creditor, kind of creditor e.g. bank vs non-bank financial institution, etc)?
40. When creditors negotiate bilaterally to restructure the loans, do they require additional security for previously unsecured loans? Since this practice may prove risky (e.g. criminal and civil liability, avoidance, etc and detrimental for the creditor in case the debtor ends up in insolvency, what measures does the creditor adopt to protect the restructuring operation?
41. Is fresh money sufficiently protected? Please elaborate, commenting on different cases.
42. Do creditors only restructure their loans against a viability analysis? If so, how is it conducted and who pays for it?
43. In the case of bank creditors: In your opinion, does the banking regulatory framework (i.e. provisioning rules, limitations to the acquisition of shares, limitation of types of activity, etc) influence the bank's behaviour?
44. Of the regulated out-of-court agreements existing in your jurisdiction, which one is more often preferred by creditors when dealing with large debtors? Why?
45. How often do creditors enter into a debt-for-equity swap? What is a creditor's typical strategy after acquiring ownership of the entity?
46. Are restructuring processes any different in cases of syndicated loans? How?
47. Not uncommonly, the solution to the distress of viable businesses is thwarted by a bad personal relationship between the main creditors and the people controlling the company. How often is the relationship between the creditor and the main shareholder/directors a hurdle to achieving an out-of-court agreement? Are there legal tools to overcome this hurdle?
48. How often is a third party (i.e. an equity investor, a fund buying the debt, a new bank financing the operation, etc.) involved in the restructuring agreement? Are there any significant legal hurdles to these operations?
49. From the creditor's perspective, what are the main problems to achieving out-of-court agreements? Do you think that insolvency law is too harsh or too lenient on debtors, or do you think it strikes the right balance?

D. Lawyers Mainly Advising MSMEs

The main objective of the interview is to gather as much qualitative information as possible concerning the behaviour of MSME debtors confronting a situation of financial and/or business distress as well as the behaviour of financial entities, employees, and tax authorities when faced with the financial distress of their debtors. Obtaining information with respect to personal or family relationships should be an additional objective of this interview.

The interviewer needs to identify the main problems faced by the interviewees in practice.

1. What information is most often requested by creditors?
2. Do debtors usually have their financial statements in order?
3. How often does financial information have to be reconstructed and prepared specifically for the restructuring process?
4. Does the lack of adequate financial/corporate information influence the debtor's choice of mechanism to tackle the business's crisis? (i.e. if the reconstruction is not feasible, the debtor may be more inclined to an unregulated out-of-court agreement)
5. In your opinion, would measures need to be adopted to tackle the legal mismatch between legal requirements for financial information and reality? (e.g. by lowering the requirements of mandatory information for regulated out-of-court proceedings or in formal insolvency proceedings; or by lowering the requirements for the smallest sector of the business spectrum (MSMEs); or by the introduction of templates for debtors, etc.)
6. Do your small debtor clients find it difficult to negotiate with their creditors? In other words, is there a passivity or lack of interest on behalf of creditors? Please elaborate concerning the different types of creditors (e.g. banks, tax, suppliers, employees).
7. Assuming your client has only one bank as financial creditor, describe the negotiation process and the bank's behaviour. Is new collateral requested? Additional or new personal guarantees? From whom? How often is new money available?
8. Are labour-related issues a problem in restructuring operations? Please elaborate.
9. Are household or family ties an issue in restructuring operations? Please elaborate.
10. If your jurisdiction has out-of-court proceedings designed specifically for SMEs, what are their strengths and weaknesses?

Appendix

Methodology of the Volume

Readers might find it helpful to understand our methodology for this volume, as it is rare that scholars from so many countries collaborate so intensively. Equally remarkable is the fact that membership of the Group has remained stable over the two and a half years of the project, with plans for another project starting in late 2018. The collaboration amongst 'the Bowen Island Group' has been intellectually challenging and satisfying. As the brief biographical notes indicate, we come from Spain, Germany, Italy, Canada, and the United Kingdom. Collectively, we bring a wealth of scholarly, law reform, judicial, and practice experience to the topic of MSME insolvency. The Bowen Island Group members have gained first-hand experience working with insolvency systems in our own countries, as well as those in Africa (Kenya, Namibia), Asia (Bangladesh, East Timor, Kazakhstan, the Maldives, Mongolia, Pakistan, Thailand, Vietnam), Europe (Albania, Belarus, Bosnia and Herzegovina, Croatia, Kosovo, Latvia, Moldova, Poland, Romania, Russia, Ukraine), the Middle East (Egypt, Israel, Jordan, Kuwait, Saudi Arabia, Turkey), Central and South America (Mexico, Paraguay, Peru), and the Caribbean (Saint Lucia).

In writing the volume, we had five in-person meetings in Spain, Canada, Japan, and the UK, and thousands of email exchanges. The collaboration commenced in Madrid in September 2015. Several of the authors had been discussing the potential for a deeper collaboration than simply an exchange of ideas and research at conferences. The insolvency of micro, small, and medium enterprises was identified as an important and timely challenge for policy reform.

The initial meeting was co-hosted by Professor Ignacio Tirado, University of Autónoma of Madrid, Spain and Professor Janis Sarra, Faculty of Law, University of British Columbia, Canada, in Madrid. Scholars took responsibility for thinking in advance about, and presenting on, the following topics: a twofold system of solution to the financial distress of MSMEs; the treatment of post-commencement finance; the problem of creditor passivity in MSME financial restructuring practice; the decision-making process in MSME insolvency; the social aspects of MSME insolvency; debtor behaviour on the eve of insolvency; the challenge of dealing with employees in MSME insolvencies; whether there should be institutions to manage out-of-court solutions to MSME insolvency; the procedural design of MSME insolvency proceedings; the problem of financial information in MSMEs; and the institutional setting in MSME insolvencies. We were joined by local scholars and practitioners from Madrid as we discussed these issues in depth.

We developed a long-form set of notes from the Madrid meeting and decided that the next steps were to take responsibility for drafting some texts for discussion, drawing on insights from the meeting. We generated a first draft outline in late September 2015 and, after various email exchanges, agreed on the content of each of the subject areas. We each contributed to a shared folder of relevant scholarship, reports by governments and intergovernmental financial institutions, and UNCITRAL and UNIDROIT documents. We undertook literature searches and examined empirical studies published by the World Bank, European

Development Bank, Asian Development Bank, and similar organizations. We shared first thoughts through exchanges by email and the shared folders. The ideas began to take shape.

In February 2016, we met for three full days on Bowen Island, a small island in the Pacific Ocean just off the coast of Vancouver, Canada. Our hosts were Professors Janis Sarra and Ron Davis at their home. There we discussed the sections drafted; debated theoretical approaches; and discussed frameworks, ideas, and practice experience. We explored why MSMEs need a special framework for addressing their insolvency. We examined various approaches used globally and the limits of public policy in multiple jurisdictions as to the treatment of MSMEs when they experience financial distress. We debated the issue of cross-over of commercial and personal insolvency, particularly in relation to micro and small enterprises; the issue of availability of discharge; the 'honest entrepreneur'; and personal liability relief. We rigorously debated the role of lenders in resolving MSME insolvency. We examined numerous studies for the definition of MSMEs for the purpose of our project. We debated the policy objectives of a special approach to MSME insolvency. It was here that the framework and key components of the volume were conceptualized and face-to face discussions over an extended few days enabled a deeper analysis. We began to appreciate the importance of presenting a 'menu' of options to national policymakers in the first instance and ultimately to the stakeholders in each distressed MSME. The 'Modular Approach' was born.

We met again in March 2016 for a full day in London, UK, at Professor Rizwaan Mokal's home, in which a long list of issues was hotly debated, including challenges in respect of information asymmetries, moral hazard issues, deemed approval mechanisms to reduce cost barriers to relief, the role of insolvency professionals and the court, and fairness as a guiding principle to an effective MSME regime. We were joined in London by Andres Martinez, the Senior Financial Sector Specialist for Insolvency and Debt Resolution at the World Bank, who was an active participant and contributor to our discussions. Having agreed generally on approach and key components of the volume, the group decided to work in pairs to produce sections of the full volume. Serious discussions were peppered with animated peripatetic walks and meals together, including at a seventeenth-century public house associated with the poet Coleridge, the portraitist Hogarth, and the highwayman Dick Turpin. We met again in June 2016 in Tokyo for half a day to discuss the draft parts and move the discussion to the next level.

We circulated a first full draft in early 2016 and began to present our ideas at major conferences and meetings: the Annual Review of Insolvency Law, February 2016 in Montréal; World Bank, July 2016, Washington, DC; INSOL International, July 2016, London; and UNCITRAL Working Group V, New York, May 2017. In early 2017, there were numerous drafts and exchanges regarding the theoretical framework for the volume, including guiding principles, drawing on the extant literature and advancing our ideas collectively. The Modular Approach was also developed more fulsomely. Many exchanges with scholars, judges, practitioners, and policymakers from around the world gave us issues to consider. We contributed to the World Bank's new Task Force on MSME insolvency, and the Task Force's First Report drew heavily on our draft volume.

The challenge was to have time to complete the volume, given our geographical locations and very busy schedules. Our efforts culminated in a full seven days on Bowen Island in July 2017, in which we discussed the full draft of the volume in great detail: every aspect of theory, policy, and practice. The meetings were based once again at the Sarra/Davis home; we worked hard, but we also brought our families—spouses and children. We would work hard from early morning to 3 or 4 pm each day, then go sea-kayaking, swimming, or hiking, and even did a singalong evening with musician friends. We cooked together—wonderful elaborate meals from different country origins, adults and children alike contributing their culinary skills. It was this integration of the scholarly and the personal that we feel resulted in creative insights and a determination to agree on the final text. From July 2017 to January 2018, the volume was completed, with iterative revisions, additions, and debates. We added country examples of how the modules could be applied in different types of jurisdictions in Africa, Asia, and Europe, in emerging and developed nations. We built a consensus on every word in the volume, each contributing insight from their knowledge and experience.

We found this collaboration greatly rewarding both intellectually and personally and venture the view that the outcome will add value to the public policy discussion.

Index

The manufacturer's authorised representative in the EU for product safety is Oxford University Press España S.A. of el Parque Empresarial San Fernando de Henares, Avenida de Castilla, 2 – 28830 Madrid (www.oup.es/en or product.safety@oup.com). OUP España S.A. also acts as importer into Spain of products made by the manufacturer.

www.ingramcontent.com/pod-product-compliance
Lightning Source LLC
LaVergne TN
LVHW011757200926
848484LV00003B/728
* 9 7 8 0 1 9 8 7 9 9 9 3 1 *